Exploring the
Islands of
INDONESIA

Exploring the Islands of
INDONESIA

*Travelers' Experiences
off the Beaten Path*

Annabel Sutton

PASSPORT BOOKS
a division of *NTC Publishing Group*
Lincolnwood, Illinois USA

All photographs are by the author

ISBN: 0-8442-9889-1

This edition first published in 1994 by Passport Books,
a division of NTC Publishing Group,
4255 West Touhy Avenue, Lincolnwood (Chicago), Illinois 60646-1975 U.S.A.
Originally published by Impact Books, London, United Kingdom.
© Annabel Sutton 1994, 1989
Library of Congress Catalog Card Number: 93-84182
Manufactured in the United States of America

3 4 5 6 7 8 9 0 VP 9 8 7 6 5 4 3 2 1

Acknowledgments

My immeasurable thanks go first and foremost to my husband, Paul Ware, who was an indefatigable source of help, advice and support during each and every stage of writing this book. Secondly, my parents, who first encouraged and gave me the confidence to start writing. My thanks, too, to everyone who read parts of the manuscript at various stages and offered constructive criticism and — and equally important — encouragement. To all those with whom I travelled along the way, but aren't mentioned by name — and to Donna for being such a great travelling companion. Also, to the Indonesian people for their boundless goodwill and hospitality. And last but not least to my publisher, Jean-Luc Barbanneau, for putting my story into print.

For Paul

Contents

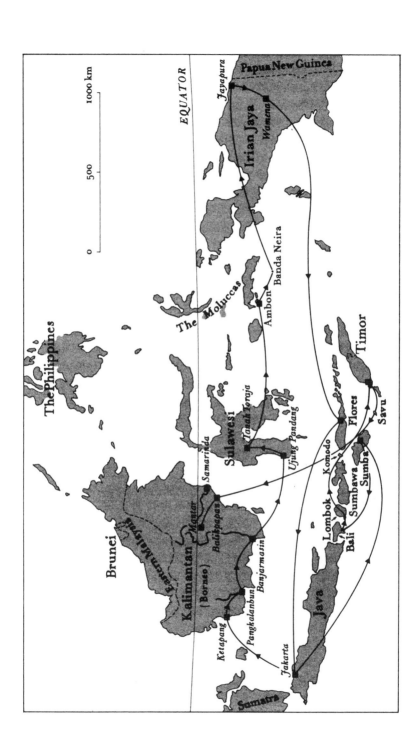

1. 'Plane is brok . . .'

South and Central Kalimantan

'*Halim*,' said the man behind the check-in counter when we arrived at Jakarta's Soekarno-Hatta airport.

'*Halim!*' we replied, thinking it some sort of formal greeting. Looking confused, he repeated the word, rather more urgently now.

'*HALIM . . .!*'

It was then that another man with several stripes on his sleeve came to our aid and explained, in English, 'You are at the wrong airport. You must go to Halim airport. Over the town. Hurry! Hurry! Or you will miss your flight!'

It wasn't a very auspicious beginning to travelling in Indonesia. We had landed the day before at Soekarno-Hatta airport and there was nothing on our tickets to indicate that our flight to Pangkalan Bun in Central Kalimantan wasn't from the same place.

Our frantic chase through the morning traffic from one side of Jakarta to another was like trying to drive across London or New York in rush-hour; and we had only thirty minutes to do it! We arrived at Halim, panting, and flung our bags on the scale. The man behind the counter looked unperturbed. 'No hurry,' he said, 'plane is brok and we are trying to mend now. There will be little bit delay.'

The concept of two women travelling together – especially when one was American and the other English – was one that Indonesians found hard to accept. Donna and I had teamed up for an indefinite period of time to travel around Indonesia together. Donna is an artist from Oregon and, before our trip, had been designing flower arrangements to finance her first love –

1

sculpture. She can be absolutely charming and very good
company, with an acerbic wit and veritable army of snappy
asides, but she is not inclined to suffer fools gladly.

We had no set schedule, purposely wanting to be flexible and
free to wander wherever the whim took us. We were attracted
towards the lesser-travelled Indonesian islands and had decided
to forsake the well-trodden tourist paths for the mysteries and
adventure of *Nusantara* – literally, 'the islands in between'.

It seemed that Indonesia was the forgotten land. A country
scattered over 13,500 islands, a thousand of which are inhabited
and three of which (Borneo, New Guinea and Sumatra) are
amongst the seven largest in the world. Home to over three
hundred separate ethnic groups in a combined land and sea area
at least as large as the USA, with the largest Muslim population
in the world, and, as we were to find over the coming months,
home to an incredibly diverse people; a kaleidoscope of cultures,
customs, religions, languages, geography and wildlife. To Donna
and I, waiting in that departure lounge, Indonesia was like a
massive chest of hidden treasure just waiting to be opened, each
island a jewel or precious stone to be picked up, turned over and
savoured.

For a race of short, brown-skinned, black-haired people, we
were something of a phenomenon. Donna is a well-built five foot
nine, with strawberry blonde hair and fair skin covered with
freckles, and I am over six foot tall. Consequently we were the
objects of great curiosity and interest wherever we went. The
departure lounge was no exception. The ten other passengers
waiting for the Pangkalan Bun flight stared at us with ill-
disguised amazement, but always smiled warmly if we caught
their eye.

After an hour Donna went in search of someone who could tell
us what was happening. Seeing her approach from the window, a
Merpati official came running out of the office waving his hands,
saying, 'Five minutes more. Five minutes more to boarding!' We
had no reason to see why he would lie to us. We were, after all,
still very new to Indonesia. An hour later we were still waiting.
Eventually a bus arrived to take us to the plane. We rumbled
across the tarmac to where the small, twin-propeller plane stood

looking like something that had been put together, badly, from an Airfix kit. We were greeted by mechanics wielding spanners and the engine still in pieces on the tarmac. The bus turned round and took us back to the waiting room. We finally left two hours later.

This was our first experience with Merpati Nusantara Airlines. There are three major airlines in Indonesia. Garuda is the large, government-owned airline and is relatively well-run. Its planes are adequately maintained and often on time. Bouraq is privately owned, but has far fewer routes than Garuda. And then there is Merpati. If you ever want to do short hops to smaller islands or places off the beaten track in Indonesia, you will almost certainly be flying Merpati. Merpati Airlines are also owned by the government but seem to be regarded as an embarrassing relative; the sort that can't be got rid of, but spends its life getting into embarrassing scrapes and difficulties. They operate a fleet of ancient CASA and Twin Otter planes and their flights are nearly always delayed, sometimes cancelled and occasionally even lost en route. A similar plane to the one we were waiting for had recently crashed in the remote mountains of Irian Jaya, another into the jungles of East Kalimantan. The latter, despite Merpati enlisting the aid of psychics, took over four months to find.

Merpati have a rule that if there has been a problem with one of their planes, the mechanic who fixed it then has to fly the next leg of the journey. With Djunardi, the mechanic, aboard, we stopped in Ketapang, on the graphically named Cape of Onions in West Kalimantan, to refuel. A group of curious children stood and stared at us from a distance as we watched the plane being refuelled with a large plastic funnel. After we had all piled back on, the pilot turned on the engines. One started all right, but the rogue engine at first refused to start and then, when Djunardi had reluctantly coaxed it into life by spinning the propeller by hand, the oil inside immediately caught fire and smoke and fumes began streaming out of it.

'Someone should write a book about this,' shouted Donna over the screaming engine. I looked in alarm at the acrid smoke pouring past the window and promised her that if we ever actually got to Pangkalan Bun I would do it. In the heat of such moments are decisions made. A few minutes later both engines were switched off and the captain, a cheerful, round-faced Chinaman, came over to us and said in forced English:

'I am so sorry. This plane it is – is – BAD.'

'We have to stay here in Ketapang,' said the stewardess.

'WHAT?' roared Donna, 'but surely there's another flight out of here? Can't we get on that?'

'Sorry, no flight today.'

'What about roads? Can't we take a bus?'

'Sorry, no roads.'

There was no other choice. Ketapang it was. We checked in with the crew at the Hotel Pasifika, a two-storey hotel with tattered striped plastic blinds on the outside. Our rooms were on the second floor, off a large linoleumed landing. Outside each room were a table and two chairs. In Indonesia, it seemed, one's room was for sleep only; one ate, drank and socialized outside.

I looked over the balcony at the scene below. Ketapang was a small, sleepy town. All along the street, bright pink bougainvillaea tumbled down from attractive balustraded balconies. On either side were shops or restaurants with living quarters on top; a grocery, bicycle shop, apothecary, clothes shop, a 'Padang-style' restaurant, and a *saté* stall selling thin slivers of barbecued meat smothered in piquant peanut sauce.

Few cars went by, but there was an endless stream of motorbikes and sturdy, old-fashioned black bicycles; the realistic alternatives for the large proportion of Indonesians unable to afford a car. It wasn't uncommon to see entire families, parents with two or three children, packed neatly on a motorbike, limbs folded in like plastic-wrapped chicken. There were *becaks* in Ketapang, too; small, hooded passenger carriages on wheels pedalled along by a muscular driver on a bicycle. *Becaks* are the cheapest form of public transport in Indonesia. These were decorated with bells, pom-poms, tassels and streamers, and made a light tinkling noise, like sleigh bells, as they passed. A man joined me on the balcony and, after carefully surveying the scene below for several minutes, nodded sagely and remarked, 'This is a small town.'

The pilot and co-pilot, Yan and Aby, were as different as chalk and cheese. Yan was Chinese, Aby Javanese; Yan was overweight, balding and sloppily dressed, Aby was slim with thick wavy hair and an impeccable dresser; Yan's character was as transparent as a sheet of cling wrap, Aby's submerged under deep, dark waters. When it became clear that we were stuck in Ketapang, Yan's reaction had been that it wasn't too bad, we could all eat (the justly famous local) lobsters! That night, after several servings of these and two beers, Yan became red in the face and animated. He had been a pilot for Merpati for eight years, he said, but he was fed up with them and wanted to move to another airline. 'Which one?' we asked politely, expecting him to reply Bouraq or Garuda. 'Pan Am,' he said expansively, making a victory salute with his right fist. As our meal progressed, I became convinced that Aby was infatuated with Donna. He hung on her every word and sneaked amorous glances at her when he thought she wasn't looking. Leaving them deep in conversation, I talked to the mechanic.

'What do you do when you're not working, Djunardi?'

'I like to read.'

'Oh? What sort of things do you like to read?'

'Only Maintenance Manual,' he said. 'Tomorrow I must to put in new engine. I have never done before so I must go step-by-step.' The rest of the crew hooted with laughter, though whether it was amused or nervous I couldn't be sure.

In the lobby of the Pasifika there was a faded painting of seven young women bathing or 'reclining' on the banks of a river. All except one were clothed in suggestive wisps of material; the other had mislaid her wisps somewhere, and exposed one breast as she swam. 'Take part in excitement with us at the Hotel Pasifika!' it said on the frame. Perhaps there was more to the Pasifika than met the eye, but as a woman I was unlikely to find out. Donna and I retired to bed without incident.

☆

Breakfast consisted of pre-sweetened coffee with evaporated milk, two thickly sliced pieces of bread with butter and sugar in the middle, and two hard-boiled eggs. Presumably the logistical problems involved in actually inserting sugar inside the shell had been the only reason the eggs came unsweetened. While I was crunching my way through my sugar sandwich, Tina, the stewardess, joined us. She was dressed in a pair of rather grubby pink pyjamas, which she didn't take off all day. She too was fed up at having to stay in Ketapang. This was the second time in a month that it had happened. Nowadays, she said, she always travelled with her pyjamas, just in case.

Yan delivered the unwelcome news that the plane still wasn't fixed. 'Well when *will* it be?' said Donna, impatiently. 'When do you think we can leave?' Indonesians rarely ask such questions. Obviously, when the engine was fixed, the plane would leave – and not before. After all, nothing would be gained by making a fuss. Such questions are the preserve of Westerners who are used to reliable timetables and immediate answers.

'Well do you think it'll be fixed today?' asked Donna in exasperation. There was no way that Yan could tell us. He didn't know when the plane would be mended, or even *if* it could be. 'Yes, I think so,' he said. This way, we were slightly appeased and would ask no more questions – for the time being.

We didn't leave that day. We had to wait until the day after, when the next scheduled plane on the same route arrived from Jakarta, to spontaneous applause from the passengers and crew. As we took off I noticed a group of people had gathered around Djunardi, who was looking doubtfully at the new piece of engine which had arrived on the flight. Tina was obviously not convinced they were leaving; she was still wearing her pink pyjamas.

☆

A large earwig crawled out of the hotel stationery of the Hotel Blue Kecubung – Pangkalan Bun's finest. I watched its progress as far as the washbasin in the bathroom, then turned on the tap. The water and earwig gushed straight down the plug and over my feet. At least there *was* a basin and a shower, even though there was no hot water. We were waiting for police permits which would allow us to travel on to the small port town of Kumai and then up-river to Tanjung Puting National Park. Borneo and Sumatra are the only places in the world where orangutans live in the wild, and at Tanjung Puting there was an orangutan research and conservation centre that we wanted to visit. As well as studying wild orangutan behaviour, the centre was also dedicated to taking those that had been kept illegally as pets and returning them to the wild.

Pangkalan Bun was your average Indonesian rural town. A dozen or so main streets with a defined 'town centre' containing shops, restaurants, banks, a market and several mosques, and the residential area nearby. Walking down the main street Donna and I were bombarded with shouts of 'Hello Mister!' (the universal call to foreigners throughout Indonesia), 'Where are you going?', 'How are you?' and several 'I luff you's from groups of young men lounging at market stalls and outside a motorbike repair shop. One little boy became so excited that he forgot what he was supposed to say. Jumping wildly up and down he yelled, 'Hello . . .' then, unable to remember the right word, came out with 'Whiteys' instead! 'Hello WHITEYS! Hello WHITEYS!'

It was in the hotel dining-room that we first met Monir. He was very young, grinned a lot and was very enthusiastic about foreigners. Newly liberated from Aby's attentions, however, Donna was not in the mood for his exuberance.

'Hello. Good eefening,' he said, 'where are you from?'

'Zimbabwe,' answered Donna with a straight face. I was to become used to this trick of hers whenever she wanted to get rid of people. Monir was not to be deterred, however. 'Where are you doing in Pangkalan Bun?' he asked. 'Maybe I help you with things. Please give me your address.'

'Address, why?'

'I would like photograph of you,' said Monir.

'But why do you need our address?'

'Please give me a photo.'

'Monir, we don't have one.'

A pause. 'Then you will *send* me a photo.'

Despite the fact that it was only July, red, purple, silver and yellow tinsel shimmered over the bar and curling crêpe paper hung limply around the walls. Plastic holly had been tucked behind all the light fittings. In a small garden outside, a deer and a stork with its head missing, both made out of reinforced concrete, stood by a pond with fake rocks around it.

We got our permits the next morning. The policeman designated the task of delivering them had the unlikely Indonesian name of Jackson ('You know, like Mikkel') and was a very cool dude indeed. He was, he told us, from Bali, but had been sent to Central Kalimantan for a few years' training. He smiled sheepishly, cracked his knuckles and made a slight adjustment to the rake of his designer shades.

As we were preparing to leave, Monir bounced up grinning. 'Please, you have a photo for me now?'

'No Monir, we still don't have one.'

'Come outside and we can take a photo for me!'

Jackson had to remove his cool shades in order to take the photograph of us with a beaming Monir. 'Don't forget my photos!' Monir shouted after the bus as we left for Kumai.

☆

The trip to Tanjung Puting by boat, or *klotok*, took five hours. The open-sided *klotok* was about twenty feet long and its roof four feet from the floor, making it impossible to stand, except at the front which was open. It was powered by a small engine and chugged slowly up-river with its owner, Pak Baso, steering with his toes as he watched from the roof for floating logs and other debris in the water. For the first few hours we passed an unchanging riverscape of dense nipa palms, their brownish grey stalks sticking straight up out of the water like the spines of giant surrealistic hedgehogs.

By late afternoon we had left the nipa palms behind and entered the world of the peat-swamp forest. The water, which had previously been muddy brown, now became tea-coloured; its hue caused by the minerals leached out of the surrounding vegetation. Not far from the water's edge, troupes of proboscis monkeys sat on the branches of tall trees, ginger coats gleaming in the sun, wearing their ridiculous bulbous 'Jimmy Durante' noses like party masks. Smaller, grey, macaque monkeys watched the boat chug past or scattered, swinging and swooping, into the jungle. White-bellied sea eagles and brahminy kites wheeled overhead, stork-billed kingfishers flashed past in a blur of red, yellow and turquoise, and an oriental darter flew, swooping, in front of the *klotok* for several kilometres; an elegant, winged escort. The light was so bright and sharp, and the water so dark and glassy, that it reflected the surrounding forest like a looking-glass. At times it was difficult to distinguish where the foliage ended and the water began. It was almost unreal, like gliding through mercury.

As the sun sank low behind the trees and the air cooled, a thin, ghostly mist hung over the river. 'Nearly there!' said Pak Baso, as we turned off the main river onto the narrow Sekonyer River. Giant reeds and palms brushed either side of the *klotok* as we carefully nosed our way through. At some points the river was so clogged with vegetation and fallen trees that it was no more than three metres wide. 'Must go very slow now because of logs in water. If we hit – *pcchha!*' Neither of us wanted to consider the implications of this word '*pcchha!*' so we fixed our attention firmly on the forest around us.

Our first sight of the orangutan research station at Tanjung Puting was of a long wooden walkway stretching from the river back into the jungle. 'Straight ahead,' said Pak Baso, 'and you will find Camp Leakey.' Camp Leakey was named after the late Louis Leakey who originally sponsored Jane Goodall's and Dian Fossey's research into the great apes, and in 1971 provided the funds for a young Canadian anthropologist, Biruté Galdikas, to come to Borneo and study wild orangutans. She has been there ever since. The camp, which is situated in a clearing in the forest, has changed considerably since 1971; what started out as one simple nipa palm hut has blossomed into a research and conservation station with approximately thirty permanent staff, a dining-hall, kitchen, staff quarters, park ranger's hut, Professor Galdikas's house and quarters for students and volunteers. At first the Professor was reluctant to put us up. 'We don't have facilities for guests,' she said, 'but as there are no students here right now, you can stay in the students' house for a few nights.'

She showed us into a spartan wooden building which contained a few fold-up beds, chairs and tables. The windows were covered with thin mesh screens and chain-link fencing. 'One to keep out the mosquitoes, the other the orangutans,' she explained. Showing us the bathroom, which was located next-door, she eyed the gaps between the wooden floorboards and said, 'Don't worry – the only snakes we get in here are baby pythons. Just ignore them!'

She swept off back to her house leaving us open-mouthed. Pythons?! In the bathroom? And we're supposed to ignore them?

'OK, Annabel,' said Donna, 'let's see your impression of someone ignoring a python while brushing their teeth. You can follow that up with an impersonation of someone remaining calm while showering with a cobra.'

I went to wash first. This was my first experience of the Indonesian *mandi* – a method of washing where one fills a plastic scooper with cold water from a large tank and chucks it all over oneself. In the tropical heat the water was by no means freezing cold, but it still took my breath away. As I was getting ready to rinse off with another scooper full of cold water, I noticed a long hairy arm reaching over the side of the hut and very gingerly picking up my wash-bag. 'Hey!' I shouted, but it was too late. Supina – a large female – had already made off with the bag and, by the time I could wrap a towel around myself and thunder out of the bathroom, she was sitting on the step outside, carefully considering how to cut the long red hair on her arm with my nail clippers.

'Invigorating?' asked Donna.

'Refreshing.' She collected her towel and made towards the bathroom. 'Oh, by the way, there's a krait in the toilet bowl . . .'

After dinner that night as we sat talking in the dining-room, a young male orangutan called Apollo Bob opened the door, climbed onto the table and, despite admonishment from the Professor, proceeded from one tin mug to another taking dainty sips of tea. He then removed the lid of the teapot very gingerly with his lips and polished off what remained in that! The Professor had a wealth of hilarious tales of mischievous orangutans, including one of an adolescent male who had hijacked the camp boat. The engine had been turned on at the time and the driver had fled, leaving the orangutan alone inside.

The Professor had reached the scene just in time to see the orangutan – having somehow slipped the gear into reverse – hands on the wheel, disappearing backwards up-river!

The sounds of the jungle – the whooping cries of the gibbons, birds singing, the steady whirring of cicadas – woke me next morning. Opening my eyes, I was immediately faced with an orangutan hanging upside down on the wire-netting looking in at me. With the orangutan hitching a ride on my back, I wandered down to the walkway where ex-captives who were still being rehabilitated were fed morning and evening. Sitting at the end of the bridge, my ears filled with the plaintive wailing of the gibbons, I watched a shimmering red sun rise from a sepia forest. It was like an old-fashioned photograph. Slowly, purposefully, the orangutans entered this timeless landscape – like ancient shadows in the mists of dawn.

Young orangutans were kept in the nursery, where they could be specially cared for. Charlotte Rose had been kept in a cage for three years before being brought to Tanjung Puting and it had been several weeks before she had dared venture away from it. Now she was making up for lost time. She was a complete klutz – flinging herself around, falling out of trees, swinging onto branches which broke under her weight and brought her and the branch tumbling to the ground. She got inside a barrel of water when nobody was looking, and ended up tipping the whole thing over; after that she rolled in some spilt kerosene and had to be marched down to the river to have it washed off. She was just plain naughty. One of the park rangers had been trying for several minutes to get her to drink some milk. Eventually she took the cup and drank the milk – only to spit it out at him the second his back was turned!

Julie was the youngest member of the nursery and, at two years old, would have been carried everywhere by her mother in the wild. All humans therefore became substitute mothers and she clung to Donna and me with her strong little arms and looked up appealingly with large dark eyes, batting her long lashes. She was adorable. If left by herself, she whimpered and cried until someone picked her up again. Even if she became interested in something going on elsewhere in the nursery and went a little closer to investigate, she would keep one foot attached to you – just in case.

That day I went into the forest to help search for wild orangutans; this takes place daily as part of Professor Galdikas's research. I was accompanied by Seha, one of the Dayaks employed at Camp Leakey as trackers. The Dayaks are the aboriginal inhabitants of Borneo, and used to be infamous as head-hunters. With the presence of missionaries and influences of the outside world, this practice has now died out. Dayaks are extraordinarily skilled in the forest. Not only do they hunt for food (originally with long pipes from which they blew poisoned darts, now increasingly with guns) and can identify the flora and fauna of the forest, they are also skilled tree-climbers and can scale a 150-foot tree in minutes. Seha told me about his older brother, who had married an American he met in camp. He had gone to America with her, he said, and at first had been very unhappy until he had discovered that he could make $50 an hour topping trees. He had come back, said Seha, full of admiration, and been able to buy himself a motorbike.

In the rainforest it is quite possible to forget where you are, who you are and what century you live in. It's a fantastic world of verticals and spirals, greens and blacks; of towering trees supported by giant buttresses and tangling vines; of brilliant coloured butterflies fluttering in rainbow bursts and phosphorescent fungi erupting from fallen trees. One might imagine the rainforest to be entirely quiet, but this illusion is soon shattered. Once the cicadas start up you could be forgiven for thinking that you had stumbled into some demented insect carnival going on in the middle of the forest.

It was as if an entire winged orchestra had set up their music stands and started playing all at once in a kind of crazy symphony. This particular orchestra had an extraordinary range, from a sound like a child blowing repeatedly into a toy horn to one resembling a fire engine or ambulance siren. Even when the principal players ceased momentarily, a steady hum pulsed in my ears, varying from a low, throbbing, pulsing whine, to a constant, thin needle of sound as if someone had left a giant flash unit switched on. Just as I felt I was becoming almost mesmerized, the distant murmur of an aeroplane broke the spell and yanked me back to the real world.

The primary rainforest at Tanjung Puting is made up of two-thirds lowland dypterocarp forest where legumes predominate, a quarter peat-swamp forest, and a small amount of tropical heath which is characterized by mossy, herbaceous matter underfoot. Every ten minutes or so, Seha would stand completely still and listen, his eyes scanning the forest canopy for sight or sound of an orangutan, while I removed fat leeches from my legs with a cigarette lighter.

'Isn't it easy to spot their red hair?' I asked.

'Not at all. Because underneath their skin is black and so they become like shadows in the forest.'

Despite searching all day, Seha and I didn't find any 'men of the forest' (*orang hutan*); only some wild deer and two baby squirrels who were chasing each other round and round a tree trunk as if they were auditioning for parts in a Disney film.

With 200,000 square kilometres being felled every year, it is estimated that by the year 2010 there will be no rainforest left outside national parks. In Indonesia, many factors conspire against the rainforest: oil and gas exploration, mining, logging, human settlement and permanent agriculture. Indonesian Borneo – now known as Kalimantan – is rich in natural resources, especially oil, gas, coal, and trees. As far back as 1846, the Dutch opened up coal mines in South and East Kalimantan, and oil exploration had started by the beginning of this century. Although permanent agriculture is the greatest threat to the rainforest, the most immediately visible is logging. The unfortunate fact is that as long as the rest of the world needs plywood and disposable chopsticks (twelve billion pairs are used each year in Japan), so the tropical hardwoods will continue to be wrenched from the rainforests.

The biggest extinction of animal life since the dinosaurs died is now occurring; half the species on earth will be wiped out in a mere hundred years. Happily, however, busy Japanese housewives are spared the drudgery of putting chopsticks in the dishwasher. Apart from the atrocity of rendering so much animal and plant life extinct, this ruthless destruction of the rainforest

13

could have global consequences. Rainforests act as gigantic
sponges which control the way moisture re-enters the
atmosphere, and ecologists believe that their destruction is
instrumental in altering the world's climate. Predictions have
been made that if current climatic conditions can be extrapolated
into the future, in one hundred years or so the world's coastlines
will become flooded, which would mean that London and Tokyo
and Los Angeles could be under water. It is something to think
about.

When I returned, exhausted, from my foray into the forest, I
found Donna completely traumatized. She had been reading
quietly in our hut, when a huge spider – at least a foot across, she
said – had crossed the floor and was now standing sentry outside
our bedroom. Donna is an acute arachniphobe. Spiders haunt her
very worst nightmares. I had to admit that this one was rather
horrible.

'Get rid of it!' wailed Donna, flailing her arms. I wasn't sure
how to. I collected the scooper from the bathroom with the
intention of scooping it up and throwing it outside, but lost my
nerve when I imagined those eight monstrously long spindly legs
running up my arm.

'For God's sake, Annabel. There's no way I'll be able to sleep if
I know it's in here.' The spider stood its ground. I picked up a
broom from the corner and poked it. It scuttled across the floor
towards the chair on which Donna was standing. She screamed. I
began to panic and chased it around the room with the broom,
finally managing to run it outside. Giggling hysterically, I
slammed the door and peeped out of the window. It was still
there on the porch and I could almost see it drumming its legs on
the floor and looking up as if to say, 'OK, you've had your fun.
Now when are you going to let me back in?'

Distant thunder rolled over the dripping forest as I went out for
my *mandi*, having made perfectly sure that the spider was
nowhere in sight. After a few moments I became aware of two
eyes peering up at me through the floor. An orangutan had found
a tin mug and was holding it out to catch the water as I washed.

The next morning I found that Apollo Bob had done a Uri
Geller on our umbrella and bent it totally out of shape. I took

the now pretzel-shaped umbrella and shook it at him. He looked suitably admonished, but his day's exploits had only just begun. The door to the bathroom could be bolted shut on both sides and as I brushed my teeth I heard Apollo Bob fiddling with the bolt on the outside. This could have been a disaster. When I had left the main hut, where Donna was still sleeping, I had padlocked the door behind me and had the key with me in the bathroom. If Apollo managed to lock me in – as he was obviously trying to do – both Donna and I would have been trapped! With a mouth full of toothpaste I rushed to the door. Apollo Bob had managed to pull the bolt slightly, but not quite far enough to stick. After frantic rattling, and to my immense relief, the door opened. Apollo Bob sat outside looking the picture of innocence. Later that morning I saw him wandering around camp with a pair of underpants on his head!

Orangutans are gentle, affectionate, inquisitive, mischievous and – extraordinarily human. Whether it was an expression or a mannerism or the particular way one was sitting, the phrase 'they're so human' slipped out time after time. The affinity we felt with them could be something to do with the fact that their genetic make-up is ninety-seven per cent similar to ours. As Professor Galdikas put it, 'When you look into an orangutan's eyes, the eyes that gaze back at you are essentially your own. It's like looking into a mirror.'

When we finally dragged ourselves away from Tanjung Puting, we were accompanied back down the river by hordes of blood-red dragonflies flitting here and there and swooping down onto the water with little splashes. Not far from the park we spotted a crocodile sunning itself at the side of the river, while nearby a magnificent heron stood on its nest. A wild adult male orangutan – distinguishable by its cheek pads – watched our progress motionlessly from the top of a tree. The whirring of the cicadas could be heard even above the chugging of Pak Baso's engine, but occasionally, when the engine was switched off to enable us to glide through a narrow stretch of water, the cicadas were quiet and the silence was extraordinary. We felt enveloped by the forest, embraced by it and completely at peace.

At Kumai we hailed a taxi back to Pangkalan Bun. Our driver

was young and over-excitable. Gripping his steering wheel, which had 'I love you, I need you, I want you' written on it, he made no effort to disguise his interest in Donna, who was sitting in the front.

'Are you married?' he asked.

'Why do you want to know?' said Donna, smiling acidly.

News of Seha's brother's good fortune must have spread. 'I want to marry rich American woman. Are you from America?'

'Yes.'

'*Waaah!* Are you rich?'

'No!'

'*Waaah!* Where are you going next?'

'To Banjarmasin.'

'Maybe I follow you to Banjarmasin . . .' He stared lustfully at Donna, who was looking out of the side window. 'Can I follow you to Banjarmasin?'

'I don't think so.'

'*Waaah!*'

'What is that – a plane or a pencil case with wings?' asked Donna, pointing towards the plane which was to fly us to Banjarmasin, the largest city in South Kalimantan. It *was* tiny, and I wasn't encouraged to see the flight attendant tinkering in the engine with a screwdriver.

It was such a small plane that all the passengers had to be weighed as well as their luggage. I stepped onto the scale and was immediately surrounded by a large crowd. '*Aduh!*' they cried, astonished, as the needle swung to sixty-five kilos. An average Indonesian family probably weighs less than that.

There was a problem. The passengers were informed that the pilot had added our combined weights and the plane was too heavy to take off. The obvious solution was for someone to volunteer to take the next flight. Nobody did. Nobody believed the assurances that another plane would be along 'soon'. The pilot disappeared. Indonesian life, culture and religion can be summed up neatly as a search for harmony. If at all possible, conflict is to be avoided and a compromise reached. Elsewhere in the world one unwilling passenger would have been excluded in the interests of the majority. But the pilot had centuries of tradition on his side. When he came back he had reached a solution. Would we all please *re-calculate* our weights, he asked. We did so. The pilot re-summed the total and smiled. Yes, that was better. Now we could take off.

'I wouldn't mind crash-landing with him,' said Donna, staring approvingly at the pilot. He didn't look old enough to refuel the plane, let alone fly it; but he was *very* good looking. I was far more concerned about his flying ability than his looks and winced as he tried to start the engine with the ignition key. When it refused to start, the co-pilot picked up the emergency axe and bashed the control panel with it. I seriously considered getting out there and then, but it was too late; the overloaded plane had already begun taxi-ing to the end of the runway. We coasted down the runway for what seemed an eternity, slowly gathering speed. Only at the very last minute, when we were just about to run out of tarmac, did the wheels lift off the ground and the plane drone into the air like a sleepy wasp at the end of summer.

We hit thick cloud just north of Banjarmasin and I looked up from my book to see both the pilot and the co-pilot on their feet and peering through the side windows of the cockpit frantically searching for some sign of the airport. The situation was so ridiculous; I couldn't help a smile.

It was the start of the annual pilgrimage to Mecca, the *Haj*, and being a strongly Islamic town (it is said that there are more *Hajis*, or returned pilgrims, per capita in Banjarmasin than in any other Indonesian city), Banjarmasin airport was swarming with good Muslims either on their way, or seeing off friends and relatives, to the Holy City of Islam. Black *peci* hats and lacy headscarves mingled with a scattering of white head-caps belonging to the privileged few who had already made the pilgrimage.

When we first saw Bill, he was berating a frightened soft drinks seller for not having a can of coke that was cold enough. Bill was a Coca Cola freak. He drank up to five cans a day. He was also a gem collector and was in Banjarmasin, he told us, to look for diamonds. Originally from Texas, he worked for an American oil

17

company in East Kalimantan and was here just for the weekend. Everything about Bill was large; his size, his personality and his voice. 'Yeah, I tell ya, soon as I heard they have real unusual diamonds in Ban-JAR-masin – almost yeller some of 'em – I got me the first plane here. I was given the name of some son of a gun who owns a diamond mine, so I was planning on lookin' him up. If you two want to join me, that's just fine.'

We piled into a taxi. 'Yep,' drawled Bill, 'the son of a bitch I have to see is one of these *Hajis*. Must mean he's made a whole bundle of money with his diamonds. Can't be cheap to fly to Saudi Arabia now can it?' We had to agree. Religion usually costs money and Islam is no exception. On the way to town we passed a crushed car on top of a concrete plinth put there as a gruesome reminder to drive safely. We also passed two young men cruising along on Harley Davidson motorbikes who looked like a cross between *Easy Rider* and the *Ramayana* epic. Their bikes had chequered Dayak baskets instead of luggage carriers and Balinese carved wooden headrests. They wore cowboy hats, levi jackets and ski gloves. 'Now those look like my kinda guys!' said Bill.

As a coastal port, Banjarmasin was trading with Arabs and had already converted to Islam by the fifteenth or sixteenth century. It established trading relations with the Dutch East India Company in the seventeenth century. Its history was one of 'trade and raid' until 1812, when the infamous Alexander Hare obtained 3,500 square kilometres of land from the then Sultan and made himself the 'White Rajah of Moluko'. He imported slave labour, had his own harem and was in the process of building a huge palace, when he was displaced by the Dutch in 1817. Today Banjarmasin and the neighbouring town of Martapura are famous for diamonds, as well as semi-precious stones such as sapphires, amethysts and agates. Surrounded by low-lying swamplands and set on and around a series of canals and waterways on which thousands of watercraft ply in and out of the city daily, Banjarmasin has spawned the nickname 'The Venice of Indonesia'. A large proportion of its population live in houses built on stilts on the banks of the Barito and Martapura rivers which converge there.

We located Bill's son-of-a-gun *Haji*, who said he would be

delighted to show us his diamond mine at Cempaka, south of Martapura. The mine was a massive gravel pit filled with water the colour of café-au-lait. To get to it from the road we had to wade across a small river. The *Haji* rolled his sarong up above his knees and strode across without a second thought. We followed much less confidently, our toes squelching rather disgustingly in the mud. Rude, corrugated iron and canvas shelters were dotted around the edge of the pit, and the place was a mass of brown water gushing from bamboo pipes, sinewy bodies and sticky red mud. Men stood chest deep in water with large conical wooden pans (*dulangs*) in which they were looking for diamonds; women picked their way through the mud carrying baskets of sludge and gravel.

'Well shee-it! Would you just look at these folk,' said Bill, a master of the sweeping generalization, 'I tell you, these Indos are such simple, unspoiled people.'

'It's like a scene from a Breughel painting,' said Donna, 'you know – one of those ones with hundreds of people busily engaged in communal effort.'

As we approached, what appeared to be four haystacks moved slowly towards us. Only as they came closer did we see that they had feet and were actually women carrying vast loads of newly cut grass. Apart from being intrigued with the diamonds, Bill was very taken with the *dulangs* and bought one from its owner for a sum which – judging by the smile on the man's face – probably meant that he could afford not to work for the next few weeks. We left virtually under siege as every other panner tried to sell his *dulang* to Donna and me!

If the mine had been straight out of Breughel, Martapura was out of a low-budget spy film. As we walked through the market, men would sidle up to us out of the shadows and pull much creased slips of paper from their pockets. 'Want to buy a diamond?' was as common an expression as 'Hello Mister' had been in Pangkalan Bun.

On the old Indonesian Rp5,000 note there is a picture of an old man sitting at a workbench examining a diamond with a magnifying glass. It is unfortunate that he has now been replaced on the new notes by Teuku Umar (a very boring Acehnese nationalist), as it is rare that one gets the opportunity to claim to have met the person depicted on a country's paper currency. But we *did* meet 'Mr Five Thousand Rupiah'. He was in a huge old diamond cutting shed at Martapura, still working at the same bench and with the shirt he had worn for the picture displayed on a hanger above his workbench. An engine outside drove an axle in the centre of the shed, which rotated a series of flywheels. The motion was transmitted by thick rubber belts and gearwork to individual workbenches, where men were polishing diamonds on wheels coated with an abrasive of diamond dust and coconut oil. The noise was deafening, even though most of the work areas were vacant.

The *Haji* was anxious to show us his workshop, so we left the noise and dust and drove to a modern, airy facility where several men were cutting diamonds with sophisticated machinery. One of them asked where Bill worked before Indonesia. 'Los Angeles,' said Bill.

'OK,' said the man, 'you take me back to Los Angeles. I very good worker, I work in your factory. Make diamonds. I drive big car and sleep on movie stars. I sleep on Meryl Streep. She very beautiful!'

'Such simple, unspoilt people!' said Donna.

The *Haji*'s anxiety to show us his workshop was, naturally, not so much for its intrinsic interest as for the fact that he had samples for sale. There were all kinds of diamonds: yellow, red, black, but Bill didn't even take out his eyeglass. 'Tourist trash!' he said.

The *Haji* looked taken aback. He talked with his assistant for a few moments, glancing every so often at Bill, who was now calmly demonstrating to one of the technicians how *he* would have cut the stone he was working on. At length the assistant said, 'The *Haji* suggests maybe you would like to have a rest now, and come to his house tomorrow. He has some gems which may interest you.'

The *Haji*'s house was a typical single-family dwelling, built out of wood with a corrugated iron roof. Inside it was split into two, with the right-hand side closed off for sleeping quarters. The left side was part room, part corridor. Chairs were arranged against

20

the walls, giving the feel of a doctor's waiting room, and at the far end a back passageway led to the kitchens. Every Indonesian house has an area at the front for receiving and entertaining guests and it is taboo for anyone not immediately connected with the family to cross the threshold into, for example, the kitchens or bedrooms beyond. I heard one story of a German anthropologist who was new to Indonesia and was eating dinner with a family in Central Kalimantan. He couldn't understand why, when he had taken the dirty dishes out into the kitchen, there had been such an uproar. He had only been trying to help!

We took off our shoes, entered the house and sat down. Dozens of children appeared and stood coyly in doorways or pressed against the walls, staring at us. Girls ranging in age from little older than the children to early adulthood also appeared, ostensibly to take care of the kids – really to stare, too. We were served thick, sweet coffee in tall glasses. At length the *Haji*'s assistant and sons appeared. The sons politely commented on how well we looked after our exhausting day yesterday, and on how well we spoke the language for people who had been in Indonesia such a short time. Eventually the *Haji* himself made an appearance. More pleasantries were exchanged. Bill was unusually calm. It was obvious he was going to play this very cool.

As if by afterthought, the *Haji* asked if we would do him the honour of glancing at a few items of jewellery his sons happened to have on them. His eldest son pulled out a long rolled-up swatch of material which had been secreted in his sarong. The rings inside were obscene; big polished pebbles (at least that's what they looked like) set in fat mountings of brass-coloured metal. Bill looked amused, but said nothing. The second son then had his turn. At least these were gemstones, though they didn't shine as jewels usually do.

'Pimp's rings,' said Bill, not attempting to disguise his contempt.

We froze. The assistant translated. He asked for elucidation of the word 'pimp' from Bill. Bill gave it. The *Haji*'s eyes narrowed. We thought he had gone too far. The room seemed quiet and stuffy, as many anxious dark brown eyes scanned the face first of the *Haji*, then of Bill, sitting there like two mirror images seen through a dark looking-glass. Then the *Haji*'s shoulders started to move, imperceptibly at first, then rhythmically, accompanied by a deep rumbling laugh. Eventually, tears came to his eyes. 'Pimp's rings,' he said in English, '*aduh!*'

The *Haji* turned to us, 'Perhaps now you would like to see what I have?' he asked, innocently.

'That's why we're here, *Haji*,' said Bill.

Bill left the owner of the biggest uncut diamond I had ever seen; gleaming yellow with individual natural crystal facets visible around its tetrahedral perimeter. To celebrate, he took us out to dinner, but the evening almost turned into a disaster. We set off in two *becaks* to a Chinese restaurant. However, when we got there the *becak* drivers informed us that as we were so heavy we had to pay four times the price we had previously agreed. We didn't mind paying over the odds, but this was ridiculous. We refused. A crowd gathered. As we were near a spot where *becaks* gathered for fares, the crowd was less than sympathetic. Voices were raised, but we had no idea what was being said. Just as it seemed that things were getting out of control, the crowd dispersed, as a policeman carrying an automatic rifle arrived to investigate the disturbance. One of our *becak* drivers was still haranguing Bill in a stream of indignant Indonesian when the policeman tapped him on the shoulder. As soon as he saw him, the man disappeared like a ruptured balloon.

'Now look here, officer,' said Bill, 'we agreed to pay these bastards Rp500 each and now they say we have to pay Rp2,000 each. That's damn disgraceful.'

Yes, he agreed, it was disgraceful. But, as in all aspects of life, there was room for compromise. Would we consider Rp1,000 to be a fair tariff – under the circumstances? He fingered his rifle.

Oh yes, we agreed; Rp1,000 was more than fair. We placed three Rp1,000 notes into his outstretched hand and walked quickly into the restaurant, not wanting to know in whose pocket the money would end up.

Grateful to be in the restaurant and not in the local hospital, we poured Anker beer into our glasses while Bill expounded his theory about policemen. Indonesian police, he said, had modelled their uniforms on those worn by the California

Highway Patrol – even down to the detail of extremely tight
trousers, which must have been excruciatingly uncomfortable in
the hot and steamy near-equatorial climate. His theory was that
it was these uncomfortable pants – mixed with a diet of coffee and
sugary doughnuts in the case of the CHP – that made cops so
damn mean! At that instant our friendly policeman walked into
the restaurant and sat down at our table, without asking
permission. He laid his rifle on the table and picked up Bill's
Nikon camera.

'I would like a camera like this.'

'And I would like a gun like that,' said Bills.

The policeman looked at Bill without smiling. He was, he said,
a boxing champion, as were all the men from his village in
Ambon in the Moluccas. Since Indonesia currently had a world
boxing champion – Elly Pical, the latest national hero who would
probably replace Teuku Umar on the Rp5,000 note if he kept
winning – who did come from Ambon, we could scarcely
disagree. Eventually, when it was established that he was going
to have to be content with just *liking* Bill's camera, he left us to get
on with our meal.

We left the restaurant in the middle of a tropical downpour.
These have to be experienced to be believed. After a fierce,
whipping wind, the rain thunders down in angry sheets, hitting
pavement and roof with extraordinary force, and if you are
unlucky enough to be caught outside it soaks you to the skin in
seconds. It can even bruise exposed skin. None of the *becak* drivers
sheltering under the awnings opposite appeared interested in us
and there were no taxis in sight. Finally we managed to hail a
bemo (the universal taxi/short distance bus of Indonesia, which
ranges from little more than a covered pick-up on the outer
islands to a luxury mini-bus on Bali).

'How much?'

'Five thousand.'

'Five thousand? Too much,' said Bill, winding himself up for a
bargaining session.

'Shut up and get in!' said Donna, already dripping.

'So, where are you guys headed next?' asked Bill, shouting
above the noise of the rain on the roof.

We told him we thought we would go to Ujung Pandang in South Sulawesi, from where we planned to go up to Tanah Toraja, home to an extraordinary culture where elaborate death rituals were still practised.

'You choose the damnedest places! Why can't you go to Bali like everyone else?'

2. Blood and biscuits

Sulawesi – Tanah Toraja

'. . . Where the buffalo foam?' mused Donna in, considering the
circumstances, a valiant attempt at humour. We were both
staring down at a football-sized organ which had once formed
part of the digestive system of a buffalo. Inside it, partly digested
grass was still bubbling and fermenting under the hot sun and the
mud-coloured organ gave occasional burps and farts, erupting a
lava of green foam.

We were standing in hell. Around us the eviscerated corpses of
six buffaloes were spread out on palm leaves. A group of about
twenty men were squatting on their haunches rhythmically
chopping with machete-like *parangs* at the flesh, pushing it into
small slippery piles of similar looking body parts. A huge pile of
yellowy intestines coiled like rope on one side. Livers the size of
small clouds were starting to harden and turn brown in the sun.
Some of the men tied up handfuls of entrails with string and
distributed them to a waiting line of people. The choicer cuts –
including the rear leg joints reserved for village notables – had
already gone, as had several large bamboo containers full of
blood for making black pudding. The air was thick with the sickly
smell of carnage. A row of severed heads stared at us sightlessly
from under a haze of flies. Mouths agape, they still had the look of
betrayed trust they had had at their death.

An old man with dark eyes, sunken cheeks and arms red to the
elbows came over and gestured to me. Small slivers of meat stuck
to his torso were being feasted on greedily by squabbling flies. All
in all I found it fairly hard to concentrate on what he was trying
to tell me.

'I think he wants a cigarette,' said Donna.

25

'I haven't got one – what shall I do?' I hissed through clenched teeth, and smiled weakly at the man. We hadn't been in Indonesia long, but basic survival instinct screamed at me that it was not a good idea to put someone standing in front of you covered in blood and wielding a *parang* in a bad humour.

'*Maaf, Pak. Tidak ada*,' (Sorry, I haven't got one) I said, trying very hard not to be sick, and was relieved when he simply shrugged and went back to his work.

We were in Tanah Toraja (Torajaland), an area nestled in the mountains of Central Sulawesi, and home to one of the strangest cultures in a nation of strange cultures. It was turning out to be everything we expected. And more.

There is a conspiracy amongst writers on Sulawesi to describe it either as 'orchid-shaped' or 'like a swastika', making it the Rorschach test of the Indonesian archipelago. Actually, it looks like a letter 'K' with the vertical stroke leaning over to the right. It is such an odd-looking island that when it was discovered by the Portuguese they refused to believe it was one island and called it 'The Celebes'. Its very long coastline coupled with its small surface area (in direct contrast to neighbouring Borneo) should have made it the most accessible of Indonesian islands from the sea, but the absence of large navigable rivers, and the rugged topography of its mountainous interior, has allowed the strange Torajan customs and beliefs to evolve in splendid isolation.

On our way to Tanah Toraja, we stopped in Ujung Pandang, near the south-western tip of Sulawesi. Previously known as Makassar, the town was once a household word in nineteenth-century Europe as the source of the hair oil that ruined many a Victorian hostess's best chair backs until 'antimacassars' were invented.

Ujung Pandang was formerly the capital of the Makassarese people. The Makassarese kingdom of Gowa was a major trading power in the sixteenth and seventeenth centuries until it was conquered by the Dutch who built Fort Rotterdam there in 1667. The Fort is still there and worth a visit. The Dutch lured the great nationalist Prince Diponegoro into captivity in 1830 and kept him a prisoner in Fort Rotterdam for twenty-six years. There was a hideous 'art exhibition' in progress during our visit of 'bijou' pastoral scenes made out of grass, sticks and plastic displayed in glass-fronted boxes. We asked several people if we could see the permanent exhibition in the museum, but were continually referred back to this collection of 'contemporary art' as being far more interesting!

Ujung Pandang is nowadays largely inhabited by the Bugis people – the original pirates of South-East Asia. The Bugis are regarded as the 'Vikings of Indonesia' and, like the Vikings, their superb seamanship took them thousands of kilometres from Sulawesi – probably as far as Australia, and certainly as far as Singapore where the famous street of transvestites named after them catered to many a sailor far from home. Torres found Bugis traders in New Guinea in 1603. While Torres had only one strait named after him, there is usually a *Jalan Bugis* (Bugis Street) in every major town throughout Indonesia, often near the docks.

We had plenty of time to look around the city, as our flight to Tanah Toraja didn't leave until the following day. We engaged a guide called Fan, who recommended a visit to Paotere harbour to see the fantastic Bugis schooners (*pinisi*) being offloaded. Several stood at anchor, their crews idly waiting for an improvement in the winds before departing. I felt as if I had suddenly wandered onto the set for a pirate movie. Craning my neck to look at the tall masts, I half-expected to see a skull and crossbones flying; as it was, a young Bugis crewman was shinning up the rigging to set a sail faster than I could thread a needle. These massive vessels, with their magnificent prows sweeping outward and upward and meeting several metres above the water, are a remnant from a bygone age. They have changed little in basic design for hundreds of years, but are still in daily use for transporting cargo from one island to another.

The atmosphere and excitement of the harbour made me half-wish that I could stow away for a trip round the islands, but Fan soon quashed that idea.

'If there is woman on board,' he explained, 'the boat will be jealous and she capsize. The only time that sometimes a woman can go on ship is if she first sacrifice a chicken to appease the boat, then – maybe she can sail on it.'

The only time he had been on board a *pinisi*, he said, a knife-fight had broken out after three days at sea because the cook had forgotten to bring the *sambal* (the chilli sauce which is used to spice up an otherwise monotonous diet of boiled rice and fish).

One swarthy boatman, lying curled up in a coil of multi-coloured plastic ropes, asked Donna where she was from. 'Amerika?! OK, I take you there . . .!' and he gave a gap-toothed grin that made him look every inch a buccaneer.

'You'd need a lot of *sambal* to get one of these to Portland, boy,' said Donna.

Intent on showing us all the wonders of Ujung Pandang, Fan suggested we go to the Bundt seashell and orchid collection. It sounded singularly unexciting, but Fan was insistent. 'Nowhere bigger than this,' he said confidently. In a sense, he was right. The seashell collection was truly astounding. Not so much for the quality of the collection as for the quantity. There seemed to be hundreds of every type, all virtually identical. We asked Fan what one particularly beautiful shell was. '*Not* the "Glory of the Seas",' he said. OK, but what *was* it? He persisted, 'Not the "Glory of the Seas". That one not, too,' he pointed at a different shaped one, 'not that one. *None* of these "Glory of the Seas",' he finished proudly, making a sweeping gesture with his arm and walking out into the orchid garden.

That evening, at the hotel bar, we were greeted by a gracious barman who told us he was from Komodo. 'I am nice to meet you,' he said effusively, smiling broadly and exposing an impressive row of teeth that would have shamed any of the dragons from his native island. 'Please sit down and drinking my special juices. I am "on the house" to newcomers.' He handed us a sinister-looking concoction in a tall glass. A wilted frangipani blossom floated on top of bright pink liquid which had things resembling small worms swimming around in it. These – to our immense relief – turned out to be slivers of coconut flesh. Some tastes defy description. It tasted thick – and sweet – and yes, pink.

A large billboard in the lobby invited us to 'tip your toes to the sophisticated sounds of Boy Fattah' while we enjoyed our dinner. Anxious to avoid this at all costs, we went to eat well before Boy Fattah was scheduled to appear. As the sky turned an extraordinary shade of coral, a *pinisi* tacked backwards and forwards trying to make its way across the harbour against the prevailing breeze. Having feasted on the sunset for twenty minutes, it occurred to us that that was the only feasting we were likely to do unless the waitress came and took our order. Donna caught her eye.

'What you want?'

'We'd like to order some food.' The waitress looked bemused. 'You *are* a waitress, aren't you?' said Donna, wondering if she had caught the eye of an unsuspecting guest by mistake.

The waitress returned a few minutes later to tell us that nothing we had ordered was available. In exasperation, I pointed to a couple at a nearby table who had just been served steaming plates of delicious smelling food. 'We'll have what they're having,' I said. The waitress looked worried, and walked off in the direction of the other table. Donna looked satisfied. 'Well at least we know that that's on tonight's men--' Her sentence was lost in a cry of anguish from the next table as the waitress wrestled with the bemused diners for their food.

At 1.30 in the morning I awoke to the sound of loud American voices. I was vaguely aware of Donna standing at the window. 'Looks like the Fleet's in,' she said.

In the street below were four large Americans in naval uniform. They were seated in *becaks* arranged in a rough laager and surrounded by a crowd of interested locals. The sailors were conducting a conversation at the decibel level necessary during test-firing of twelve-inch naval guns. 'You a baa-ad muthafukka, you know that? A baa-ad, baa-ad, muthafukka!!!' The sailor to whom this was addressed chuckled appreciatively. It was evidently a compliment. Another sailor struggled out of his *becak*. None of the Americans was less than six foot tall; this one was at least six foot three. He was also very drunk. He swayed a little, then walked up to the 'muthafukka' and put his hands on his hips. At this an appreciative ripple ran through the audience. Indonesians do not put their hands on their hips while talking – it is the attitude of defiance in Indonesian *wayang* (puppet) plays and means contempt for the person to whom you are talking. 'You ain't nuthin', man! You ain't nuthin' but nuthin'! I *own* you,

29

man!' In comparison to what had previously been said this seemed relatively mild, but evidently it wasn't. 'Muthafukka' got out of his *becak* with considerable difficulty. He was slightly shorter than his antagonist, but had muscles like a weightlifter. When it was test-firing time he obviously carried the twelve-inch shells to the gun. He pointed in the other man's face – another thing Indonesians don't do. 'You don' say that, man, you don' say that! Uh, no man, you don' say that . . .!'

The two men danced round each other, adopting menacing poses from kung-fu movies and weaving and bobbing. The crowd were loving it. Suddenly both men seemed to lose impetus. They returned to their *becaks* and slumped inside, the wind evidently having gone from their sails. At this point, the *becak* drivers offered to take them somewhere where – drunk and incapable – they would probably have their wallets stolen. They agreed with as much collective free-will as a swarm of lemmings heading for the cliff. 'Anchors aweigh, guys!' said Donna, as we watched their *becaks* disappearing round the corner.

The next day we took the Merpati flight from Hasanuddin airport to Pongkitu. As in the United States, airports in Indonesia are often named after people. Hasanuddin was the Sultan of Gowa, who resisted the Dutch attempts to gain a spice monopoly in the seventeenth century. Who Pongkitu was I have no idea. The flight took only half an hour, but it gave us a good preview of the sort of landscape we were to look forward to. Our little plane hummed along, passing a giant's jawbone of jagged limestone peaks on either side. In the valley below, the outlines of thousands of rice-terraces looked like a patchwork quilt crafted in myriad shades of green and yellow. And in the midst of it all were clusters of traditional Torajan houses and rice-barns.

The 'airport' was a level piece of ground between the mountains; the 'arrivals lounge' a cattle-byre with a huge black and white buffalo in it. Tanah Toraja is one of the most beautiful and prosperous regions of Indonesia. At a cool, high elevation, set in the valley of the sinuous sparkling Sadang River, the area is a mass of emerald rice-terraces carved between craggy limestone mountains. The area is so fertile that alternate fields will be golden with rice ripe for harvesting, while adjacent fields will be still green and others still being planted out. The Torajan people are mostly farmers, cultivating more than enough rice to sustain their families for the year. Their day starts before dawn when they wend their way to the *padi*-fields and ends when they return home at sundown.

Rice cultivation in Indonesia is as varied as the people, but certain general beliefs hold. One is that only women should transplant the young rice shoots from the nursery (a small square of the *padi* that is replanted with seed at the same time as the seedlings are transplanted to the main *padi*), because they will endow part of their fertility to the ground. Another is that rice should be harvested stalk by stalk with a small wooden-backed razor held hidden in the crook of the hand so that the rice goddess can't see it coming! In Tanah Toraja, they gather the rice together in sheaves of about twenty stalks which are then arranged on the ground in fan shapes to dry. Just outside our hotel were several attractive golden 'haystacks' of rice – about four feet high – which had been stacked preparatory to cracking the husk from the rice and winnowing the grain from the chaff.

A large black buffalo standing nearby was having a very hard time reaching the short grass. Life had dealt him a cruel blow by endowing him with an extraordinary pair of down-turned horns, which were magnificent but utterly impractical as they hit the ground each time he bent his head to graze. For the Torajan people the buffalo is a symbol of wealth and status, which rises proportionately with the number of buffaloes a family possesses. The more buffaloes sacrificed at your funeral, the better 'afterlife' you will have. Even among buffaloes, however, there is a class system. Black-and-white buffaloes command prices ten to twenty times the price of an ordinary plain black buffalo, while pure white ones – which are very rare – are almost invaluable and *cannot* be sacrificed.

According to Fan, there is a legend which explains why the white buffalo is so revered. Long ago, apparently, a King of Tanah Toraja had to make a very long journey. In his travels, he came to a river which was so wide he couldn't cross it. A white buffalo appeared and told the King he could ride on his back, on the condition that the King must promise never to kill a white

31

buffalo. In Tanah Toraja, white is the equivalent of what blue is to British royalty or purple was to ancient Rome. It is the colour of aristocracy. Nobles of the *puang* or highest caste are said to have 'white blood'. They are forbidden to eat not only the meat of the white buffalo, but also white chickens and – for some unexplained reason – the giant river eel.

All this is part of *Aluk Todolo* (literally, 'ceremonies of the ancestors'), which is the animist religion of Tanah Toraja. Following the arrival of Protestant missionaries in 1913, most Torajans converted to Christianity, and some to Islam, but as we were to find repeatedly throughout Indonesia, the original beliefs remain solid and unchanged.

We were staying in a hotel built in the shape of a traditional *tongkonan* house. These are massive, wooden structures that look sturdy enough to survive for centuries, and are so skilfully crafted that they are constructed entirely without the use of nails. Raised off the ground on tall piles, the most stunning feature of the *tongkonan* house is its mighty roof, which sweeps upwards at either end like a magnificent pair of buffalo horns and is painstakingly constructed with layer upon layer of split bamboo.

There are numerous theories as to why the people of Tanah Toraja should have built their houses in this extraordinary way. The most common explanation, and the one that Fan gave us, was that when the ancestors of the Torajans came to Sulawesi, they dragged their boats up onto the beach and slept under them, which, in his words, 'give rise to this architect'. An alternative story – and one which goes down well with the 'is God an astronaut?' crowd – is that the original inhabitants of Tanah Toraja came in spaceships from the Pleiades. Their houses are shaped like the starships in which they made the journey. We tried this one on Fan, who looked at us incredulously, then giggled in an irritating way for the rest of the day.

The first traditional Torajan village we visited was Nangalla, which had a veritable fleet of *tongkonan* houses – fourteen in all – arranged in a line. Many were so old that they had vegetation – ferns mostly – growing out of the roofs. Each house had a central front pillar to which dozens of bleached white buffalo horns had been attached. Fan was ready with an explanation: 'Every time there is ceremony and buffalo is killed, the family keep the horns and attach to the house. So everyone can see how rich they are. Also it is symbol of fertility and strength,' he added uncertainly, 'I think.'

No *tongkonan* house is complete without the decorative carvings which cover the exterior. These are mostly geometrical, but are interspersed with the recurring motifs of buffaloes, chickens and other symbols of Torajan life. The designs are painted in four colours: black to symbolize death and the underworld; yellow which is associated with the blessing of gods; white which is the symbol of purity and the upper world; and red, denoting human life, which strikes a balance between the others.

Facing the houses, looking like a row of stocky *tongkonan* offspring, was a line of rice-barns. The rice is stored about two metres off the ground in an enclosed storage area which stands on six stout pillars. These are extremely smooth and slippery, making it impossible for mice and rats to climb up to the stored rice, unless they happen to have a set of mini-crampons handy! Each rice-barn has a sturdy platform underneath which the corpse is placed during funerals but, more routinely, where village men gather for meetings. Fan explained that each pillar was reserved for men of differing rank to lean against. Because heaven is believed to be to the south, only the village chief is allowed to lean his back against the southernmost pillar.

We were immediately surrounded by a group of excitable children, and it soon became clear that they were very used to having foreigners around. For some reason, more than any other part of Indonesia, Tanah Toraja is very popular with the French. One little girl grabbed Donna's hand and, looking up appealingly at her with huge dark eyes, said, '*Je t'aime maman, avez-vous les bonbons?*'

'I'm not French,' said Donna, 'and I haven't got any damn bonbons.'

Undeterred, the little girl let go of Donna's left hand, ran round, grabbed her right hand and said, 'Mommy, I love you. Give me sweets.'

'Look, kid, I haven't got any.'

'Give me sweets! Give me pencil! Give me money!' said the

little pest. 'Give me tupperware!' Tupperware? I was still
pondering where she had got that one from when Fan ushered us
away. 'Come, we must go to see the gravies at Lemo. Come!'

Torajans believe that when they go to the heaven they call *puya*,
they will have the same level of prosperity as they had on earth.
Also, it is believed that your riches *can* be taken with you, so many
valuables, as well as practical items like hats and baskets, are
buried with the coffin. After an elaborate funeral, the dead are
taken to their final resting place, the location of which will vary
depending on the wealth of the deceased. The higher the grave,
the more prized the location, as the deceased will be nearer to the
upper world (and further from the reach of grave-robbers!) At
Lemo village there is a massive limestone cliff, into which dozens of
square tombs have been chiselled. Each tomb has its own wooden
door, making the cliff face look like a child's advent calendar.

Also chiselled into the cliff are several 'galleries', inside which
stand wooden effigies of the deceased called *tau-tau* (meaning not
quite human or puppet-like). They stand motionless, gazing out
from their galleries like ghostly spectators at a football match that
will never be played. *Tau-tau* function as the representative of the
dead person and the receptacle for its spirit, should it ever wish to
pop back to earth for a visit.

The *tau-tau* are dressed in the deceaseds' clothes, which are
changed from time to time by relatives when they disintegrate
with age. Sadly – and suggesting that nowadays tourist dollars
are more prized than traditional spiritual values – many of these
wonderful effigies have been stolen to sell to wealthy tourists. In
fact Fan informed us that several of those at Lemo had
disappeared just before our arrival. Unfortunately, the *tau-tau*
cannot simply be replaced with copies. An elaborate ritual has to
be gone through, and *tau-tau* spend the lying-in period between
death and burial with the deceased.

Fan took us to see many 'gravies'. Many, like those at Lemo,
were chiselled into the cliffs, while others hung from the cliff on
scaffolding platforms. We also went to a large water-scoured
limestone cave containing hundreds of coffins. The wooden
coffins and sarcophagi eventually rot, of course, and the cave was
so full of skulls and bones that it looked like the site of a gruesome

genocidal massacre. One coffin had a macabre skull half-emerging from a hole in the bottom, giving a hideous toothy grin, while a partly decomposed skeleton festered, covered in dust and cobwebs, in another.

Babies (or, as Fan put it, 'children without teeth') are buried inside specially hollowed trees. The ones we saw grew in the midst of a bamboo copse, and had white and yellow epiphytic orchids growing from them. It was rather peaceful except for the zinging – not to mention stinging – of monstrous mosquitoes, who had appointed themselves guardians of the tombs.

☆

That night at the hotel we met Gail. Gail was a Californian in her mid-forties, twice-divorced, and was travelling with a tour group. The group consisted of two married couples and a single man – Charles – who, Gail was convinced, was a sex-fiend and had joined the tour with the express intention of getting her into bed. In hushed, conspiratorial tones, Gail described how he was always following her around and how he had tried several times to sit next to her on the bus and *engage her in conversation.*

'Kinda hard not to on a tour isn't it?' said Donna, but Gail ignored this.

'I tell you, he's only after one thing . . .'

'A glance at your guidebook, perhaps?' I said, but Gail chose to ignore this, too, and rattled on at length about all his supposed attempts at seduction.

The Charles of Gail's fantasies looked terribly meek and mild and, we noticed, kept his nose firmly stuck in a book – though whether this was because it was a particularly good book, or he was trying to avoid Gail, we were never sure. We soon tired of Gail and her pathetic fantasies, and retired to bed.

'Put me down if I ever get to be like that, will you?' said Donna.

Next day we went to the covered market at Rantepao. Markets are fun just about anywhere in Indonesia, and filled with colours, textures and activity. Returning the friendly smiles and greetings that we had now come to expect from the infinitely hospitable Indonesian people, we wandered through the huge market with the aroma of coriander, turmeric and ginger tickling our nostrils, feasting on the diversity of sights around us. Stall after stall was filled with colourful vegetables: aubergines, bright red and green chilli peppers, tomatoes, cabbages. Others sold water melon, pineapples, apples, rice, eggs, maize, chicken pieces, beef and goat meat. In addition to plastic household goods, there was ironware for sale, too, particularly swords and *kerises* (snake-shaped ornamental daggers). Men walked by toting frothing bamboo containers of *balok* (palm wine, called *tuak* elsewhere in Indonesia) like rifles.

A variety of banana called *unti darek* was also for sale. We had seen it growing and remarked on the flower, which is yellow instead of the more common dark blue. The bananas themselves were unusually fat, and had very thick skins. Unlike pineapples, bananas are indigenous to Indonesia and there are hundreds of weird and wonderful varieties available – from tiny finger-sized ones to some the size of one's forearm, and from bright red, through the more usual yellow, to brown covered with hair! There is a saying in Indonesia that 'a banana tree will not bear fruit twice', which is the equivalent of the English 'opportunity only knocks once'. Fan told us about a tree in North Sumatra which actually *did* bear fruit twice. It caused so much excitement amongst the superstitious locals that a village elder had had to cover the second crop with a white cloth to calm fears of an impending catastrophe!

Markets are often the place to see traditional textiles and basket-ware, and the strongest, most durable hats in Indonesia were for sale in Rantepao. Hat design varies greatly from island to island. In many parts of Indonesia they don't wear hats at all, just headscarves tied in a variety of unlikely ways. Torajan hats are the classical shallow conical shape and are completely waterproof and insulated from the sun by having an underlying coarsely woven layer with another finer layer on top. The best ones were reputed to come from a nearby leprosy village, though the vendor from which I bought mine denied this vehemently; presumably because he thought I wouldn't buy it if I thought it had been made by a leper!

Dozens of little pigs lay on the ground with their legs trussed with bamboo twine, and squealed pathetically as they were taken away to an untimely death. These, Fan told us, were ready to be taken to a funeral as sacrificial gifts.

'Fan, is there any chance of *us* going to a funeral?' asked Donna. One of our aims was to see how much of the original animist religion still existed, so we were eager to witness a funeral.

'I'm not sure,' he replied, 'you'll be very lucky to see one, but I'll ask around and see if there will be one coming up.'

At Kete'kesu, the dark, rather forbidding houses contrasted starkly with the rich golden piles of freshly gathered rice which lay drying in the last rays of the dying sun. This particular village had 'traditional' souvenir shops operating from the traditional houses. I bought an ebony cane from one old lady, who was so pleased by the sale that she invited us into her house. For dwellings which looked so huge from the outside, the actual living space inside is comparatively cramped. It was sparsely furnished with just a table, a stool and a large bed. On the other hand, it shared one important characteristic with all the other traditional Indonesian houses we were to visit: it was wonderfully cool.

☆

Back at the hotel we found Gail still obsessed with Charles, and armed with more imagined evidence of his evil intentions. She had been out for a stroll the previous night, she said, and when she came back into the hotel had found him '*in the reception, reading*'. Donna and I looked at each other aghast. As the light in the rooms was so bad – and it was notably brighter in the reception area – it made perfect sense to *us* that if someone wished to read, they would do so there. But Gail was convinced that he had been waiting there all night ready to jump her when she came in from her walk. Poor, meek Charles! He didn't look capable of jumping a place in a queue, let alone the formidable Gail.

That night the management of the hotel had rather mistakenly decided to put on a 'cultural evening', and we watched uncomfortably as two old men shuffled about in warrior dress giving belligerent grunts while waving their swords in the air. I only hope it was a mockery; I would hate to think of that as being an authentic Torajan folk dance.

Fan arrived the next morning looking noticeably pleased with himself. 'I have found a funeral for you!' he announced. 'It is some way from here and so we must leave straightaways.'

The trip there was arduous and bumpy, but it gave us a chance to experience more of the spectacular Torajan scenery; golden *padi*-fields, sparkling riverwater, and lines of jagged hills becoming progressively bluer in the distance. I was a little concerned that we would be intruding at such an intimate and private ceremony, but Fan assured us that our presence would not be resented, but would rather reflect well upon the family giving the funeral.

A line of people dressed in black were slowly wending their way through the *padis* when we arrived, walking towards a distant village, which had been draped with red banners to indicate a funeral was taking place. Some carried pigs like those we had seen in the market, trussed and swinging from long bamboo poles which they carried over their shoulders. Others bore chickens and smaller gifts. We joined the solemn procession.

'No way! I can't go in there!' cried Donna suddenly with her hand over her mouth and her face visibly pale despite the heat. 'I just don't think I can handle it.' Buffaloes are always slaughtered at Torajan funerals, and as soon as we had entered the village we had been confronted by the sight of six of them on the verge of being sent to graze in the vast *padi*-field in the sky.

A steady procession of guests streamed into the small village in two parallel lines – one male, one female. They all wore black and the women's heads were covered with black shawls. Two small children stood at the entrance of the village to greet them. The little girl was immaculately made-up, her hair swept back under a bandanna of red and gold. She had on a royal blue sarong and blouse, with a bright beadwork necklace which ended in tassels. An enormous *keris* in a gold sheath was tucked into her belt, which she fiddled with constantly, though I noticed she never removed it. Indonesians, like Gurkhas, believe that certain knives have magic properties; if you remove a *keris* from its sheath, you have to touch a wall or something hard with it – otherwise it will look for flesh.

A 'professional mourner' with a primitive PA system played

wailing noises which, we were told, was 'sad music'. He broadcast these by pointing his microphone at an old cassette-recorder with fading batteries. The feedback was excruciating. Every so often he would be handed an updated list of mourners from the ledger desk and would read out their names (and, I assume, gifts) over the public address system.

Despite Donna's reluctance, Fan ushered us in past a table where gifts from the visiting relatives were being entered into a ledger, and on into the house of the man who had died. Donna committed an understandable faux pas by commiserating with the widow on her husband's death. 'Illness,' hissed Fan. 'They believe that until the funeral is over he not "dead" yet – only very sick.'

'Well, someone in there is,' said Donna, holding a tissue over her nose.

Torajans consider that when someone dies they are still in the world of the living. They have a delightful expression for this: *unnelong lendong*, or 'lying waving like an eel'. The corpse is even served three meals a day and occasionally friends or relatives will drop in for a chat and a cigarette! As we were later to find with the Dayaks, a person is not buried immediately after death. Not only must all kinds of rituals and ceremonies be conducted before the deceased can journey safely to the 'afterlife', but in practical terms the family must have time to collect sufficient funds to hold an adequately elaborate funeral and feed and entertain the hundreds of relatives who will attend. In this particular case, the man had been dead for a little over eighteen months, though it is not unknown for a body to lie waiting for many years for its transportation to *puya*, 'the land of souls'.

The body had been wrapped in many metres of cloth, presumably to prevent it from smelling too badly, though Torajans take other steps to prevent the inevitable smell of the decomposing body from permeating the household. When someone is about to die, a magician is hastily summoned. He catches the last dying breath in a bamboo tube, the mouth of which is then covered with a piece of black cloth and thrown into the forest. As the smell has been removed to the forest, the family will not be bothered by it.

'Quite logical really,' said Donna, and suggested that we do the same with our laundry at the hotel.

Fan started to describe a special functionary who is deputed to deal with maggots, but the concept was wholly too horrible to contemplate and we stopped him before he could elaborate.

We witnessed the bloody and horrible slaughter of the buffaloes from a temporary shelter for guests, which had been draped with red cloth for the occasion. Each animal was carefully positioned to face south, after which its throat was cut with a *parang*. This, to our dismay, was done by hacking at it several times rather than by cutting it smoothly. After the sacrifice of the first bewildered buffalo, the human corpse was thrown into the air to release its spirit, and then placed with its head towards its ultimate destination (*puya*). This, I have to confess, we missed, as we were busy trying not to throw up while the rest of the buffaloes were slaughtered in a bloody, struggling frenzy, and bamboo containers were forced into their carotid arteries to collect the blood.

While this carnage was going on, we were offered tea and biscuits. It was as if the ghastly scene unfolding before us was just an everyday event – which, of course, it is for the Torajan people. Donna and I felt as shocked and sickened as if we had wandered into a scene from *Hallowe'en, Part X*. We nibbled numbly on the biscuits and sipped the sweet tea, which Donna pointed out was really quite appropriate as it was an age-old remedy for shock.

One of the other guests was an army officer who had flown in from some remote island posting, as he was a distant kinsman of the deceased. As we watched the guests still trickling into the village, the army officer suddenly came out with a quite unintended *double entendre*, which caused us both to choke on our biscuits. He uttered in English what we took to be a complete non-sequitur: 'We Toraja-men are very proud of our cocks!' After a moment's shock, I realized that he wasn't attempting to brag to the two foreign women sitting beside him, but was referring to the men filing past with cockerels tucked under their arms as gifts. Donna and I started laughing, which must have seemed extremely rude, and then, to make things worse, Donna made the mistake of trying to explain what we *thought* he had meant. Not knowing the technical vocabulary, Donna got herself hopelessly involved in an absurd – and most embarrassing – pantomime. It was shortly after this that we decided to leave. The quasi-human screams of pigs being butchered wafted across the *padis* as we walked back to the road.

That night I went for a walk in the cool evening air before dinner. It was Sunday and a nearby church was resonating with hymn singing that sounded like a Maori choir. Fireflies were nestling in the trees as people walked home from the fields carrying cut rice in strong baskets on their backs. I stopped to watch a man and his wife pounding coffee in a large wooden mortar, as a large black sow nearby was giving apparently endless birth to a huge litter of piglets. In the distant green *padis*, two children were wending their way home on the backs of two black buffaloes, and I was struck by the undeniable magic of Indonesia – the timelessness, the natural beauty, the grit and determination of its people, the diversity of its culture.

We noticed that Charles was absent from the table at dinner that night. Gail waved at us and gave us a knowing look. The poor man was probably resting in a state of nervous exhaustion, but Gail soon confided her latest theory. 'He's gone too far this time,' she said.

'Where is he?' Donna asked with feigned interest.

'*In his room!*' said Gail meaningfully.

'Oh.'

'Oh, indeed!' exclaimed Gail.

'Oh, indeed, what?' I said irritably.

'Well, don't you see?' said Gail. 'He's obviously waiting for me to go there . . .'

'Why don't you?' asked Donna.

'Because he won't open the door,' said Gail.

☆

We arrived half an hour before our flight was due to leave from Pongkitu airfield. His duties as guide now over, Fan left us standing there feeling rather foolish, with the thought occurring to us that we had only his word that a plane was going to arrive to pick us up! The scheduled departure time came and went. The only flying object that hove into view was a black-naped kingfisher, which was greedily watching multicoloured dragonflies flit over the field. Finally a plane appeared on the horizon, landed and disgorged several passengers. It took off again almost immediately with us on board, but heading north, rather than towards its scheduled destination of Ujung Pandang.

Ten minutes later, we began an unscheduled descent towards a large grassy field on which several horses were grazing. We were, apparently, at Masamba. A cluster of houses near the field spewed forth several hundred people, mostly children, who swarmed towards the plane even before it had taxied to a halt. From the midst of the throng came the unmistakable shape of an Indonesian VIP (dressed in a politician's safari suit and looking as if he had attended too many official luncheons), who strode purposefully towards the plane and got on board.

The children, already over-excited to the point of hysteria by the plane's arrival and the politician's visit, suddenly spotted Donna and me and erupted into totally uncontrolled screaming, which went beyond delight into fever. Though we didn't realize it then, the next time that would happen to us it would end in bloodshed. As soon as a path could be cleared through the mob, the plane took off, now heading in the right direction.

Our trials were not yet over, however. We had a long wait at Hasanuddin airport for our flight on to Ambon. I was peacefully ensconced in the departure lounge trying, with the aid of a dictionary, to translate a copy of Agatha Christie's *Sepuluh Anak Negro* (literally translated as 'Ten Negro Children') which I had just bought at the bookstall, when I heard Donna's voice raised in alarm from the other side of the security gate. She had suddenly realized that she had left her carry-on bag behind at the check-in desk and had gone back to retrieve it. Unfortunately, in trying to explain what she was doing in her hazardous Indonesian, she had said: '*Saya hanya mencoba mencuri tas ini.*' ('I was just trying to steal this bag') instead of '*Saya hanya mencoba mencari tas ini.*' ('I was just trying to look for this bag').

'For God's sake, Donna, are you trying to get us arrested?'

'Well, of course not. Anyway, they wouldn't have arrested me. They don't do that sort of thing to tourists.'

Or so she thought. As we sat patiently waiting for the flight to be called, a young policeman was just arriving for work at Ambon airport. He was not in a good mood, and our arrival would give him just the excuse he needed to take his ill humour out on someone else.

3. Over the volcano

The Spice Islands

'Choice is simple. You get back on plane and fly back to Ujung Pandang or I will arrest you.'

The surly young policeman's lip curled into a smile. He leaned back in his chair and closed our passports with an air of finality. I looked at Donna. She was sweating so much that the perspiration was dripping in a steady stream off the end of her nose. We were standing in a stuffy, unairconditioned office at Ambon airport; so tiny that there was room only for a small wooden desk, a chair and us. However, news of this confrontation between the local police and two *touris* had spread like a contagious disease, and dozens of people had crammed into the miniscule room, while others leaned through the open door watching the exchange with what I felt was some sympathy for us.

According to the policeman, the Moluccas was a 'closed area' and we needed a *surat jalan* (travel document) even to leave the airport. Our plane from Ujung Pandang had hit tremendous turbulence; the sensation of which was similar to being caught in the wake of a speedboat in a dugout canoe, except, of course, one feels a lot more vulnerable at 27,000 feet *above* sea level! As a result, our nerves were strung pretty taut by the time we landed, and this confrontation with officialdom was the last thing either of us felt able to cope with.

In stilted Indonesian, I tried to plead our case: 'We only want to stay in Ambon one night; we're going to Banda Neira tomorrow. It's cost us a lot of money to get here. We can't just turn round and go back. You must let us in!'

He shook his head. '*Tidak bisa.*' (Not possible.) Despite this, I thought I had noticed a flicker of interest when I had mentioned

44

the word 'money'.

Donna looked as if she were about to collapse. The crowd murmured and shifted uneasily. We appeared to have reached an impasse, so, clearing my throat, I said quietly: 'Er, maybe we could, er, *find* a *surat jalan* here in this office . . .'

The implication was clear. Without looking up, rolling his pen systematically between two fingers, he replied: '*Mungkin*' (which means both 'possibly' *and* 'probably' in Indonesian!), and waved the crowd out of earshot. Donna perked up slightly. 'Well that's more like it! How much would one usually, er, cost?' she asked.

'That depends . . .'

We looked at each other. I took two notes out of my wallet and laid them down on the desk. The policeman re-opened our passports, copied down our names and dates of birth and handed them back to us.

'But what about the *surat jalan*?' Donna asked. The policeman looked surprised.

'*Tidak usah.*' (Not necessary.)

Donna was just girding herself for a very unwise argument, when a young man with bad skin, shifty eyes and a marked family resemblance to the policeman bustled into the tiny office. 'Come, come! I take you into Ambon City in airport limousine.'

'No, that's OK,' said Donna smiling. 'We'll take the bus.'

At this, the policeman stood up and, in a way that suggested there was no room for argument, announced: 'No, ladies. You will not take the bus. You will take my brother's limousine. And I think the price for you will be Rp15,000.'

'Fifteen thousand . . . !' burst Donna in a cascade of sweat and frustration. I knew that if we stayed in that office any longer, Donna was bound to lose her temper and most certainly succeed in her ambition for the day in getting us arrested, so I hastily bundled her outside. The policeman's brother followed. 'That my brother, the policeman. He is very very kind to help you, I think. Yes, he is very kind man.'

Only with the wildest stretch of the imagination could the scrap metal heap on wheels in front of us ever have been called a limousine. The only thing it had in common with our mental image of one was that it was very long. It was also very brown. It had been very recently painted a nauseating milk chocolate brown both outside and in (including the vinyl seats) and it still reeked of paint fumes. The body had been welded together from dozens of small pieces of scrap metal and looked more like a piece of Donna's sculpture than a working vehicle. The seats weren't attached to the floor, neither of the passenger doors opened properly – one was permanently stuck shut, while the other could be opened only from the outside – there were no mirrors, no speedometer, no horn, precious little tread on the tyres and, from the way we veered across the road, questionable steering.

Heading away from the airport towards Ambon City, we passed by now familiar scenery: lush vegetation, banana and coconut trees, bougainvillaea, fields of tapioca and small wooden dwellings. Occasionally, we approached strips of brand new tarmac where repair work had recently been finished and it was plain that these were to be used at all costs, even when they were on the wrong side of the road! From the number of people and animals sitting, walking, lying and pedalling in the middle of the road, traffic was obviously infrequent. As we had no horn, our driver adopted the dangerous – and often near fatal – strategy of driving up behind pedestrians, cyclists or dogs at speed and applying the brakes at the last minute. The ghastly screeching sound was then supposed to alert them to our presence – albeit almost too late.

The short car ferry trip across the bay to Ambon City cuts half an hour's drive and was infinitely preferable to the paint fumes. Ambon Island (also known as *Nusa Yapoona* or 'Dew Island' because it is so frequently immersed in fog) is the capital of the Moluccas. Nowadays just a forgotten cluster of islands straddling the equator, these were once the fabled Spice Islands where nutmeg, mace, cloves and cinnamon grew, and to which traders from all over the globe were lured by the huge profits to be made from the spice trade. The Moluccas (or *Maluku* in Indonesian, from the Arabic word meaning 'land of kings') are scattered over a vast sea area half as big again as Kalimantan, but comprise only about four per cent of Indonesia's total land area. It was these 'East Indies' that Columbus was searching for when he unwittingly discovered the Americas in 1492 and called the inhabitants 'Indians'.

Ambon is a tiny horseshoe of an island just south-west of Seram. Seram and Ambon islands themselves were never notable as spice producers, and Ambon achieved its strategic importance only after the Portuguese built a large fortress there in 1574. It soon evolved from being the preserve of a few missionaries to the administrative centre of the entire region. Three centuries of close association with the Dutch began with their ousting of the Portuguese in 1605. In fact, the Dutch liked to think of the Ambonese as their most loyal subjects and this led Soekarno (the first leader of Indonesia after independence in 1945) to christen Ambon *'Anak Maluku Bukan Oneka Nederland'* or 'the children of the Moluccas are not Dutch puppets'! Despite this, a minority of separatists caused problems for the central government right up to the 1970s.

We checked in at the innocuous Hotel Amboina and went out to explore the town. It is said that Ambon used to be a 'charming coastal port with tree-lined shady promenades'. However, thanks to extensive bombing during and after World War Two, much of its charm has disappeared into dull, grey concrete blocks. Many trees have survived the onslaught of time and strife, though, and the streets are dotted with beautiful frangipani, oleander, bougainvillaea, jacaranda and red flame trees. At the end of a large sports field stands a statue of the only Indonesian national hero who was once a sergeant in the British army: Pattimura, who led a rebellion against the Dutch in 1817. Pattimura is depicted as a Rambo-style warrior, brandishing a massive sword in a suitably rebellious gesture. The sword, however, has unfortunately been cut off in its prime – the victim, apparently, of a low-flying army helicopter!

That evening we ate in the Amboina, where Donna was unable to resist the dubious temptation of a 'Honki Burger' and I chose the even more alluring 'Honki-Tonki Special'. Our flight to Banda Neira left at the crack of dawn the next day. Originally scheduled to leave at 8.00, we discovered while reconfirming our tickets that Merpati's schedule had changed and the flight would be leaving at 7.00 instead. This was no problem, but unfortunately we had

arranged for the infamous airport limousine to pick us up at 6.30.
We would now have to leave at 5.30. 'No problem,' said Donna
optimistically. 'Hey, there's bound to be buses or taxis around
early in the morning.'

At 5.00 the next morning I opened the curtains and looked out
of the window. It was a damp, grey, silent morning and as yet
barely light. One or two people passed by on foot, but there was
not a car, bus or even a bicycle to be seen. I had a queasy, sinking
feeling of foreboding about missing the flight. Our optimism
fading, we packed our bags and went to check out. The lobby was
in total darkness except for an illuminated aquarium in one
corner shedding a ghostly pale purple light onto a potted palm
next to it. I rang the bell on the reception desk. A young man,
who had been asleep on one of the sofas in the lobby, jumped to
his feet and stared at us groggily. 'Check out?' inquired Donna,
'please? NOW!'

The young man continued to stare for a few seconds, then
walked slowly over towards the reception desk where, without a
word, he disappeared through the door behind it. I looked at my
watch. It was already 5.30. As Donna dealt with paying the bill, I
peered anxiously out of the door. The activity outside had
increased to a few bicycles and one packed *bemo* heading in the
wrong direction, but nothing that would get us to the airport. As
I was considering offering a quick prayer at the large Catholic
church across the street, the familiar squeal of smooth rubber on
tarmac announced the airport limo, which miraculously
appeared, rattling and shaking, round the corner.

I felt like embracing the policeman's spotty brother, but
instead hastily informed him about the time of our flight. '*Aduh!*'
he exclaimed, looking at his watch and running his fingers
anxiously through his thick black hair. If we thought he had
driven badly the previous day, that was as nothing compared to
his display of utterly manic driving that morning. As passengers
in the back, we felt like we were on one of those horrible rides at
an amusement park where you hurtle towards things at great
speed and veer away only at the very last minute. At that time, in
the cool of the morning, there were many more people and dogs
flirting with death in the middle of the road, which made our

journey proportionately more nerve-racking!

After five minutes I was relieved to see that we were approaching the turn-off to the ferry, but Mad Max drove straight past it. 'Hey! What about the ferry?' I shouted over the screaming noise of the engine.

'No ferry. No ferry!' he shouted back, hunched over the wheel. 'Ferry no go until 7.00.' Oh God! We were going to have to drive all the way round the peninsula. I closed my eyes and took deep paint-scented breaths to try and calm myself.

We skidded to a stop outside the airport at 6.45, rushed to the check-in counter, where we were greeted warmly by the waiting Merpati official, and bundled straight onto the plane, which in minutes was buzzing happily over the deep blue waters of the Banda Sea. When things went well, it was hard not to have a soft spot for Merpati.

Gazing out of the window, I reflected on the place we were about to visit; so tiny as regards land mass, but so significant historically. Apart from having a delightful taste and aroma, nutmegs and the fibrous mace which surrounds the nuts were vital as a natural preservative in the days before refrigeration. As a result of their indigenous trees, the Bandas and their affable peoples were subjected to frequent attacks as the Dutch, Portuguese and British wrangled over the spoils, each wanting to gain control of the islands and monopolize the highly lucrative spice trade.

Before the arrival of the Europeans in the sixteenth century, there were five kingdoms of Banda. The ruling *orang kaya* (rich men) supervized the sale of nutmegs and mace to traders from Malaya, India, China, Arabia and Java. By the time the spices reached Europe, they had passed through many hands and increased in price many times.

I was shaken out of my reverie by Donna jogging my arm and pointing out of the window. There, so close below that it looked as if it was just about to scrape the wing of the aircraft, was Gunung Api (Fire Mountain), the beautiful, perfectly symmetrical volcanic cone which comprises one of the five main Banda islands. The small plane circled the volcano and finally came in to land at Banda's tiny, uneven airstrip.

As we walked into the airport building, a man grinned to us from behind a desk which had 'Information' encouragingly displayed over it. 'Hello. Hello!' he cried, 'you need hotel? I can take you to very good hotel.' We thanked him, but explained that we had already been recommended one. 'No problem,' he said. We should have been warned; nothing in Indonesia is ever that simple.

He led us outside to where a single decrepit vehicle stood disintegrating in the sun. The driver – also apparently disintegrating – was slumped over the wheel. He was roused from sleep with difficulty, and our bags stuffed into the taxi, which was push-started into life. Five minutes later we rumbled into the little town of Banda Neira along narrow dirt streets, passing crumbling stone buildings, a Chinese temple, a cinema and the fish market, before the engine finally puttered out in front of a hotel. Unfortunately it wasn't the hotel we wanted. It was, as the information man had said, a very nice hotel – the Maulana Inn – but we nevertheless insisted he took us to the hotel that had been recommended to us.

There then followed a farcical drive at high speed around the tiny streets of Banda Neira, the methodology of which became clear only several days later; the information man was actually an employee of the owner of the Maulana, who incidentally also owned the 'hotel taxi' – and, as it turned out, most of Banda. Despite the fact that there were no other vehicles in sight, our taxi driver insisted he was 'unable to stop' at all but one of the hotels on the island 'because of heavy traffic'. Needless to say, this hotel was also owned by his boss. Our lightning tour ended up back on the steps of the Maulana.

The Maulana Inn was a replica of an old Dutch *perkenier* (the name given to licensed Dutch planters) villa; two storeys high, with grey stone slab floors, an arched facade facing the sea, under which one could sit, eat and drink, and spacious, airconditioned bedrooms with attached bathrooms. Luxury indeed by the standards we were expecting. We were shown to a room on the second floor, described by the receptionist as the 'big fat room' – appealing in itself. Undoubtedly the most alluring aspect of the hotel, though, was its location; built right on the seafront, next to the harbour, with an outstanding view over the Banda Strait to

Gunung Api six hundred metres away, the tip of which was now immersed in a thin wisp of cloud. The only luxuries missing were hot water and a shower, but otherwise, relatively speaking, the Maulana Inn was five-star. It was expensive, however: $45 per day. We inquired about a discount and were told that we would have to wait for the 'Boss' to come back and ask him.

While we sat with a beer and awaited the boss's arrival, Donna picked up a copy of the *Jakarta Post* which was lying on the table. 'Listen to this!' she said. 'The dead body of a ninety-year-old woman has just been found after *seven months* . . . I quote: "The woman, named Icih, had been staying with her only daughter. The family told the police officers who checked the house yesterday that on June 17th last year Icih had told them that she wanted to *take a nap* and had asked them not to disturb her. The family claimed to have done as she had wished . . .". Now there's an understatement!'

By the time the owner showed up we were so taken with the location of the hotel and lulled by the gentle lapping of the sea – and perhaps the beer – that we were charmed rather than suspicious when he immediately agreed to our request for a hefty discount. The owner, Des Alwi, turned out to be a celebrity in himself. He had, at one time, been one of Mohammed Hatta's protégés. Along with Sutan Sjahrir, Hatta, one of Indonesia's charismatic young nationalist leaders, was banished by the Dutch to Banda Neira in 1936. It was obviously hoped that the serenity of the islands would help to calm their political passions. While there, they became very attached to the five children of a local Arab family – the Baadillas – one of whom was our host, Des Alwi. After Ambon fell to the Japanese in 1942, Hatta and Sjahrir escaped from Banda taking three of these children (Des himself followed later) with them to grow up as apprentice nationalists in Batavia – now Jakarta.

After Indonesian independence was proclaimed in 1945, Hatta became vice-president to Soekarno, and Sjahrir served as prime minister. Sjahrir sent Des to be educated in England, and he worked for the Foreign Service in London and Geneva before returning to Indonesia. Disenchanted with Soekarno's policies, he joined the Permesta Rebellion in the 1950s and became its official spokesman overseas. When the rebellion collapsed, Des moved to Kuala Lumpur to wait out the demise of the Soekarno regime, where he became a close personal friend of Tengku Abdul Rahman, the prime minister of Malaya, whom he had known in London. In recent years, he has taken great steps to improve life on his native islands. Not only was he responsible for building the airstrip and setting up a communications system, he has also put a great deal of money and energy into developing Banda for tourism.

This famous man now stood before us in a crumpled batik shirt half tucked into a pair of ill-fitting, baggy trousers, a navy blue sea captain's hat at a jaunty angle on his head and a pair of grimy, light blue espadrilles. 'But of course we can give you discount. Yes, that is no problem. You have already seen the room? Is very good here; you can do whatever you want – relax, snorkelling, climbing up our volcano over there . . .', he indicated the smoking volcano with an elaborate gesture. 'Yes, it's initiation to living in Banda. Everyone who stay here must get up at 5.00, swim over to the volcano, and then run up the volcano and down the other side, hee-hee-hee-heeh.' He finished his sentence with a wheezy chuckle, sounding exactly like Dick Dastardly's cartoon dog, Mutley. 'No, no, don't worry – that is joke; but seriously, many guests have climbed the volcano and lived to tell the tale.'

Later, as we were sitting on the verandah enjoying a cup of tea and Dutch cakes, Des swept outside saying, 'Come, come, I will take you to see my nutmeg and cinnamon plantation over there on the other island.' He pointed towards Gunung Api island at the base of which was a small village and Des's huge plantation.

Nutmeg trees themselves are unremarkable, but hanging from the branches were dozens of round, pale yellow fruit the size of apricots, looking like primitive Christmas baubles. Des reached up and picked one of the fruits and split it open. Inside was a small, dark brown nut – the nutmeg – covered with bright red shiny fibre. 'Now this,' said Des, peeling the fibre from the nut, 'this is what everyone is wanting and what all the fuss was all about. This is the mace and, as you can see, you don't get very much of it from each fruit, so is very expensive, yes. The price has recently risen from $8 a kilo to $80, I think. Here, smell this.' The red fibre had the unmistakable, freshly scented aroma of mace. 'It's very nice, yes?'

'You know why the nutmeg is so highly prized?' Des asked, as we walked on towards his cinnamon plantation. 'Because it keep the food fresh. Even nowadays, they use the nutmeg in tinned goods – as a preservative, yes. Actually, even the flesh you can use – we make into jam – or we dry, and sell dried and candied in the market. Many many uses for the nutmeg.'

The cinnamon 'sticks' that one buys in a supermarket come directly from the bark of the cinnamon tree, called *kayu manis* (sweet wood). The bark is peeled off and dried in the sun. As it dries, it curls up and acquires its distinctive shape.

On the way back to the boat we passed some mango trees with dozens of savaged, half-devoured fruit on the ground oozing dark yellow flesh. Des grimaced at this. 'Ah, I love to eat the fresh mango, but unfortunately so does the *cus cus*.'

'*Cus cus*? That's an Arabian dish isn't it?' said Donna.

Des wheezed with polite laughter, 'No, it's the tree kangaroo we have living here on this island, but they are hard to spot. They stay high up in the trees – the bloody things.'

Des told us about his recent trip to London where he had been attending his class reunion at the Central London Polytechnic in Regent's Park, where he had taken a course in telecommunications. It all seemed rather incongruous, standing under a mango tree on such a remote, exotic island, discussing the early morning rush on the Baker Street tube!

Later that afternoon we strolled up to the museum. It was an arduous hike – almost one and a half minute's walk from the hotel! The building itself was an attractive old Dutch villa which had been recently restored and was surrounded by an attractive, green wrought-iron fence. Supported by a series of curled white pillars, the roof covered a wide verandah and a series of tall doors flanked by decorative wooden shutters. An old iron Raffles-type streetlamp stood watch outside, while inside a small collection of artefacts from Banda's past – furniture, pistols, coins and a cannon or two – lay on display, lovingly cared for by an aged curator and his family.

The most eye-catching of these was a horrific painting of 'the massacre of the *orang kaya*'. This major event in Bandanese history – which occurred on the night of May 8th, 1621 – was ordered by a Dutch Governor General who believed that the *orang kaya* were leading a conspiracy to kill him. The unforgettable painting shows a gargantuan Japanese mercenary standing knee-high in blood, gore, dismembered limbs and bodies.

Back at the hotel that evening we met the two other guests: a young, chic French couple called Jean-Marc and Françoise. Jean-Marc was charming, friendly and outgoing and spoke excellent English. He was, he explained, just coming to the end of his 'military service' in Jakarta. His family had pulled the right strings and he had managed to avoid the compulsory year's conscription in France by 'doing his time' instead as an assistant cultural attaché at the French Trade Commission in Jakarta. He lived in a huge house with three other bachelors, drove a car with *Corps Diplomatique* numberplates, dined out at the best restaurants, frequented all the Jakarta night-spots and was basically thoroughly enjoying himself!

'Of course, it eez a tough assignment. I mean, I am not allowed to leave Jakarta at all during my fourteen-meunth term of service.'

Donna and I exchanged glances.

'But, luckily for me, it doesn't mean anytheeng – I 'ave been to Bali at least eight times already . . .' Jean-Marc laughed good-naturedly.

Des joined us as we sat on the terrace. Despite his best efforts, he always looked as if he had just got out of bed, or had crumpled his clothes into a ball and stamped on them before getting dressed. As he entertained us with tales about the Banda Islands and his role in their history, he demolished a vast bowl of salted peanuts on the table beside him. Without pausing in his commentary, he would seize a handful in one hand and then pop them into his mouth one by one between syllables.

'Banda was always ruled by the *orang kaya*, the Council of Five, . . . and now I am the leader of this. Whenever we have special religious festivals, then always the Bandanese people must take offerings to the graveyards of the *orang kaya* (pop, crunch) who, as you know, were massacred by the Dutch. We have found already fourteen graveyards on the islands, but actually (toss, pop) we only know for sure who is buried in three of them. But these graves are very important for the people of Banda, yes (crunch, crunch). And now let us eat. The food is ready, I think.'

We approached the dinner table with trepidation. The regional cuisine of the Moluccas is derived from sago and has been compared to wallpaper paste, so we were delighted by the variety of dishes before us: bean soup, rice, tomato salad, corn fritters and fresh tuna fish that had been prepared as the Japanese delicacy *sashimi*. This was obviously Des's favourite. He spent several minutes painstakingly mixing up a special *sashimi* sauce made from soy sauce, ginger and mustard, and devoured the fish with audible enthusiasm.

In our room that evening we tried to make ourselves comfortable on beds which were so excruciatingly lumpy that Donna was moved to suggest that nutmegs had also been used to stuff the mattress. She was re-reading the section on food in our guidebook. 'Hey, listen to this! It says that there's a particular banana here called the *pisang raja*, which can grow up to half a metre in length. And get this! It also says that Ambonese women aren't permitted to eat this banana, because it's thought that it'll wreck their marriage. The mind boggles!'

A tremendous din woke us early next morning. Out on the street a jeep was passing with several young men on it waving flags and banging tin lids together. The noise was incredible.

'What on earth is that row for?' Donna asked one of the hotel staff.

'The day after tomorrow the new Governor of all Moluccas is coming to Banda, so it is to stir up everyone into action to clean their garden and make the town clean for his visit.'

With further sleep impossible, we walked up to Fort Belgica. This pentagonal fortress, built in 1611, must in its day have been a very impresive sight, standing solidly on its high plateau and commanding fine views of the surrounding seas. Its massive outer walls and towers, built from black volcanic rock, have well withstood the ravages of time. We ascended a fern-covered staircase to the top ramparts, but apart from a couple of

discarded cannons pointing forlornly out to sea from the broken
battlements, all other evidence of habitation is gone or covered
with vegetation. Any section of wall not smothered in ferns and
creepers is plastered with graffiti.

In the centre of the fort are the remains of an underground
tunnel, which led to the even older Portuguese Fort Nassau,
which lies in a far more advanced state of deterioration a few
hundred metres down the hill. It was here that the infamous
'massacre of the *orang kaya*' took place. As we stood on what must
have been the very spot, Donna read out the grisly account of the
massacre (recorded by naval lieutenant Nicholas van Waert)
from Willard Hanna's book *Indonesian Banda*, which we had
bought at the museum:

> The condemned victims being brought within the enclosure, six
> Japanese soldiers were also ordered inside, and with their sharp
> swords they beheaded and quartered the eight chief *orang kaya* and
> then beheaded and quartered the thirty-six others. This execution
> was awful to see. The *orang kaya* died silently without uttering any
> sound except that one of them, speaking in the Dutch tongue, said,
> 'Sirs, have you then no mercy?' but indeed nothing availed. All that
> happened was so dreadful as to leave us stunned. The heads and
> quarters of those who had been executed were impaled upon bamboos
> and so displayed. Thus did it happen: God knows who is right.

The tiny town of Banda Neira is full of the atmosphere of a
bygone age. Most of the houses are restored or reconstructed
perkenier mansions, their common features being attractive
painted wooden shutters, deep overhanging roofs supported by
pillars, and thick, whitewashed stone walls. However, many
others have sadly deteriorated. In some cases only the odd wall or
row of pillars still stands, but one can still catch a glimpse of the
grandeur of the past; an impression of how the place must have
been a hundred years ago, with the magnificent buildings in their
well-kept gardens, thriving on either side of avenues of brilliant
red flame trees. In one's mind's eye one can almost see elegantly
dressed *perkenier* wives gliding down the main street with parasols,
or sipping their tea and taking delicate bites from their Dutch
cakes in the afternoon . . .

On the way back to the hotel we stopped at the large white

Catholic church. Though the present building dates only from 1852, when it was rebuilt after the original was destroyed by an earthquake, this is the site of the oldest church in Indonesia. There are two stone slabs in the floor at the front of the church. One reads: 'Herelieth the body of Mr John McLeod, late of the Royal Navy, who departed this life on the 14th Day of April Anno Domini 1800. Universally regretted by numerous acquaintances. Aged 27 years.' The church too adhered to the same architectural style with an overhanging roof supported by four massive columns. The old Dutch clock at the front is stuck at five past four. Not, apparently, time for tea, but the exact moment the Japanese invaded the island.

The waters around the Banda Islands are famous for their beautiful 'sea gardens' and spectacular coral reefs. When we got back, Jean-Marc was looking for us. 'Des has offered to take us snorkelling. Do you want to come?' The only reservation I had was that I had heard there were sharks in these waters. I asked Des about it. He vehemently denied that there were any sharks within a hundred miles of Banda. In fact, the very last thing I heard before tumbling over the side of the boat into the pellucid aquamarine waters was Des saying reassuringly, 'There are *absolutely no sharks* in these waters. Don't worry.'

The first thing I saw was a shark! It wasn't more than a couple of metres long, and swam around me curiously as if wondering how long I was going to interrupt it at its favourite feeding ground. With the theme music from *Jaws* coming unwelcomely to mind, I could very easily have panicked, but in fact felt extraordinarily calm and compelled just to float quietly and watch the shark, which eventually moved away to another patch of coral. I decided not to mention this to Donna. If I had, I am certain I would never have got her within a Great White's length of the sea again.

Françoise was determined to return to Paris with an even darker tan than she had already acquired, so that afternoon Des arranged for his speedboat to take the four of us over to a tiny island – called *Pulau Pisang* or Banana Island – which had a white sandy beach which was very conducive to sunbathing. The boat would leave us there and collect us a few hours later. From a distance, Banana Island – or what we thought was Banana Island – looked like a half-submerged wine bottle discarded and left floating by a Gulliver-sized hand. We spotted a tiny speck of white sandy beach from a long way off, but the driver shook his head and kept going. We all assumed that he was going the wrong way and demanded truculently that he turn and take us towards the beach. Ten minutes later he very reluctantly dropped us off.

After about half an hour of busying ourselves laying out towels under the shade of a mangosteen tree (except Françoise), covering ourselves with sun block (except Françoise), shaking the accumulated sand off the towels, finding our books and so on, it came to our attention that there was distinctly *less* white sandy beach than there had been when we arrived. None of us had even considered the possibility that the tide might be coming in. No wonder the boatman had been so reluctant to drop us off, but of course the *orang putih* (white people) thought they knew best. I walked along the beach, which was completely deserted except for a few dark volcanic rocks which had tumbled from the cliffs above and lay littered about the beach like giant bath sponges. The beach abutted sheer cliffs and, from the water mark, it was obvious that when the tide was fully in it covered the sand completely. If the boat didn't come back for us soon, what then?

As the minutes ticked by and the waves swept in relentlessly, we were forced to retreat further and further up the rapidly dwindling beach. We scanned the horizon for any sign of the returning boat, but it was still hours before it was due to collect us. Jean-Marc went in search of an escape route, while Donna and I sat and quietly panicked and Françoise laid herself out on the last remaining sunny bit of sand. Had we not been about to perish there, the beach was a fascinating place to sit; masses of beautiful butterflies danced in the air, a frigate bird soared above and a tiny kingfisher laboured diligently nearby, diving again and again into the sea from an overhanging branch. In the distance, the outline of Gunung Api persisted on the skyline. As I gazed across the turquoise sea I thought I saw a speck bouncing along on the water. Could it be the boat? I looked again and couldn't see it. But there it was again, a few seconds later. I was overcome with relief. Days later, and in a different frame of mind, Jean-Marc suggested that Des had decided to send back the boat to ensure that we were alive to pay for our rooms.

Des joined us later as we sat recovering on the verandah drinking some tea. 'Please, please drink lots of this tea. The Operation Raleigh people came to stay a few months ago and brought all this bloody tea. I don't know how to get through it all.'

As the next day would be fairly quiet – the Governor was due to arrive the day after – we had talked about trying to climb Gunung Api.

'So Des, what do you sink if we want to climb up ze volcano tomorrow?' asked Jean-Marc.

'Yes, of course it can be done. The record you know is thirty-nine minutes, which was done by one of the Operation Raleigh people. But he was very annoyed because actually our guide, you know, he got there just one second before! It will be a nice day tomorrow. No wind or rain.'

'Yes? 'ow can you tell?'

'Look over there past the volcano. If you can see the island of Seram in the distance, the weather will be bad tomorrow. It will be very windy, yes. And rain too.' Des slurped his tea. We strained our eyes, but none of us could see an outline of an island. So it was decided. We would tempt fate and climb Gunung Api the day before the Governor's visit and pray to the appropriate gods that it would shirk tradition and not choose tomorrow to erupt as, according to Willard Hanna, Gunung Api had a nasty habit of demonstrating a show of strength whenever a new governor made a visit to Banda. Hanna describes the arrival of one such governor in April 1824:

> The arrival of the Governor General, his wife and his large entourage
> . . . at four in the afternoon on April 22nd, was signalled, not
> altogether auspiciously, by one of the sudden eruptions of Gunung
> Api which major Dutch visitations seemed habitually to trigger. Just
> as the Eurydice was sailing past little Pulau Pisau . . . approaching
> the anchorage situated almost at the base of the volcano, flames
> leaped from the crater and smoke blackened the sky. The Eurydice
> turned back to Pulau Ai, returning to Neira the following morning

when the situation seemed less alarming. Volcanic rumblings nevertheless all but drowned out the salutes fired from the fort and the rather worried speeches of welcome. Billows of smoke and vapour, streams of molten lava, showers of stone and ash, all served, as the Governor General remarked, to make the visit 'most unforgettable'.

It was pitch dark when we stumbled downstairs at 5.30 the next morning. Jean-Marc was raring to go, but Françoise looked less than enthusiastic. From the moment our feet touched ground, it was obvious that Jean-Marc was intending to try to beat the thirty-nine minute record. I looked up apprehensively at the tip of the volcano. It gazed back stoically from all of its 665 metres.

The first twenty or so minutes were easy, but then we encountered conditions that stopped even Jean-Marc in his tracks and made what was supposed to be a pleasant morning's climb into an exhausting and strenuous exercise. In an attempt to make the ascent easier (or else it was some kind of sadistic joke), someone had worked tremendously hard to cover the thin dirt trail with small basalt and pumice stones. No doubt this was advantageous during the wet season, when the trail would become muddy and slippery, but otherwise the stones had exactly the effect they had been put there to avoid. They were so light, and we were climbing at such a steep angle, that no sooner had one taken two steps upwards, than one invariably slipped one step backwards.

I now know what it feels like to be one of those wretched hamsters running around endlessly on a wheel and never getting anywhere! Françoise scrambled up in front of me, muttering to herself in a constant stream of disgusted French and dislodging torrents of small stones which I then had to avoid.

The other Banda islands – Run, Ai and Lonthor – spread out below us. The British occupied Run and Ai in the seventeenth century. However, in a very ungentlemanly act, the Dutch destroyed their nutmeg plantations, which had the desired effect of preventing the British from trading, as well as causing widespread famine amongst the locals. In the Treaty of Breda in 1667, the British officially abandoned their claim to Run, while under the same treaty the Dutch relinquished their claim to a small island called Manhattan in what would one day be the

USA. Looking at the tiny jewel of an island with typical West Coast bias, Donna said, 'I'd say the Dutch got the better deal.'

'I just can't think why I agreed to do this,' Françoise complained sulkily, examining her shins for cuts and bruises. Jean-Marc sighed resignedly and glanced at his watch.

'Well,' he said, 'we're already way over the thirty-nine minutes and I don't think we're even halfway yet.' We all looked up at the tip of the volcano seemingly miles above, none of us relishing the prospect of another hour's exhausting struggle up – and downwards.

Eventually, two and a quarter hours after we started, we reached the summit, though even then we were unable to see the crater, which fell away on the northern side of the volcano. It was noticeably cool at the top, and the cold breeze brought with it gusts of hot, sulphurous steam. The ground felt hot underfoot and the smell of brimstone stung our nostrils. Clouds had formed while we had been climbing, and the spectacular view that we were to be rewarded with at the top eluded us. The clouds were so thick that it was as if someone had abruptly turned on a dry-ice machine and enveloped us in a swirling mist. As we gazed into misty nothingness, the wind suddenly blew a gap in the clouds and there, just for a split second, was a glimpse of the deep blue sea and islands beyond. It was like being in a strange dream and having one's vision blur mysteriously, only to clear again a few seconds later.

The enormous sulphurous crater was steaming benevolently like an old man puffing on a pipe. Inside it looked as if bright yellow powdered poster paint had been scattered over an old, well-used palate stained with splashes of red, ochre and orange. The vegetation on the north slope was almost jungle-like. Large trees, vines and creepers towered and twisted above us on either side of the steep, muddy trail.

The descent was almost as hard as the ascent, and I frequently had to grip on to a sturdy-looking branch to prevent myself from slipping. I lost count eventually of the number of times I fell because the branch was not as sturdy as it had looked!

I didn't see the spider until the last minute. 'Be careful!' shouted Jean-Marc, 'there's a *huge* spider right by your head!'

Donna screamed. I shot a glance sideways and there it was – an alarmingly large black and red spider inches from my right eye. I screamed too and jerked aside so suddenly that I slipped and careered luge-style down the muddy trail. There were hundreds of webs spun across the trail, all with attendant spiders. Donna was a nervous wreck by the time we reached sea level.

Outside the Maulana Inn, a wooden hoarding had been erected with *'Selamat Datang'* (Welcome) printed carefully in large black letters. It was obviously brought out for special occasions to welcome whichever eminent visitor was coming to Banda, but this time, looking very much like an afterthought, the words *'Pak Gub'* (an abbreviated 'Mr Governor') had been scrawled in untidy writing at the end of the sign! *'SELAMAT DATANG – Pak Gub'*.

The rousing awakening the day before had clearly been effective as the town looked pristine; the dirt streets still showing the streaky marks of having been hand-swept with brushes made from long thin twigs. As the most influential member of the community, Des was to greet *Pak Gub* at the Maulana Inn and take him and his entourage on a tour of the Banda Islands.

As far as we were concerned, the best part of the Gub's visit was that, to mark the occasion, three traditional Bandanese warships, called Kora Kora, were to be brought out to greet him. I asked Des about them; 'Ya,' he said, 'in olden times, each Kingdom of Banda had its own Kora Kora, and they were used to defend a particular village against intruders, and to attack other villages and so on. They would also be used to carry the noblemen, sultans and important people about the places. Nowadays, we use only for special occasions like this, or for important ceremonies, and also twice a year there's a big sporting event called the Kora Kora race where six boats race against each other around the islands – just like your Oxford and Cambridge . . .'

On the morning of the Governor's visit, I awoke early to the faint sound of drums and singing in the distance. Stepping out onto the balcony into brilliant, clear, early morning sunshine, I looked in the direction of the sound and there, rounding the bend in the Strait, were the three Kora Kora warships. Des's description had made them sound impressive, but nothing could have prepared me for this truly magnificent sight. Despite the heat, the sight of the Kora Kora, coupled with the rather eerie sound of the singing, sent shivers running involuntarily down my spine.

The three ships, one blue, one green and one brown, flags billowing in the breeze, approached relentlessly. The bare-chested oarsmen plunged their paddles into the water for two strokes, then held them upright and let the boats drift for a few seconds. The brilliant sunshine caught and highlighted the colours of the boats, flags, men's turbans and clothes, which were in turn reflected in the steel grey water, sparkling like forbidden jewels in a treasure chest. It was dazzling. I imagined myself a villager in olden times faced with the sight of these imposing ships and knowing myself to be on the brink of attack.

'Well, at least you'd go in style,' said Donna, who had joined me. 'Chippendales should sign these guys up.'

Each boat was about seventy feet long and looked rather like a cross between a gondola and a Viking longboat. They were very slender – less than four feet across at the widest point – and looked extremely unstable. Each Kora Kora had thirty oarsmen, two musicians, two men to bail out water, a captain and a helmsman; it was remarkable that they stayed afloat at all with all those men aboard. As the three Kora Kora passed in front of Gunung Api, they looked like parts of some strange, misplaced Canaletto painting. They did a brisk circuit past the volcano, turned round, and came to rest in front of the Maulana Inn, where they, like everyone else, waited for the Governor's arrival.

The boat from Lonthor village was by far the most impressive. Its elaborately carved and painted figureheads depicted birds, ginger flowers and nutmegs. Relics from past warfare – a helmet, sword, spear and shield – were attached to the front of the boat and the sides were decorated with carved images of tuna, barracuda and other fish. Large colourful flags representing the Kingdom's colours and crests billowed in the wind from a total of eleven flagpoles.

The musicians sat at the front, one beating a drum and the other a series of gongs. At the other end, the helmsman sat

wielding a large oar. The captain gripped on to the central
flagpole and shouted orders to the oarsmen. They all wore orange
turbans, shirts and sarongs, and sat hunched, muscles flexed – a
vision of strength and concentration.

One and a half hours passed and there was still no sign of the
Governor's plane. Dozens of police and uniformed officials had
gathered, and a small traditional orchestra – or gamelan – had
been bonging away for hours at the water's edge. By this time, in
Britain, everyone would probably have packed up and gone home
grumbling, but, being Indonesia, everyone patiently waited – and
waited – and waited. Occasionally someone would utter a small
sigh and look resignedly up at the heavens, but nobody became
impatient. Impatience is an emotional speciality of those of us
from the west, and, true to our origins, the only impatient ones
there were Jean-Marc, Donna and I, who had been slowly baking
up on the roof of the hotel hoping for a bird's eye view of the
Gub's arrival. The only one of us who was really happy was
Françoise, who had a perfect opportunity to add another layer to
her tan.

Earlier that morning the boat that was to take the Governor on
his tour around the islands pulled up in front of the hotel. For
almost an hour one of the boat-hands busied himself cleaning out
the engine, which had resulted in a hideous oil slick. As if this
weren't unsightly enough, a huge passenger ferry, en route for
Ambon, had docked at the harbour in the middle of the night,
and a considerable amount of jetsam – banana skins, cigarette
packets, plastic bottles, coconut husks – had been tossed out of it.
This had all accumulated in the same oily waters in which Pak
Gub's vessel – freshly painted, pristine and flying brand new
decorative flags – was now waiting.

As official host, Des had put on his best finery. This consisted
of a pale grey safari suit, but, we were amused to see, even this
was drastically crumpled and looked as if it had been lying in a
drawer for years and needed a good iron. Pak Gub's arrival – over
two hours late – was rather an anti-climax. Instead of the
grandiose figure I had been expecting, he looked more like a
Japanese tourist on a golfing holiday, in white slacks, a short-
sleeved shirt and a beige pork-pie hat! He was accompanied by a

vast entourage, all of whom, after the usual protracted hand-shaking and photograph-taking ceremonies, squeezed onto Des's boat for their trip round the islands. We watched in amazement and some trepidation as yet another smiling official stepped unsteadily onto the already overladen boat, and were convinced that it would never make it round the islands without capsizing and depositing its important load into the Banda Sea.

The Kora Kora led the procession of boats away from the harbour towards the clearly visible island of Seram, and within five minutes they had rounded the corner in the strait and were out of sight. Only Gunung Api was left, silently smoking and looking on with an air of superior smugness, having seen governors come and go for centuries. But perhaps it, too, was unable to believe the man in the pork-pie hat really was the Governor. It was a few months later that the realization must have set in as the volcano responded with a terrifying eruption that led to the evacuation of the entire island group.

Much, much later, when we were convinced that Des's boat – and its important cargo – had sunk to the bottom of the Banda Strait, it returned looking more like a vessel crammed full of refugees than a tour boat out for a joy ride. The illustrious party disembarked looking crumpled and tired. Pak Gub was seen off at the airport and Des returned insisting that we all partake of several more cups of his Operation Raleigh tea. A strong wind started up, gusting round the hotel and blowing over several potted plants and a rattan chair.

'Hey, zat is my towel!' cried Françoise, as she watched it being ripped from where it had been drying on the balcony and deposited in the strait a hundred metres away.

'Is the monsoon winds,' said Des. 'Very strong, yes. Sometimes they go on for several days.'

As we were all supposed to be leaving the next day, this was bad news. There was no way that a small aircraft could take off or land in these winds. They continued to rage all night, bringing stinging sheets of rain that lashed against our windows. Just when I thought they had quieted a little, another tremendous gust would send something else crashing downstairs.

Our flight was supposed to leave at 8.30am, and even though

the wind was showing no signs of abating, we were picked up at 7.00 by the Merpati bus. Earlier that morning we had all been presented with our bills. To our surprise, and Jean-Marc's great angst, we had all been charged every time Des had 'offered' to take us somewhere on his boat, or suggested that we use it to take a trip. So much for our 'discount'. Once tax and a hefty service charge had been added it coincidentally came to within a few rupiah of the original sum! Jean-Marc was hopping mad. 'Ze man is a swine – he can be sure zat I will be telling all the people I know in Jakarta not to come to his stingking hotel . . . my God, what a bastard . . .!' Des was conspicuous by his absence.

Our bags were carefully weighed when we were checked in at the airport by another of Des's employees. Jean-Marc asked the bemused man acidly whether perhaps he might like to weigh his wallet too, to see how much more he could extract from it.

The wind was beginning to die down as we, and the other yawning passengers, sat and waited; the air heavy and languid with boredom. Many hours late, the plane eventually landed and expelled its cargo of fifteen grinning Japanese tourists, all of whom felt impelled to take several photographs of each other getting out of, in front of, and beside the plane. It made all of us feel extremely grateful that we were leaving. As one passed us, his camera made a loud beeping noise. 'That's to warn him that he hasn't taken a picture for over a minute,' commented Donna. Before we got on the plane, Jean-Marc told the Merpati agent that it was absolutely imperative – a matter of French National Security – that he, as a member of the French Trade Commission and a personal friend of the ambassador, make the connecting Garuda flight to Ujung Pandang.

As we approached for landing at Ambon, we could see the plane for Ujung Pandang, which was clearly waiting for us. The only setback, and a point that Jean-Marc had neglected to tell the Merpati man in Banda, was that he didn't actually have tickets for the flight! Françoise and Jean-Marc rushed into the terminal, while Donna and I stood guard by our plane waiting for our luggage. Just as we had collected all our bags from two bemused airport workers, who were used to people waiting in the arrivals hall for their luggage rather than hovering around for it on the tarmac, Jean-Marc and Françoise ran back triumphantly waving tickets, grabbed a bag and rushed to the plane.

Donna and I were left wondering why we bothered to book flights well in advance when it was obviously much more fun getting on at the very last minute! Jean-Marc and Françoise were on their way to Bali. We later heard that when they arrived in Ujung Pandang they headed straight for the transit lounge still hand-carrying their check-in baggage. Jean-Marc waved his tickets (which were actually to Jakarta and dated a week later) and his diplomatic passport and insisted – in a way that only Jean-Marc could – that he be given a boarding pass for the flight to Bali, which was leaving in five minutes. Somehow he got away with it and he and Françoise rushed onto the plane before anyone realized they didn't actually have a ticket.

When Jean-Marc had heard that we might be going to Jakarta, he had insisted that we stay at his house and, if he was away, use his room for as long as we liked. He scribbled a note on the back of an envelope to introduce us to his three house-mates, and to ask them to accommodate us for as long as necessary.

During our four-hour wait for our flight to Jayapura in Irian Jaya, we saw our entrepreneural policeman, now sporting a pair of designer sunglasses. He grinned at us. 'I wonder where he got the money for those . . .' said Donna.

'Well, if the police in Jayapura are anxious to get some too, they're going to be disappointed.' We had *surat jalans* with us, as we knew Irian Jaya to be a restricted area. We had our guidebook and our dictionary; we felt ready for anything.

4. 'Killer dude! Catch a wave'

Irian Jaya

'Seven people were killed and twenty-three seriously injured when a Twin Otter plane crashed in the mountainous part of Indonesia's easternmost province of Irian Jaya, Monday. This was the fourth air accident and the second involving a Twin Otter in less than a week . . .'

I stopped Donna in mid-sentence. 'Do you *have* to tell me that now?' She was quoting from an old *Jakarta Post* she had found in the seat pocket of the plane that was taking us to Irian Jaya.

The island of New Guinea (of which the Indonesian province of Irian Jaya makes up the western half) is the world's second largest island and it remains one of the least explored places on earth. When the Portuguese discovered the island, they gave it the name *Ilhas dos Papuas*, the 'Island of the Fuzzy-Hairs'. It was the Dutch who called it 'New Guinea', because the people reminded them of the black-skinned natives of Guinea, Africa. At the end of the nineteenth century, the island was divided between Dutch, German and British rule. After World War One, Australia controlled both the British and the German territories which, in 1975, became known as Papua New Guinea. The Dutch retained control of West New Guinea until 1963, when they were forced to hand the territory over to Indonesia, and Soekarno – with his love of acronyms – dubbed the territory Irian (*Ikutlah Republic Indonesia Anti Nederland*; 'Follow the Republic of Indonesia against the Dutch').

It was believed that, over time, the population of West New Guinea would come to identify with the Indonesian Republic, but the *Organisasi Papua Merdeka* (OPM or 'Papuan Freedom Movement') continues to resist Indonesian state control.

In the central highlands of Irian Jaya is the Baliem Valley. At an altitude of five thousand feet, this beautiful, fertile valley lay undiscovered until 1938, when the explorer Richard Archbold travelled to New Guinea to collect specimens of alpine flora and fauna. During a reconnaissance flight, he discovered the ten-by-forty-mile valley of the Baliem River, and saw clear indications of habitation – thatched huts and irrigated fields. Those inhabitants were the Dani tribe, and their emergence from the Stone Age began only with the appearance of missionaries in the mid-1950s.

Our first sight of Irian Jaya on our approach into Sentani airport, Jayapura, was of cloud-encircled, tree-clad mountains sloping straight into the sea on one side, and into massive Lake Sentani on the other.

I looked at the people around me at the airport. The Irianese – black-skinned, broad-nosed and frizzy-haired – really did look 'Papuan'. They were hirsute, too, a physical characteristic we hadn't until then associated with Indonesians. My first impression was of how fierce and threatening they looked, and this feeling wasn't diminished when a tall, broad policeman with flashing black eyes and flaring nostrils grabbed me roughly by the arm and pulled me towards his office. He wanted to see our *surat jalans*.

'Please, I will help you.' A short, paler-skinned man rushed to my rescue and ushered me out of the office. A bizarre encounter followed with the policeman alternately bellowing threateningly at the man, then tossing his head back and laughing loudly; hitting him hard in the stomach with my passport, and slapping him good-naturedly on the shoulder. Finally, the man emerged, smiling, and introduced himself. His name was Freddy and he would be happy to guide us to the Baliem Valley. Freddy looked like a 1950s British 'Teddy Boy'. He had slicked-back hair with sideburns and wore dark glasses, baggy black trousers tapered at the ankle, leather loafers and white socks. He informed us that he spoke Indonesian, Dani, German and English, but he gabbled so fast and so incomprehensibly that it was hard to tell exactly which he was speaking at any given moment.

Churches dominated the landscape as we drove into Jayapura. There are said to be at least three thousand expatriate

missionaries in Irian Jaya; its 'savage natives' are obviously felt
to be good candidates for conversion to civilized Christian values.
We stopped at the museum. It was run down and its collection of
Dani artefacts neglected, but Donna was drawn to some primitive
pottery, which inspired this mystifying conversation with the
woman in charge:

'Can we buy pottery like this?'
'Yes. In Ambon.'
'Oh. But this notice says the pottery was made locally.'
'Yes. In Sentani.'
'So, you *can* buy it locally?'
'No. Only in Ambon.'

Jayapura is Irian Jaya's capital and largest city with about
thirty thousand inhabitants. Built by the coast on a series of hills,
it is pretty at night with its lights twinkling and reflecting in the
water, but is otherwise unremarkable. We stayed at a hotel in the
centre of town, opposite a large mosque. A cinema close by was
showing 'made-for-video' type films: the ones that aren't good
enough to be screened in cinemas in the Western world, but form
the major part of the Third World's exposure to Western culture
– specifically sex and violence. All over Indonesia, cinemas
invariably advertise the worst kind of sadistic 'action' movies and
the public laps them up. Seemingly, the bloodier, the better. It
was an aspect of Indonesian life that we found hard to
understand and a little difficult to accept.

It was Saturday, and we shared the hotel restaurant with three
officials from the Governor's office who had just finished work for
the week. They sat laughing and joking at a table already covered
in empty beer bottles. When two bottles arrived, unordered, at
our table, the men rose to their feet and made their way
unsteadily over to us. 'We are happy you are come to our
country, Irian Jaya (pause) . . . which is a part of Indonesia. We
buy these beers for you . . .' Without finishing the sentence, the
men reeled out through one door, only to reappear seconds later
through another. They returned to our table, '. . . you are so very
welcome in our beautiful country. You know, we all working for
the peace in the world . . .' Again they exited and reappeared
through the original door; it could have been a well-rehearsed

comedy routine, '. . . black and white together . . .' There was
much shaking of hands before they departed for the third – and
final – time.

'They're here very often,' said Freddy, as if that explained their
behaviour. 'Tomorrow we must leave very very early to get to
Wamena. I think you must be ready at 4.30 in the morning.'

There was no danger of us over-sleeping. At four o'clock the
beautiful tenor voice of the muezzin drifted across on the wind
from the mosque and into our semi-consciousness. Five times a
day, the muezzin calls Muslims to prayer by chanting the verses
of the Koran over a loudspeaker. The singing is plaintive and
rather eerie. If nothing else, it is this sound which assures the
non-Muslim traveller that he is in a foreign land. It is also one of
the universal sounds that links Indonesia's scattered parts; it can
be heard from Sumatra to Sulawesi, Kalimantan to Komodo,
Jakarta to Jayapura.

Indonesian Islam is much more moderate than the
fundamental forms found in its Middle East heartland. Muslim
women in Indonesia are allowed much more freedom and are
shown more respect than their Arab counterparts; they aren't
obliged to wear veils over their faces, though the more devout do
cover their heads with shawls. The fanatical Shi'ite form of Islam
of, say, Iran doesn't fit the Indonesian ideal of striving to
maintain harmony and social order. This is not to say there aren't
enclaves of strict observance throughout the country, but, for the
most part, Indonesian Muslims are very relaxed about their
religion and pre-Islamic beliefs still thrive in many places in
parallel with Mohammed's teachings.

The Muslim population in Indonesia is somewhere over ninety
per cent. Christians make up the second largest religious group,
and the Balinese are Hindu, but perhaps the biggest group of
non-Muslims is the substantial proportion of the population
(especially those living in isolated areas) who still adhere strongly
to animist beliefs in which ancestral spirits play an integral part
in daily life.

Waiting for our flight to Wamena in the Baliem Valley, Donna
and I played 'spot-the-missionary'. Even disguised in cowboy
hats and Hawaiian shirts, they are unmistakable. Their tidy

wives and children, their air of piety and their sensible shoes give them away every time. 'Nerds,' said Donna. The missionaries were obviously not trusted by the local police; their bags were thoroughly searched for arms and subversive literature for the separatists, while we walked through unmolested.

Missionaries are adept at replacing outmoded, home-grown beliefs with their own pre-packaged, alien religion. 'So is that symbolic or what?' Donna pointed to one who was carrying a Rubbermaid plastic broom in his luggage – on his way to an area where people still used natural tools.

☆

At Wamena, the fresh, cool air slapped us in the face the instant we stepped off the plane. Seconds after we landed, a gigantic pig wandered onto the runway and lay down to sleep. A siren sounds to announce the arrival of planes and to warn people (and pigs) temporarily to vacate the runway. Even though one is forewarned, the sight of Danis wandering around the airport almost naked takes some getting used to. They are 'phallocryptic' and the men wear *kotekas*: long hollow gourds worn over the penis, secured around the testicles, and tied round the chest with string.

Freddy explained that the size and shape of the *koteka* depended on which tribe the man belonged to.

'It's not the size that counts,' I said.

'Oh no?' said Donna, giggling. Freddy blushed. The majority wore the long, thin *kotekas* of the Dani; the short, fat ones belonged to the Lani, and others attached around the body with rattan hoops distinguished the Yali tribe. One of the problems with Freddy was that halfway through many of his explanations he would lapse into giggles – especially when he started to explain that men kept paper money, tobacco and even sweet potatoes down their *kotekas*.

Married women wear specially woven orchid-fibre skirts and girls wear grass or raffia skirts. All are bare-breasted. As we carried our bags to the car, we were watched by a ferocious-looking Dani warrior. Feeling quite nervous under the scrutiny of his gaze, I hazarded a weak smile and his face instantly lit up with the broadest grin I have ever seen; all eyes and teeth, dimples and creases.

The Baliem Cottages Hotel had obviously once been relatively luxurious. With domed, grass roofs in the style of Dani huts, each circular cottage formerly had washbasins, baths and hot and cold running water. Times had changed. They did still have washbasins, but ours hung down at a 45-degree angle from the wall. We also had a huge bath which had been filled with cold water from a well several days before and was now doubling as an olympic-style swimming pool for scores of aquatic insects. A large stone had been used to stop up the plughole. There were numerous dead insects of unknown species on the beds and – to Donna's horror – spiders hanging in dust-encrusted cobwebs from the ceiling.

The path through the hotel grounds was in constant use by villagers on their way to or from market, and we felt like exhibits in a zoo as everyone who passed came up to the large window and peered in. After half an hour it was covered in smear marks at varying heights, where women and children had pressed their noses against the glass to see in better. Dani men (who were far more interested in their own appearance and adornments than in us), would glance at their reflection in the window and adjust their *koteka*, or primp their hair as they passed.

Walking into the market was like going into sensory overload. An amazing, earthy scene unfolded before us – a sea of wide-featured, expansive faces and a jumble of near naked bodies, sinuous legs, bare feet and large hands. Women sat on the ground selling sweet potatoes, tomatoes, maize, garlic, sugarcane, tobacco, cabbages, onions, chillis, spears, string bags, bananas and pineapples.

Men sat around in huddles; some on the ground, others lining wooden benches worn smooth by thousands of naked bottoms. Some were clothed, most were not. Several wore string or plastic bags on their heads; one walked by with a pig on a lead. Many wore beads, bracelets, cowrie-shell necklaces or had feathers in their hair. Their black eyes and dark, bushy eyebrows made them look fierce, warlike and alarming, until they smiled that fantastic, glittering, mischievous smile.

Irian Jaya

In other parts of Indonesia, baskets are used to carry goods from village to market – the Dani use string bags, or *noken*. Woven by hand, usually with yellow, red and black stripes, the long handles are worn over the top of the head and the bag dangles behind the body. Vegetables, pigs and even babies are carried in this way, often simultaneously. Even when they are not actually in use, the women wear them draped across their shoulders like a shawl.

I stopped to watch a man roll a cigarette. Taking a wad of leaves out of the end of his *koteka*, he peeled one off, licked it and rolled it up and down on his leg. Then he added a pinch of dried tobacco, rolled it up, licked it again, stuffed the wad of leaves back into his *koteka* and lit up.

Every so often we saw glaring examples of two worlds meeting head-on: a naked Dani carrying a bright, gleaming tin of coke in his tatty old string bag; another digging a hole with a brand new metal spade, but squatting and using it in a sideways chopping action as if it was a stone adze.

The scenery around Wamena was almost alpine and characterized by fir-like casuarina trees, rushing rivers, tall mountains, stone walls, even woolly sheep from an Australian aid project. Women sat washing yams in the river, poppies and hollyhocks proliferated by the side of the paths. And the Dani strode like proud living fossils through the landscape.

According to Freddy, there were only two Muslim villages in the Baliem Valley, the rest being animist or Christian. This, despite an Islamic teacher training college in Wamena. Part of the problem with converting the Dani to Islam is the high value they place upon pigs; tribal wars have frequently started over the ownership of animals the Koran derides as 'unclean'.

Around the perimeter of the first Dani village we visited was a tall fence topped with sharpened wooden stakes. The entrance was a tall stile designed to keep the villagers' pigs inside the compound. The village was almost deserted; the women were in the fields or at the market. The Dani are polygamous, a man having as many wives as he can afford. Freddy told us about one chief who had had fifty-six wives. The women leave the village early to work in the 'gardens' cultivating sweet potatoes – their staple diet – while the men stay at home and have a hard day rubbing pig grease in their hair and fashioning it into 'dreadlocks' ('What is this – the original mousse?' said Donna), or decorating themselves with feathers or cowrie-shell necklaces. Many Dani men have beards, but it is considered most becoming if the beard starts around the jaw line, which makes them look rather like garden gnomes! They spend hours plucking the hair from their face with tweezers made from split reeds. This is often done in mutual grooming sessions.

The apparent indolence of Dani men is misleading. Before 1950, inter-tribal wars were commonplace in the Baliem Valley, and the role of Dani men was to safeguard their families from attack. They spent much of their time on the lookout for raiders from the tall watchtowers which once dotted the landscape. The last serious outbreak of tribal fighting took place in 1968, since when the government – with help from the missionaries – have managed to bring the fighting virtually to an end.

The village chief appeared from the men's hut at the far end of the village. He wore a black plastic bag over his hair and looked as if he could be waiting to go under the drier at a hair-salon. (The natural vanity of these delightful people is so great, that had a hair salon been available he no doubt would have been waiting to do just that.) Holding out a large, rough hand he whispered '*La 'uk*', the Dani greeting between men and women. We shook his hand and returned the greeting. The hands and fingers were coarse and bony, but the handshake was as gentle as a child's.

'Come,' said Freddy. 'Come and see cooking hut.' This hut stretched the entire length of the village. It took a few minutes for our eyes to adjust to the darkness, but as they did so we could make out four smoking fires along the centre with cauldron-shaped pots beside them. It was completely blackened with smoke inside. An old woman was sitting on the straw, making a string bag. She was covered in light-coloured mud from head to toe and looked as if she had some disfiguring skin disease.

'Why do they do that, Freddy?' Donna whispered, staring at the spectral figure.

'Yes, sometime they do that if they are in mourn for someone.

And, you see, then, if they are all cover in mud, the spirit of the dead person cannot find them and give them problem.'

Attracted by the sounds of squealing, we returned to the daylight. A man and a woman were holding a small pig on their laps. A small fire smouldered beside them, and they were using a stick to smear pig fat over the skin which had become unhealthy. This was being done with great care and tenderness. 'The Dani like their pig,' said Freddy. 'Sometime they treat same as children. Sometime better maybe!'

Like the Torajans with their buffaloes, a Dani's wealth is measured by the number of pigs he owns, but attachment to the pigs goes way beyond their economic value. They really do seem to love them. Pigs are cuddled, stroked, fondled on laps, carried around in string bags. We even saw a piglet suckling at a young woman's breast.

The men's hut is sacred, and accessible to males only. When conjugal relations occur, a man will go to the woman's hut and he and the wife of his choice will wander out to the fields together. Small boys may sleep in the men's hut, but little girls must stay with the women. The men's hut, despite being only ten feet high, is divided into two, with sleeping quarters on top and a fireplace on the ground level. The men sit and talk there; the fire provides warmth during the cold nights and the smoke keeps insects at bay. All the huts are strewn with dried grass. Special 'spirit stones' are kept in the men's hut also; carefully wrapped in banana leaves and tied with string and kept for ceremonial purposes.

Despite the missionaries, the Dani are still largely animist and worship the spirits of their ancestors who, they believe, live in stones, trees, flowers – all natural things. If there was one underlying thread to our journey, it was that this belief was common to every island we visited. According to Dani beliefs, the first man and woman were created from a large stone. The stone was white and so the man was given the name Tebhe (meaning white skin). The woman was beautiful and was given the name Hesage. They covered themselves with mud as protection from the rays of the sun, and at night they went into a cave that God had made for them. When their children were born – in this same cave – they had black skin to protect them from the sun, and they built houses with roofs shaped like their parents' cave.

When the children were old enough to marry, Hesage and Tabhe were turned into sacred stones, which the children called Wesa. Even today, there are Wesa stones in all Dani houses and sacred places, and it is forbidden by tribal law (and accepted by Indonesian law) to remove even a fragment of them. The Dani rub the stones with pig fat to keep the spirits calm. Sometimes, the spirits within the stone may lose their strength, after which they are no longer considered sacred and may be exchanged or sold.

On the way back to Wamena, we were faced with the first of many terrifying bridges. This was a long, swaying, suspension bridge made from branches, vines and wire, and it stretched endlessly like an enormous cat's cradle over the rushing Baliem River. We crossed one at a time. The high wind and strong current resulted in an alarming optical illusion; if you looked down (and you had to, so as not to put your foot through one of the many gaps), you had the distinct impression that the bridge was moving sideways. Slowly, clumsily, we edged across. Feeling an enormous sense of achievement at having reached the other side in one piece, we were immediately shamed by an old Dani, who – though unable to walk on terra firma without aid of a large stick – sprinted across in seconds. He reached the other bank and gave us a broad smile before continuing on his way.

Back at the Baliem Cottages, we were the objects of great interest to an old man with a white beard and half a soccer ball on his head. He smiled and waved at us, then squatted down on the ground, took a small hand-mirror out of his bag and carefully examined his rugged face. I watched him for some minutes, intrigued, then turned away. When I looked back he was gone – as suddenly as he had come.

'Can't we get any beer, Freddy?' we asked at dinner.

'No. No alcohol here – no beer or whisky. The government doesn't allow. They say they are primitive, the tribesmen, and we don't want them to go out of the control. If we give them drinks, they will get crazy and silly and do the fighting all over again.'

Freddy also told us about 'Operation Koteka' – the government's unsuccessful attempt at 'civilizing' the Dani in the early '70s. They had hoped to persuade them to abandon their grass huts, and exchange their *kotekas* and grass skirts for some nice dresses, T-shirts and shorts. To this end, they distributed clothes and built them modern huts. The huts were never used, as they had corrugated iron roofs which made them too hot in the sun and were too noisy in the rain. And they let in mosquitoes. As for the clothes, said Freddy, nobody taught them about taking care of them, so they wore the same things day in day out until the clothes disintegrated.

We did visit villages, particularly around Wamena, where the Dani were clothed. It is hard not to sound patronizing, but the clothes were tattered, torn and grubby and it made them look wretched and poor. Those without clothes looked so much more dignified and gracious and proud. Missionaries and the government serve very important functions for the Dani – distributing medicines and eradicating internecine warfare – but, on balance, are the Dani really any better off? They had managed perfectly well for centuries without outside intervention.

During our stay in the Baliem Valley, we were only too aware that we were contributing to the Dani's exposure to outside influences. I felt constantly guilty about it, but at the same time hopeful that the people we visited realized that we were there just because we found their culture so fascinating, rather than as emissaries of the world of Rubbermaid brooms.

One effect of outside intervention is that diseases like flu and pneumonia are now the Dani's biggest killers. Before 1938, the Baliem Valley was virtually disease-free, the biggest threat to health being arrow wounds and respiratory ailments caused by sleeping in unventilated huts full of woodsmoke. Judging by the number of snotty-nosed, constantly sniffing children, this continues to be a problem today.

☆

It was cold in the morning. Dani men walked briskly past, hugging themselves for warmth. We set off early towards Pugima, travelling the first fifteen minutes of the journey by truck. To start with we bounced along muddy tracks, but suddenly came to a beautifully smooth bit of road. I was impressed.

'What a fantastic bit of road this is!' I exclaimed.

'We're on the runway, you fool,' said Donna. Freddy giggled.

When the 'road' ran out, we set off on foot on a path polished like marble by generations of leathery feet. People passed us on the way to market carrying wood, rattan, vegetables. The mountains swept up from the valley floor, sweet-potato gardens were protected from hungry pigs by wooden fences or stone walls. Wild strawberries grew at the side of the path. Villages dotted the landscape. We visited a few, but felt uncomfortable inside; the villagers wanted to pose for money. No sooner had I raised my camera to my face, than they put two fingers up and rubbed them together. This was a sign for wanting Rp200. Paper money only, of course, as coins tended to rattle uncomfortably in a *koteka*!

The first village we stayed in was one of those built by the government during Operation Koteka. The huts were rectangular, much larger than traditional Dani huts, with rusting corrugated iron roofs. Inside was a table, two wooden benches, a cracked mirror and a strange selection of reading matter: a child's exercise book full of Indonesian history, a Roman Catholic prayer book and litany in Latin and Indonesian and a copy of *The Carpetbaggers*.

We went to wash in a natural spring, which flowed from a small cave full of stalactites, and returned to find a Dani warrior sitting in the hut. His right hand was wrapped up in a filthy bandage. He had cut it with a *parang* when he was working in his garden, he said. I asked him how many days it had been sick. He had no idea. Had it been sick for a long time, I asked him. He nodded gravely. I put on some antiseptic cream and a clean bandage, and he left.

Dani have a very distinctive smell; an earthy combination of woodsmoke, sweat and horse leather. When they passed us on the trail, they always left the faintest hint of their scent on the air afterwards. It was far from unattractive. 'Someone really should patent this,' said Donna. "Eau de Dani" or "Dani for Men". They'd make a fortune.'

That night, the hut was packed with men, women and children, the warm yellow light from an oil lamp spreading over their dark bodies like melted butter. They sat and watched us as we talked to Freddy.

'About three months ago all chiefs in Baliem Valley go to Jakarta. I am interpreter. They met the President to talk about government.'

'What did they wear?'

'They must all buy dress. Outside from Wamena they cannot use *koteka*. But in hotel, every day they take off dresses and put on the *koteka*. Sometimes in Jakarta we out walking and they have to use the shoes, but they never use shoes here, so after two hours they take off, and walking around Jakarta, they walk in the Monas (the National Monument known amongst Jakartans as 'Soekarno's phallus') and all around without shoes!' Freddy giggled.

'What did they think of the planes?'

Freddy giggled again. 'Well, you know, here they know only Merpati. So when they see the Garuda plane, they tell me they have found Merpati's big brother!'

Towards the end of this story, one of the men took out two slender pieces of bamboo attached with string, and started to play them like a jew's harp. The *twangg twangg yingg yongg* reverberated in the night like an aboriginal call across the Dream Time.

As the government had neglected to provide the Dani with bathrooms in their new huts, I wandered out to find a suitable place for a pee. The music followed me out of the hut as I picked my way gingerly through the compound in the dark. Suddenly I heard a rustling to my left. Whirling round, the fading light of my torch picked out a pair of gleaming eyes and then a huge smile in the blackness. My heart thudding, I forced a smile and a weak '*La 'uk*'. I scanned the countryside with the beam of my torch, frightening two Dani women who were squatting nearby, but eventually found a suitable spot and was disturbed only by a massive sow snouting around in the earth.

☆

The sun shone thinly and the air was crisp when we started out north the next morning towards Suroba village, picking our way around sweet-potato gardens fenced with stone walls, through pampas grass and over tiny log bridges over irrigation channels. The slate grey mountains in the distance looked magnificent; the foothills deep green and rock-strewn like Cornish Tors.

Dani women looked ragged and dull in comparison with the men. They rarely wore anything other than their grass or orchid-fibre skirts and a string bag hanging over their shoulders, though they did sometimes find things to wear around their necks, and seemed to be particularly fond of shiny objects. One old woman was wearing a heavy-duty zipper, which was attached to a piece of string and hung down between her breasts. Safety-pins and paper-clips were in vogue, too.

Freddy pointed out a vine growing by the side of the path. 'This *koteka*-tree,' he said. We looked at the small gourds hanging down from the vine. 'The men they come and choose what size and shape they like. Then they pluck from tree and they dry in hut.'

Donna pointed to one particular fruit which had grown into a corkscrew shape. 'That one just for tourists,' said Freddy, 'Dani like them long and straight.' Donna gave a knowing smile.

The village at Suroba nestled near a river at the foot of limestone cliffs, and consisted of six huts in a large grassy compound. The huts had been made of wood lashed together with rattan and they had grass roofs and straw on the floor for sleeping on. The chief, Pua, came to greet us.

'My, but that's a fine specimen of a man!' said Donna in a husky voice.

She was right; Pua *was* magnificent. A young man in his early thirties, he wore a crown of striking red feathers around his head, out of which protruded three long feathers, black in front and red ones at each side. A long, rectangular 'bib' made from hundreds of cowrie shells hung from his neck to past his navel, and he had smeared pig grease blackened with soot on his forehead. Above all, he had an air of natural grace, which would have been as much at home on Windsor's polo ground as in a compound of grass huts in Irian Jaya.

While we were resting in our hut, a commotion started outside. A paunchy, middle-aged Dani wearing a pair of slacks, sneakers and a pork-pie hat like Pak Gub's was in heated conversation with Pua. This was Bohorok, said Freddy. A very famous chief. '*That's* a Dani chief?' said Donna. Neither of us found this easy to believe. The story goes that in 1972 Bohorok had met and married an American called Wyn Sargeant. She had written a book about 'her life among the savages', which had caused embarrassment for the government and resulted in her deportation. When they had been married, there was a huge feast and many pigs had been given as gifts by neighbouring village chiefs. Now that Wyn had left him, tribal etiquette dictated that Bohorok return these pigs. He had asked Freddy many times if he knew her address in America so that he could write and ask her to send the pigs to him!

Bohorok was complaining to Pua that he wanted to have foreigners staying in *his* village and wanted us to go with him. Pua stood on a small grassy mound, very much the superior in the exchange, with a collective force of village elders grouped around him. Harsh words were exchanged, and in those moments it was easy to imagine how terrifying the Dani could be in an aggressive show of strength. Next to Pua and the others, Bohorok looked ridiculous. Eventually he left the village grumbling to himself.

That night we were treated to an Edinburgh Rock sunset; the sky was splashed with pastels – duck-egg green, sky blue, pale pink and ivory. In the glow of the oil lamp and with mugs of tea in our hands, we sat and listened to Freddy as he told us about four Javanese students who had come to Irian Jaya to climb snow-capped Mount Puncak Jaya (at 16,532 feet, the tallest peak in Indonesia) earlier in the year. They had had seventeen porters and carried with them a radio powerful enough to contact Jakarta direct. When they disappeared, a search party, which included Freddy, was mobilized to look for them. They had looked for days without success, until a woman tipped Freddy off where to search. Next day, the party had gone to the cave she had suggested, and had found the bodies of the students and all but three of their porters. They were all dead; riddled with arrow wounds. Freddy's theory was that they had been killed for their radio.

'Their *radio*?'

'Yes. Don't forget OPM. A radio like that could be very useful.'

I dreamed that night of being under attack from Dani

guerrillas who wanted my Walkman, and woke the next day to
the sound of pigs snuffling and grunting outside the hut. A thin
mist hung around the hills and the sun was just coming up, as I
stumbled outside and wandered down to the river to wash. A
woman with a child on her shoulders walked past, the child
bobbing up and down, her orchid skirt swinging. These skirts are
extraordinary looking garments. They are made from scores of
thin strands of plaited orchid and fern fibres – yellow, red, black,
maroon – and rest on the hips well below the navel. On a
woman's wedding day, she must stand still (usually with a string
bag over her head!) for up to twelve hours, while her husband
fashions the skirt onto her. From that day on she will never
remove it. Women develop callouses on their thighs which help
keep the skirt on, even when they lose body fat as they become old
and frail.

The life of Dani women is, without doubt, extraordinarily
tough. Not only must they work hard all day in the fields, bear
children (although a Dani man may have so many wives that
each may only bear one or two), serve their husbands *and* wear
these uncomfortable skirts, but also, when a relative dies, a
woman must have one or two of her finger joints amputated to
appease the spirits. She is struck on the elbow, which causes her
lower arm to become temporarily numb, and a stone chisel is
used to cut through the bone and sever the joint. This is a
practice that both the government and missionaries have tried in
vain to eradicate; almost every woman we saw in the Baliem
Valley had finger joints missing – even the young ones.
Occasionally, the men subject themselves to voluntary
amputation, too; they cut their ears off horizontally above the
aural opening when their parents die.

'Do you like to see a pig-feast?' asked Freddy. 'There is one in a
village near here.'

'Of course! What's it for?'

'It is for an important event – a marriage, death, something
like that.'

'Well, if it's finger-licking good, I hope we still have fingers to
lick,' said Donna.

We reached the village by walking in the shadow of

overhanging limestone cliffs. It was a scorching hot day and flies
buzzed around us; I was reminded of the film *Picnic at Hanging
Rock*. By the time we arrived, the ceremony was already in
progress, and the village was packed with over a hundred people.
The men sat in groups at the far end of the village, near the men's
hut, grooming each other. Women were nursing babies, cradling
piglets and dogs, chatting and smoking. One old woman had so
few fingers left that she had to hold her cigarette between her
toes. Others were thronging in from the fields, their string bags
weighed down heavily with sweet potatoes, cabbage, maize and
other green vegetables just picked for the feast.

In the centre of the compound a fire was raging, in which
dozens of stones had been placed. We entered the village just as a
pig was about to be killed. One man held its back legs and
another its head, and it was held aloft at chest height for the chief
of the village to shoot with his bow and arrow. The chief was an
awesome individual with a pig bone through his nose and a
striped orchid-fibre cap topped with a cassowary feather. His
shot was deadly accurate, and the pig died instantly. Its ears and
tail were cut off and taken to the men's hut, where they would be
kept as a reckoner to the number of pigs that particular village
had killed.

Then, using a bamboo blade as sharp as any master chef's
carving knife, the three men set to butchering the pig carcass on a
bed of banana leaves and ferns; innards placed on one pile, meat
on another, bones on another. The intestines were then taken to
the river to be washed by the children. Everything was to be used.
'Everything but the squeal,' said Donna.

A pit had been dug and filled with freshly cut grass, banana
and squash leaves. Using tongs made from long poles split at the
bottom, six men levered and collected the hot stones from the fire
and carefully placed them around the sides of the pit. Once this
initial layer was in place, grass and leaves were packed on top
and then the women took over, carrying stones from fire to pit
and packing on more grass. In between the layers of hot stones
and grass, sweet potatoes and vegetables were lain, as if the
women were preparing a giant, green, crunchy lasagne.
Gradually, the hole became a mound, and was built up and up

until it was as tall as the women making it. Finally, the pig meat was put on the top and the whole thing was wrapped up tightly with grasses and rattan rope. The process had taken almost an hour. It was left to steam for two hours. 'Bit different from microwaving a hot-dog, isn't it?' said Donna.

While waiting for the haystack to smoulder and the food inside to cook, the Dani stamped up and down the compound, singing. Actually, it was more a series of guttural shouts, wails and whoops. They began to work themselves into a frenzy, jumping high into the air. An old woman with stick-like limbs, bent double with advancing years, got into the prevailing fervour more than anyone else and sang with gusto in her thin voice.

'What are they singing about, Freddy?'

'They giving thanks that they are strong and will have foods to eat.'

'And the dancing?' I said, thinking the stamping movements to be significant of some ancient tribal ritual.

'That just to keep warm!'

While we were sitting by the women's hut, a Dani – whose name I learned was Himan – came over to me with a striped bracelet woven from black and yellow orchid fibres. We exchanged greetings, and shook hands. He held out the bracelet. He wanted to put it on my wrist. However, the bracelet was far too small to fit over my hand. Himan fetched two of his friends and between the three of them they forced the bracelet, centimetre by painful centimetre, onto my wrist by wrapping lengths of grass twine around it and tugging down on them. Himan sat next to me and smiled.

'Now you married to Dani man,' said Freddy, shaking with laughter.

'What? You're kidding!'

'I wonder if Pua's got any of those bracelets?' mused Donna.

The haystack was dismantled by the women; smouldering rocks and grasses were tossed aside, and the pork, sweet potatoes and vegetables taken out. Bending over the steaming pit, their dark string bags tumbling over their shoulders like giant spiderwebs, picking out the sweet potatoes with disfigured fingers, they looked like so many witches bent over a cauldron.

There was a definite pecking order as regards the distribution of food. The meat was distributed by the chief first to the men and to selected women – probably his wives or favourites. Then the women filled string bags with sweet potatoes and gave them to the chief to separate up; some for storage in the men's hut, some for the women's huts. Bags of sweet potatoes were also presented to visiting dignitaries, including us, and after this everyone else had their share.

Back at Suroba, Pua told Freddy that he had taken a great liking to our striped umbrella. Freddy passed the information on to us.

'Pua, he say he want your umbrella. He will give two pig – like this one (he pointed to a small pig) – swap for umbrella.'

'What are we going to do with two pigs in our luggage?' said Donna dismissively. However, when we left the village, I noticed that the umbrella was missing and Donna had an orchid-fibre bracelet on her wrist!

Our next port of call was Jiwika village. From there Freddy wanted to take us to Aikima to see the 250-year-old mummified body of a much revered village chief. We stayed in a guesthouse called the La'uk Inn which was run by a Christian teacher. Guest-books often make for extremely entertaining reading; we glanced through the one at the La'uk Inn. One page was filled with twenty-three Swiss names and addresses, but all had declined to write any comments. 'Neutral to the end,' Donna said. The next visitors had written, 'We are very thankful that we missed the group above!'

'Ayal Telem' from Los Angeles felt inspired to comment, 'Killer dude! Catch a wave!', while a police officer from San Francisco had written: 'If all the people in San Francisco were like these villagers, I'd be out of a job.'

Some visitors seemed more interested in saving money than having a good time. 'Mans François', a student from Monaco, had written at length, obviously incensed at what he had witnessed: 'Don't go to Aikima, it's a fucking place where the favourite game is to rob tourist with their mummy. So please look at the picture in your guidebook and you will save at least Rp3,000. You can go to the mountain for the salted springs, it's

OK, but don't give them money for a picture. Smile and give them *kretek*.' He finally thought to add, 'Have fun and enjoy yourself but don't forget that they are human beings.'

☆

Early next morning we started the long hike up a steep mountain path to the brine pool at Iluerainma. Having staggered up to the top, past pandanus palms, moss forest and rhododendrons, we were rewarded with the sight of a very dull pool of stagnant water. If you dip in a finger and lick it, however, it doesn't disappoint – it really *is* full of salt. Every day, a steady trail of Dani women wend their weary way up to this natural well. Strips of banana palm – which have first been beaten dry of fluid – are put in the water to soak up the brine. Once they are fully saturated, they are taken back to the village and dried in the sun. A few days later, they are burnt and the salty ash which remains is mixed with water and made into a paste. This paste is then wrapped in banana leaves and left to harden into a solid block, which can then be grated directly onto food.

'Now I think you are ready to see mummy,' said Freddy. We had mixed feelings about this. It was the most 'touristy' thing in the Baliem Valley and for this reason we were reticent. But it sounded so extraordinary, that we put our feelings aside and let Freddy take us there. No sooner had we stepped into Aikima village, than we knew that our gut feelings had been right. The villagers were the only people we had come across so far who weren't friendly. Even the dogs were unfriendly and barked at us and snapped at our heels. We had to pay Rp5,000 each to see the mummy. Mans François would have been delighted to know he had got a reduced price.

The mummy – which was called Werap – was kept in the men's hut and was brought out carefully and placed on a wooden chair. Adorned with a large shell necklace and a moth-eaten feather crown, this amazing figure, blackened from centuries of residence in smoke-filled huts, crouched, unseeing, on its chair, knees bent up to its face, its hands loosely wrapped round its ankles. Parts of the body had been clumsily repaired with leather and nails or stuffed with grass. Somehow it looked indescribably sad; this once magnificent Dani chief – the Pua of its day – now brought out to order as a tourist attraction.

Back at Jayapura, Freddy took us to swim at Base G, the beach near which General MacArthur had his wartime headquarters. The beach was a crescent of pale yellow shelly sand with coconut palms and inviting turquoise water. We walked round a rocky headland and surprised a group of European tourists, who were skinny-dipping in the sea. Their indignant squealing and rushing to cover themselves seemed faintly ridiculous after the dignified nakedness we had encountered in the Baliem Valley.

5. Basilican spies and dirty little mice

Flores

Loud singing and raucous laughter emanated from the cockpit.
The pilot and crew of our Merpati flight to Flores were obviously
in high spirits. Ahead was the island of Flores, getting closer, but
the plane showed no sign of descending. I looked anxiously out of
the window and saw the single runway at Maumere airport, now
clearly visible below. Suddenly an anguished shriek came from
the cabin and the plane nose-dived downwards at such a steep
angle that it was only my long legs that prevented me from
disappearing under the seat in front. The plane screamed
towards the runway, pulled out with a gut-wrenching swoop, and
landed – heavily. The singing, which had ceased for the descent,
started up again.

Donna and I were on our way to Komodo – an island between
Sumbawa and Flores – to see the Komodo Dragons,
extraordinary giant lizards, which can grow to a length of twelve
feet. We had decided to fly to Flores and work our way back to
Komodo, taking a bus from the eastern town of Maumere to
Labuhan Bajo on the west coast, and then catching a ferry from
there to Komodo. We didn't know much about Flores, except
that there were three famous crater lakes at a place called
Kelimutu, and that a good deal of traditional weaving was still
done on the island – something that Donna, with her love of
'textures', was anxious to see.

As we were waiting for our bags, a smiling, middle-aged Italian
came over and introduced himself. His name was Luciano and he
ran a hotel not far from Maumere. Would we like to stay? He
could give us a lift there. A large crowd stared as we followed him
to the hotel mini-bus. Luciano explained that watching the twice-

weekly flights land was a local pastime, as the general consensus was that sooner or later one would crash. Our safe touchdown had disappointed the pundits, who were convinced that years of patience were finally to be rewarded.

'I'm afraid the bus-a was involved in a (pause) slight accident last week. One of our boys, he came into the collision with a large tree. Resulting, the bodywork is not, er, quite as-a she should be,' stammered Luciano awkwardly.

'Hey, no problem!' said Donna, opening a door which promptly came off its hinges and fell onto the ground. Luciano shuffled his feet uneasily.

'Please,' he said, gesturing for us to get in. The door was hastily replaced behind us. As the back door was jammed shut, our bags were squeezed in through the back window, as was one of the boys. Luciano and the driver got in the front.

The engine roared into life immediately. The driver beamed broadly at Luciano. Triumph was short-lived, however, as the gear-lever knob came off in his hand. It was passed to Luciano, who hastily put it in the glove compartment. He laughed nervously as the bus back-fired and we pulled out of the airport. The road was narrow and dusty and only partly paved. In a little under an hour of driving, we passed less than a dozen vehicles. Most people were walking, though some swayed along on ancient black bicycles. A few were on horseback, which was something we hadn't yet seen in Indonesia, but were to become accustomed to.

'Welcome to Flores!' shouted Luciano over the noise of the engine, 'this is what we call the "Inter-Flores Highway".' We laughed. 'Yes, yes, I know. Is joke, si? But is the only road on the island; 640 kilometres from one end to the other.'

The scenery was starkly arid. It was the end of the dry season and most of the fields were tilled and awaiting the first rains; some had shrivelled cobs of corn ready to harvest. Bare, dry earth and sparse yellow grass stretched on either side of the road. In the distance, green mountains were softly turning hazy purple in the late afternoon sun.

The hotel buildings – a large, airy clubhouse and guest bungalows set just back from the beach – were all made of local materials and in the local style. As the passenger door again hit the dirt, the noise disturbed a flock of small, brilliant yellow birds and a family of monkeys appeared in a nearby tree to see what the fuss was about. Our small bamboo and coconut-palm bungalow felt strangely primitive – though in the most comfortable way. Disturbed by our entry, several light grey *cicak* (pronounced 'chickchack') lizards scuttled across the walls and ceiling.

That night, Luciano and his family had arranged what they called 'a happening' for us on the beach. As Flores has a chilling history of human sacrifice (the practice of killing a child and burying the corpse under a corner post of a newly built house for good luck was reportedly still occurring as little as twenty years ago), we were somewhat alarmed to see that preparations involved digging a grave-shaped pit in the sand. The pit was filled with coconut husks, which were then set aflame. When the flames had subsided and the husks reduced to smouldering charcoal, a huge fish was placed on top of the coals. Sand was then poured over the lot and the fish was left to cook.

When the fish was dug out of the pit I expected it to be like a cinder; instead it ran with juices. The night was cool; the waves lapped gently onto the beach, cicadas chirruped in rustling palm trees behind us. In front of a crescent of flaming bamboo tapers, a group of Floresian men and women dressed in hand-woven sarongs sat on the sand and started to sing a strangely haunting melody. They sang many songs; songs about fishing, songs about harvesting corn, songs about waiting for the rains to come. One accompanied a kind of limbo dance, in which the object was to dance not under, but between, two bamboo poles, which were banged together on the offbeat, trapping one's ankles if one got out of step. Somehow, the silly Italian operatic song about a funicular railway '*Funiculi Funicula*' had sneaked into their repertoire. Luciano laughingly denied responsibility for this. He said that the people had been taught the song so long ago by Italian Catholic missionaries, that now they refused to believe that it didn't originate in Flores!

Missionaries came early to Flores. The Portuguese discovered the island in 1512 and called it *Cabo das Flores*, or 'Cape of Flowers'. By the mid-sixteenth century, there was a Portuguese mission in Larantuka, which had become a centre of Catholicism. Today, the population of Flores is officially eighty per cent Catholic, though we were to find out that animism, the original religion, is still practised by a large proportion of Floresians, especially those living in the more remote areas, who are thus less accessible to missionaries' influence.

As I was being lulled to sleep by the sounds of the sea, a *tokay* startled me. The *tokay* is a much larger lizard than the *cicak*, and the sound it makes is reminiscent of the exclamation an adenoidal child in an American sit-com might make when he realizes he has done something wrong. 'Uh-oh!' The sound is also extraordinarily loud; as if the *tokay* is calling into a mini-megaphone. 'Uh-oh! Uh-oh! Uh-oh! Uh-oh! Uh-oh! Uh!' After an indeterminate number of cries, the lizard will sometimes finish with an extra 'Oh!' as if suddenly it has forgotten what it is calling for and why. 'Nobody told us the room came equipped with a "gecko-blaster",' muttered Donna sleepily.

'Ah yes, the *tokay*,' said Luciano at breakfast the next morning. 'You have to listen very carefully to the little fellow. If he calls seven times, it means wealth, five times means happiness, six times, it means that the last thing that was said was true, more than seven times it was false, and eight, well, who knows! It is said that some people use him to make a decision. When the *tokay* begins to call, they will count yes and then no for each cry until the last one decides it.'

Being the only guests at the hotel, we had the undiluted attention of all four waiters. Hovering discreetly as we ate, they watched us like hawks and swept to the table bearing more food before we even had a chance to put our forks down. Should we (heaven forbid!) refuse a third helping, there would be a ghastly ruckus in the kitchen and Luciano would hurry out to see what the problem was.

'What's-a wrong?' he would ask, shuffling his feet and pulling at his beard anxiously. 'You didna enjoy the food we make-a for you?' We would quickly assure him that the food was absolutely delicious; which it always was, there was just too much of it.

'So then! You'll-a want some more!' and he would march back to the kitchen, rubbing his hands in a satisfied manner. We looked at each other helplessly, feeling like naughty school-children who had been caught not eating up their spinach and blancmange!

But this was not all. Every morning while we were having breakfast, Luciano's twenty-year-old daughter, Nicoletta, would come to our table to give us the intended menu for the day. Unfortunately, her grasp of the English language left much to be desired. Donna and I listened in horror as she informed us that we would be enjoying a meal of 'dirty little mice' for lunch. 'Is OK?' she asked, 'you like?'

'Oh yes, very nice,' we replied through forced smiles, and then had a hasty conference between ourselves as to what it could mean. It turned out that they had managed to buy thirty small corn cobs (maize) at the market!

When we weren't sleeping off our prandial excesses in our hut, we would be on the beach, which was like a page out of a holiday brochure; miles of black volcanic sandy beach, dark blue sea, a gentle breeze in the coconut palms – and us frolicking around in the surf, snorkelling and sunbathing. When the sun and sand got too hot, we would retreat under a large umbrella made of coconut fibres and watch the world go by.

The beach was a constant thoroughfare for the many local people who made their living along the shore. Most of the one million Floresians live simply; making their living from fishing, hunting and farming. Floresians are an attractive mixture of Melanesian and Indonesian peoples, tending more towards the stocky build, wide flat noses, frizzy hair and very dark skins that we had seen in Irian Jaya. Men, women and children in colourful hand-woven sarongs passed back and forth; some carrying baskets filled with shellfish they had found on the reefs, others *parangs* to chop bamboo or palm leaves. One small boy struggled by with a heavy green plastic bucket. A small dog trotted behind him. He disappeared down the beach only to return ten minutes later singing loudly with the bucket over his head, the dog still following behind.

Luciano was obviously a frustrated master chef. He would tantalize us with recipes which he would make for us if only such-and-such a vegetable, meat or other ingredient became available in the market. As we sat cradling cold beers in the clubhouse, he described a mouth-watering recipe for kingfish – thinly sliced and marinated for twenty-four hours in lime juice and garlic – which had been suggested by Prince Bernhard of the Netherlands when he had stayed at the club. He wasn't a bad name-dropper, either.

'Aaahhh, if only we had a Kingfish,' sighed Luciano, his eyes raised to the heavens as if in a dream where he was about to make the first incision with the paring knife . . .

Later, as we were sitting on the beach making plans to leave for Komodo at dawn the next day, a small, rough dugout canoe appeared in the distance, being paddled by a muscular fisherman with a large afro-haircut. It came closer and closer, until eventually the man leaped out and pulled the canoe up onto the beach. He bent down and picked up a huge fish, well over a metre long, and held it aloft proudly for us to see.

'*Apa itu?*' we asked him. 'What is it?'

'*Ikan Raya,*' he replied. 'Kingfish.' We stayed another day!

The sunsets from the beach were classics; the sky turning to glowing orange, blood red or gold, behind an outline of silhouetted palm trees; the mountains fading into the middle distance and children splashing about in the surf. It was like stepping into a travel poster for a tropical paradise.

☆

At breakfast the next morning, Nicoletta approached our table, beaming. 'Good morning! Good morning!' she cried. 'Is a lovely day, no?' We agreed that it was and waited apprehensively for the day's menu. 'Tonight you know you 'ave ze big fish?' We nodded. 'An' for lunch we make for you special porridge of sporty meat with chopped Basilican spies.' Donna choked on her pineapple. Before we could ascertain what this appalling-sounding concoction was (game stew flavoured with basil), Nicoletta excused herself with a mumbled apology about 'the dam . . .'

Next to the club, just along the beach, ran a small creek which, as it was the end of the dry season, was dry. On the other side of this creek was land, which was variously described by Luciano as belonging to either a 'minister of the government' or a 'disgraced ambassador'. At any event, he was Luciano's arch enemy. He had constructed a dam, according to Luciano, in order to divert the water during the impending rainy season so that it would flood out the club. Luciano's every waking moment – not spent torturing us with gourmet food – was devoted to devizing ways to counter this threat. He had mobilized the local villagers to build *another* dam to divert the water from upstream back onto its rightful course. He daily entertained a prosecuting magistrate from Maumere in the hope of burying the 'government official' under a rainstorm of writs. He had even engaged the services of the local witchdoctor to put a curse on the dam!

Finally, we decided to make the long journey to Komodo while there was still time to get across Flores and over to 'the island of dragons' before the rains came. As the standard form of public transport were huge open trucks with no seating – the passengers standing for hours swaying to and fro in the dust – we chartered a battered old mini-bus. Our first destination was the little village of Mone – a day's bumpy ride from Maumere – where we could stay overnight at a mission, before going on to the volcanic lakes at Kelimutu.

Travelling on the 'Inter-Flores Highway' was an experience in itself. Over most of its length it was unpaved. Far narrower than an English country lane, it frequently dissolved into little more than a track as it wound relentlessly through the mountains. Our driver's technique at blind corners did not involve slowing down, but rather clamping one hand on the horn while steering with the other. The only problem with this was that he was then unable to hear the horn of any approaching truck whose driver was employing the same technique while hurtling towards us from the other direction! In this event, both vehicles would screech to a halt and heated arguments would ensue as to who should give way.

Most of the bridges were being repaired simultaneously before the imminent rainy season. Only two or three men would be working on each bridge and, as they had no heavy machinery, this meant that two of them would be engaged in carrying heavy stones to the third, who would then cement them in place. At this pace, none of the bridges looked as if it would be repaired before the *following* rainy season, let alone this one. In the meantime, our bus was forced to leave the road and bump across the dry river beds and up the bank to the opposite side. Inevitably, we got stuck, and we had to get out and fetch banana leaves to jam under the wheels to provide traction.

When we weren't helping to pull huge boulders out of our path or push the bus up steep river banks, the journey was very rewarding scenically. It was beautiful driving through the mountains, glimpsing the sea sparkling in the distance. We passed small villages built from bamboo and coconut palm; children carrying long pieces of hollow bamboo, which they use as a receptacle for water; women returning home from the fields balancing huge baskets of vegetables on their heads.

At one of these villages we stopped to buy some coconuts for the journey. Immediately we were surrounded by a gaggle of curious villagers, none of whom responded when we tried to talk in *bahasa Indonesia*, the national language. It was rather disconcerting after the ready friendliness of the other islands.

Six bone-crunching hours later we arrived at Mone. The mission was a bright white, red-roofed, church-shaped building set amidst fertile hills. I was, by this time, suffering from an extremely heavy cold, which had started in the morning and had become progressively worse. I seemed doomed for a miserable evening, until one of the mission workers suggested that I try some locally-distilled brandy called *arak*. This concoction is made from sugar palm and is about 110° proof! It tasted foul, but after several glasses we were both way beyond caring about my cold or our uncomfortable iron beds.

We were woken at day-break by the sounds of the weekly market, which was setting up in the field just outside our bedroom window. Throughout our entire travels in Indonesia, neither Donna nor I could resist a market. The bustle, chatter, textures and colours fascinated us. On a scale of one to ten, this one was at least a nine. People had journeyed many miles to sell their produce and buy goods that were unavailable in their remote villages in the surrounding hills. Some came by foot or on horseback. Others poured off open trucks. More and more people streamed onto the field. Some set down woven mats or simple palm leaves, thereby claiming a small space for their produce. Others weaved between the crowds, stopping to chat or to examine a giant cabbage or a pile of green and red chillis. Women with skins the colour of roasted coffee squatted by their goods, children cradled in their arms or laps, eyes squinting in the bright sunlight as they talked to a friend or prospective customer. Most people were wearing traditional, hand-woven sarongs around their waists or draped over their shoulders, and many protected themselves from the sun by wearing elaborately folded tea towels on their heads.

The usual assortment of items were for sale – potatoes, bananas, coconuts, cabbages, dried fish, beans, rice, pulses, spices – but our eyes were drawn to the bamboo fence at one side of the field along which were draped dozens of locally woven *kain ikats* – the traditional tie-dyed fabrics for which Eastern Indonesia is famous. The styles in Flores are quite different from those we later saw in Sumba and vary markedly from village to village. The relative isolation of much of Flores allows the styles to be far less under the control of the dealers, who purchase much of the output of East Nusa Tenggara at budget prices and then sell at mark-ups of 400%–500% in Bali. Historically, Flores *ikats* were for the people. In Sumba, they were for the royal and rich families; only the King and his retinue, for example, were allowed to wear the *hinggi kombu* (the red, white and black patterned cloths). I shocked one of the salesmen by buying a black and blue striped sarong. These are men's colours and such a sarong should not even be *chosen*, let alone worn, by a woman! After the sale, however, he insisted that all his friends be photographed with me while he stood at my side – his head barely on a level with my shoulder.

By now it was approaching 8.00am and we had to leave in order to reach Kelimutu before the clouds did. They tend to roll in by mid-morning and envelop the volcano. On the way up to Kelimutu, Flores began to live up to its name as the Isle of Flowers. Brilliant red and apricot hibiscus, deep purple, red and pink bougainvillaea, the scarlet thin flowers of the lipstick plant, tiny purple jarong flowers, wild water-melon and fragile passionflowers bloomed in abundance. The landscape was accentuated by glittering streams, terraced *padi*-fields and traditional villages with tall palm roofs.

We stood staring down at the volcanic lakes in awed silence. At 1600 metres, in the caldera of the volcano, lie three massive craters containing deep lakes of different colours. Two are so close that they are separated only by the thinnest rim of volcanic rock. Close, but remarkably different. One was a deep turquoise, the other a deathly milky white. The third, a little distance away, was a dark, inky black. Films of sulphur precipitated on the surface, bubbling up from below. Every now and again small stones became dislodged from the crater wall and fell almost silently into the opaque waters beneath. A lizard scuttled in the dust nearby; a hawk soared way above us on the thermals; the sun blazed. Still, we stood and stared, unable to speak. I looked at Donna. Despite the heat she was as deathly white as the lake.

'You do realize,' she whispered, unable to avert her gaze from the two liquid skeleton eyes below, 'that this place incorporates two of my greatest phobias – heights and deep water?'

'At least there are no spiders,' I said helpfully, but there was no reaction. The lakes appeared to have mesmerized her. I pulled her away from the edge of the crater and sat her down on a rock, while I looked up Kelimutu in our guidebook. It seemed that the lakes had taken on these colours after an earthquake in 1982. Before that, one had been blue, one red and the other white. Even further back in time, in the 1930s, they were reportedly blue-green, deep green and red. According to local legend, the lakes are the final resting place of departed souls. The black lake is home to those of sorcerers and the elderly, the souls of the young and pure of heart reside in the turquoise lake and the white one contains the souls of departed sinners and the general hoi polloi.

The original religion of Flores, called *Nitu*, is remarkably similar to many of the pre-Hindu animist religions of the entire archipelago, and is based on the belief in the souls and spirits of one's ancestors. These reside not only in distant volcanic lakes, but also in trees, rivers, mountains or stones. Relatives are buried not in cemeteries, but around one's house to keep them near at hand, and if the spirits wish to contact their living human descendents, they will send snakes – particularly pythons – as messengers. At a museum we visited a few days later, we saw photographs taken a year or so previously of a family home with a python coiled up in one corner. It had just appeared one night, slithering its way into the bosom of the family, so to speak. Far from being frightened, the family – despite being 'good Christians' – were honoured to be chosen and left food out for the snake. After a week, the python left as suddenly as it had appeared. As Luciano had commented, 'The people of Flores are eighty per cent Catholic and one hundred per cent animist.'

Clouds rolled in and obscured the mountain tops and, as we scrambled down the rocky path to the bus, I turned back and saw that the volcano and its mysterious secrets had become quickly enveloped in swirling cloud.

After several hours of being bounced around in the bus and screeching around knife-edge ridges, it started to rain. It occurred to us that conditions could only get worse. We stopped to consider our options at what our driver assured us was the 'best restaurant' between Mone and Labuhan Bajo. The food was not merely inedible; it was indescribable! We were told that it was sago, but it looked and tasted more like some industrial waste product. Rain was pouring off the roof into big tin buckets, and didn't look as if it was going to stop. Suddenly a small boy came running into the restaurant, completely drenched and breathless. He garbled something excitedly to his father, who came over to our table to relate the news. The rains had caused a huge mudslide, and the road a few kilometres on was blocked. 'But,' he assured us, 'it may be cleared soon.'

'How soon?' I asked.

He shrugged. 'Maybe this week. Maybe next.'

So much for Komodo. We paid for the mostly untouched meal, returned to the bus and turned back for Maumere.

We arrived back completely exhausted. As we flopped down onto the chairs in the clubhouse, Luciano scurried out of the kitchen to greet us.

'Welcome! Welcome!' he cried. 'You have arrived at-a the good time. Today I have bought the fresh turtle meat at the market. I will make-a you the best meal you have-a ever tasted. A leetle herbs, a leetle garlic . . .' And he swept back to the kitchen to don his chef's hat and sharpen his knives.

Neither of us had ever contemplated eating turtle before, but anything would be better than our unappetizing encounter with sago pudding.

The turtle was a delight. Luciano had surpassed himself. We ate it all, which made him very happy. During the meal we noticed a hermit crab which had taken a wrong turning from the beach, ended up in the clubhouse and was obviously having difficulty finding its way back again. It would stop still for a few seconds, trying to take stock of its position, and then career wildly sideways in whatever direction it had decided on. As it was making no progress at all, we decided to intervene and help it on its way, to the astonishment of our usual mélange of silent waiters. As well as hermit crabs and orchestras of fiddler crabs on the beach, there was one particular species of land crab which occupied burrows near our hut – and they would frequently challenge us with up-raised claws over who had right of way on the path.

That night we became acquainted with the soon-to-be-familiar portly figure of Father Bollen, who resembled the English actor, Robert Morley. He had been in Indonesia for a quarter of a century and lived at a large Catholic seminary at Ledalero, where he described himself as a 'social worker'. He had a habit of chain-smoking *kretek* (clove) cigarettes (during our hour's conversation with him he smoked an entire pack), and he reeked of sour, stale smoke. In his guise as social worker, Father Bollen told us, he encouraged his flock to adopt various untraditional practices, such as terracing their hillside smallholdings to prevent soil erosion, and using birth control. The latter surprised us. 'But I thought you were Catholics?' said Donna, rather tactlessly. 'Oh ja,' replied Bollen, 'but we only allow the mucus method.' Neither of us had heard of this form of contraception, but it sounded too disgusting to pursue further!

We went to visit him at the seminary, as we had heard that the nearby village produced weavings. Bollen confirmed this and, giving the signal to one of his domestic staff, said, 'In fact, I believe they are doing so just now.' The servant sped off and

Bollen took us on a long circuitous route, presumably giving the weavers time to set up their spinning wheels and looms. On seeing us, six women just happened to start performing simultaneously all the steps necessary to produce an *ikat*. One was crushing the seeds out of raw cotton on an old-fashioned mangle, another spinning it into thread on a wheel which was turned by foot, while, on a frame, the long threads were being bound with coconut fibres to produce the desired pattern. An older woman with several ivory bracelets on both wrists was in charge of the dyeing process. She was stirring a pot over a fire, in which threads were undergoing coloration from red dye made from *mengkudu* root and *loba* bark. Nearby, other pots contained blue, yellow and green dyes, which were made from indigo flowers, seed pods and green leaves.

'*Ikat*' means 'to tie', and *ikat* cloths are fashioned by binding the warp threads tightly with grass or palm-leaf fibres, to create a dye-resistant pattern. Sometimes the patterns are recorded on paper or palm leaves, but more often than not, the weaver knows by heart which areas and individual threads need to be bound. Gazing incredulously at the sea of tiny knots stretched on the wooden frame before us, it was hard to imagine the skill involved in tying the knots precisely and evenly enough to form the intricate patterns, let alone doing it from memory.

After they are bound, the threads are dyed. Cheap, easy-to-use chemical dyes are widely available in Indonesia now, but though they are often used to make textiles to sell, most weavers refuse to use them for cloths that will be kept in their own families. The dyeing process is often a closely guarded secret, surrounded by superstitions and taboos. To ensure success, certain rules must be obeyed. In some parts of Indonesia, for example, the enclosure where the blue dyeing is done is absolutely off-limits to men. In others, menstruating women aren't allowed to dye cloth lest their 'impure' state disrupt the process.

The processes of binding and dyeing can take months – even years – depending on the richness of colour desired. Once this is finished, the actual weaving begins. Throughout Indonesia, the 'back loom' is the one most commonly used. A young woman sat at one of these, bracing her feet against a tree and controlling the tension of the threads by leaning backwards or forwards against a back brace. Every few seconds she would raise the warp threads with a long, slender piece of ebony and then slip the shuttle containing the weft threads through. It was slow, painstaking work. An *ikat* woven in this way can take weeks, whereas a factory-made cloth can be finished in a matter of hours.

The finished sarongs had wonderfully rich colours and elaborate, mostly geometrical, designs which, we were told, were very private to their creators. Passed down through the generations, nowadays only the old village women are said to know what they really mean. Most motifs have developed from animist beliefs, and revolve around fertility symbols, hence the recurring symbols of man and woman, animals, birds and flowers. The one that Donna was particularly taken with was, according to Father Bollen, an incongruous mixture of fertility symbols and gambling dice!

The museum attached to the Catholic seminary housed everything from mastodon teeth to brand new Australian coins; it had ivory, jewellery, shells, Ming pottery and albums of photographs of *ikat* designs from all over Flores. It was here that we saw the picture of the family with their python guest. The curator of the museum, a busy little man with long, crooked fingers, took another album down off a shelf and blew thick dust off it. Looking nervously over his shoulder to see whether any of the 'fathers' were around, he opened the book and showed us faded colour photographs of various piles of rocks and caves from very remote villages. These, he whispered, were sacred animist shrines; magic places where, for example, the rice or corn spirits dwell and can be summoned when necessary. There had been a number of ceremonies recently, to incite the rains which had been late. There was no doubt, even with extensive missionary influence, that the ancient pagan religion was alive and well.

On the way back we noticed a large crowd gathered at the side of the road. At its centre was a woman surrounded by a circle of other women, while nearby was another – less well defined – assemblage of men. A pile of possessions stood by the road. Our driver stopped to find out what was happening. It appeared that the woman had had enough of her husband's philandering and was going to divorce him. Marriages in Flores involve the payment of a 'bride price' in ivory, silver, money or livestock. Divorce is rare, as it involves repayment of the entire price. Whatever the eventual outcome, the village had decided that this matrimonial dispute was good viewing and had turned out in force to watch.

The next day – Friday, our last day in Flores – was market day at the small village of Wainara. We walked there with Luciano. There was a permanent market-place where the majority of produce was sold, and also a large animal market where a selection of dejected horses stood for sale, with their heads bowed, along with goats, chickens and pigs. Most of the Flores Muslims are fishermen and live on the coast. Catholics and Muslims usually live peacefully together, but occasionally violence breaks out. To reduce friction between the religious communities, the authorities had forbidden people to allow their pigs to roam freely (as this would offend the Muslims), so those for sale in the market lay on their sides, with trotters trussed, pitifully awaiting their fate.

The beach market was the most interesting. Here, people from the smaller islands off the coast would sail over in their boats, bringing their produce with them. According to Luciano, the reason the market is held there, rather than at the official market-place, is because the islanders are lazy and refuse to haul their goods any further than the beach! Small outrigger canoes lined the water's edge, and people were disembarking with baskets of dried, salted fish, while others approached the shore. The land around the coast was very dry. There were none of the fresh, crisp, green vegetables that we had seen in the fertile mountain area at Mone. The staple food was maize and dried fish, and both were there in abundance. We could locate the dried fish with our eyes shut, the smell was so pungent. The lack of variety in their diets caused many people to look ill-nourished and, according to Luciano, vitamin deficiencies were responsible for the leg and spinal deformities that were rife on the island.

A white-haired old man squatted on the ground, holding up two yellowing elephant's tusks for us to see. In the past, ivory was used widely in Flores to make bracelets such as the ones we had already seen on the wrists of older women. These formed part of their 'bride price' and were presumably originally brought by Bugis traders from Sumatra. A few yards away a local 'medicine man' was working himself into a verbal frenzy, trying to convince a large crowd that had gathered around him that his foul-looking potions would cure everything from boils to malaria. Some worked, Luciano said, but others were downright dangerous!

As we walked back to the club along the Inter-Flores Highway, the morning wore on and the sun rose higher and hotter and we sought the shade of the palm trees. Not one vehicle passed us during the half-hour walk. Luciano pointed to a small house near the beach. A child had died there recently and had been buried under the house, rather than in the garden as an adult would be; a modern vestige of the old practice of sacrificing a child and burying it under the foundations for good luck.

As we walked on, he regaled us with other stories of local lore. 'Recently, a man here cause an accident and kill another man. You know the first thing he does? He runs helter-skelter to the police to beg to be put in jail, because he knows that the first thing the family of his victim will do is to look for him and decapitate him.' And worse. 'If they're really terribly angry with him, they will hack him to death and eat his liver!'

That afternoon Father Bollen drove up to the club shrouded in *kretek* smoke, and asked us if we were interested in joining him on a short trip to Kampung Baru, a *transmigrasi* village of recent immigrants from the overcrowded island of Java. We had thought Bollen a little strange, and this jaunt confirmed our opinion. The road to Kampung Baru was appalling, with huge potholes and the road metal often disappearing altogether, leaving only a deeply rutted muddy track. This, however, did not deter Father Bollen, who drove at least sixty kilometres per hour all the way. He, too, refused to slow down on blind corners, or over bumps, or anywhere. It was as if he was racing to get to the *transmigrasi* before they could be converted to Islam or *Nitu*! As we flew over the bumps, Mad Father Bollen (as we have called him ever since) would shout 'Hoop-la!' and chortle with emphysemic laughter, the inevitable *kretek* stuck firmly between his lips. We gripped on for dear life in the back of the jeep as we were bounced and shaken about, our heads hitting the roof whenever we went over a bump.

As we raced through low-lying mangrove swamps, Bollen slammed on the brakes in order to show us a couple making salt by boiling seawater. This process must be one of the most arduous and least rewarding occupations on earth; it takes litres and litres of water to produce even a few grammes of salt. They were boiling the water in big vats. When the solution became supersaturated brine, they poured it through large funnel-shaped baskets from which it evaporated to precipitate 'stalactites' of salt.

An air of poverty hung over the entire process. The couple were not expecting visitors, least of all white visitors with cameras. They greeted our arrival with classic displacement behaviour; evidently too frightened to admit to themselves that we were there, they simply refused to acknowledge our presence. When I caught the woman glancing at me from a distance, I smiled, expecting the usual Indonesian response of a smile returned with interest. Instead she quickly averted her gaze, stared at the ground and started shaking with fear. We left as hurriedly as possible, feeling more like intruders than we ever felt in Indonesia before or since.

Every few kilometres we would come across one or two country people on their way back from the market. At the speed we were travelling we would spot them only at the last moment, whereupon Mad Father Bollen would slam on the brakes and we would end up in a crumpled heap against the back of the front seat. Father Bollen would give a quick 'Hoop-la!' and then offer a lift to whoever we had just nearly run over. Probably under the impression that they would be safer *inside* rather than outside, the people would usually accept, with the result that there were soon nine of us crammed in the jeep, plus three chickens and a small pig. This did give us some extra cushioning, though we nearly crushed two betel-mouthed old ladies who had had the misfortune to sit between us and the front seat.

On our arrival at Kampung Baru, we learned that the priest we had journeyed so long – and so uncomfortably – to see wasn't there. We asked at the church when he would return.

'Oh, soon,' came the inevitable reply. 'Would you like to wait?'
'How soon?' I asked.
'Oh, he'll be back for the service,' they said.
'When's that?'
'Sunday.'
We declined the offer and bumped our way back to the club.
When we reached the salt-makers' camp the people had gone, but
a monitor lizard about a metre long was walking across their
encampment, tasting the salty air with its long forked tongue. We
thought of Komodo, which had slipped from our grasp. 'Imagine
one of those four times the size . . .' said Donna. We looked at
each other, both of us thinking that, but for bad timing, we could
have reached Komodo by now.

Donna turned to Mad Father Bollen and asked if he had ever
been to Komodo.

'Oh no!' he replied. 'They're all Muslims there!'

'But what about the dragons?' I asked.

'Dragons? Hoop-la!' cried Mad Father Bollen, as we hit yet
another bump.

☆

After our experiences of the difficulties of travel in the rainy
season, we decided it was time to take advantage of Jean-Marc's
offer of hospitality in Jakarta. By the time we arrived there, we
had been on three long flights, all of which had been delayed, and
were on the verge of total exhaustion. The taxi driver managed to
find the address that Jean-Marc had given us, and the *jaga*
(security guard) let us in without question. Jean-Marc was away
– again! – and his house-mates all out for the evening and the *jaga*
didn't know what time they would be back. By now it was 9pm
and for all we knew, being young bachelors about town, they
could be gone all night, so we placed Jean-Marc's note
prominently on the table for them to see and decided to go to bed.

Some hours later we were awakened by a furious banging on
our door and a voice shouting, "Ooo are you? What do you want
'eere?' It was like something out of *Goldilocks and the Three Bears*;
they had returned home to be informed by the *jaga* that their
'guests' had arrived and were sleeping upstairs. Not expecting

visitors, Jean-Marc's friends had rushed upstairs to find out who the hell these strange people were sleeping in their house. Once we explained who we were, and they had read the note, they were terribly apologetic and insisted that we get up and have some dinner with them.

One of them, Alain, was going to Banda in a few days' time and was only too happy to ply us with questions about the place. Yes, the snorkelling was fantastic; yes, the Maulana Inn was a great place to stay, but watch for Des and his optional extras; yes, the food was wonderful; yes, the scenery was great too.

A silence fell. We could hear the night traffic of Jakarta honking and squabbling outside the high security fence around their house.

'Zen what are you doing here?' asked Alain, with a wry grin.

Donna and I looked at each other. He had a point.

6. The early tourist catches the worm . . .

Sumba

Jakarta gave us an opportunity to recover during the rainy season when much of Indonesia is inaccessible, as well as to plan our next moves. By February, our efforts were directed towards one goal – finding out the date of the 'Pasola', an ancient pagan ritual which takes place annually in Sumba. Despite its size, Sumba is largely ignored by tourists to Indonesia. It lies far south of Flores, west of Timor, and is just too much out of the way even for those more adventurous folk who are travelling through the islands of the Nusa Tenggara chain. In centuries past the island was known primarily as a source of sandalwood, slaves and horses. Even then, it was off the beaten path and escaped the influences of the Hindu, Muslim and Christian religions that marked its neighbours. As a result, its ancient pagan culture remains preserved. Well over half of the population adheres to the animist *Merapu* religion, which reveres and worships ancestral and land spirits.

We had heard about the Pasola during our travels and it sounded intriguing. It marks the start of the rice cycle and, correspondingly, the animist New Year, and the date varies each year according to solar and lunar calendars. The first – and the true pagan – part of the Pasola centres on the arrival on a certain beach of thousands of small, multi-coloured sea worms (called *nyale* in Sumbanese). These worms are said to have magic properties, and their size and shape will predict the outcome of the rice harvest. The rest of the Pasola is given over to spectacular jousting matches, which take place between hundreds of horsemen from rival villages and have evolved from real tribal warfare that took place in Sumba in days gone by.

The major problem confronting us was finding out exactly when the Pasola was to happen. Donna and I must have gone to every travel agent in Jakarta. None had even heard of the Pasola, let alone when it was scheduled to take place. Several hadn't even heard of Sumba. 'Why don't you go to Bali instead?' they said. Clearly we were wasting our time. However, we did manage to get the phone number of the Government Tourist Promotions Office for East Nusa Tenggara, in Kupang, Timor. This sounded hopeful.

The ensuing attempts at getting a straight answer about the date of the Pasola encapsulates everything that is at once infuriating and endearing about Indonesia. I was told that the Pasola (they had heard of it – that was a good start!) was definitely set for March 23rd, eight days after the full moon in the second solar month. That same afternoon, we received a telegram from a hotelier we had contacted in West Sumba, informing us that the Pasola would take place on March 20th. As if this didn't confuse matters enough, one of the more enterprising travel agents had also contacted the same Tourist Office in Timor and called with the news that they had given her a definite date for the Pasola: March 15th! In the end we opted for a date somewhere in the middle and – discovering that Merpati (of course) flew once a week to an airstrip in Tambolaka, West Sumba – we booked ourselves on that flight. All we could do then was hope for the best.

I should have guessed that something was wrong when an official at the airport asked us where we were going, and laughed derisively when I said Tambolaka. Did he know something we didn't? If he did, we weren't to be in the dark for long.

'Flight to Tambolaka cancel,' stated the man at the Merpati check-in counter. 'Plane brok.' Good old Merpati.

'Déjà-vu airlines,' sighed Donna.

The next direct flight wasn't until Saturday, by which time we would be too late for the Pasola. I felt desperation creeping over me like a malaise.

'How about try Bouraq?' he suggested. The Bouraq desk didn't open for two hours, so we fortified ourselves with some Bali coffee – strong, black and sweet – at a small stall nearby. One side of the

counter was cluttered with large plastic sweet jars, overflowing
with chiclets, bars of chocolate, fried bananas, chewing gum and
so on. On the other side was an impressive, large, tiered glass
case, which was completely empty except for one expired box of
Kodacolor 100 and two bent toothpicks.

Eventually the Bouraq officials arrived. Donna insisted she do
the talking. She flicked through her dictionary as the officials
behind the counter looked on with an air of gleeful expectancy.
Taking a deep breath and looking confident, she said in a loud
voice the equivalent of: 'Excuse me, sir, what time does the
lobster machine leave?' The officials looked alternately puzzled
and frightened. Indonesian for aircraft is *pesawat udara*, literally,
'air machine'. The word for lobster is *udang*. Donna had read the
adjacent word in the dictionary by mistake. We were in luck.
There was a flight to Mau Hau on the east side of the island at
midday. We bought two tickets.

Our flight was only half an hour late and we finally landed in
Sumba that afternoon. We were the only foreigners on the flight
and, obviously smelling of innocence and quick money, quickly
attracted a bevy of taxi drivers and representatives from hotels,
trying to drum up business . . . 'Where are you going?' 'What will
you do here?' 'Here for Pasola? Ah yes.' 'Stay at Hotel Elim. Best
hotel in Sumba!' 'Losmen Surabaya. Give you good price!' A
scrawny man with high cheekbones and the pale milky blue eyes
of a man who is nearly blind, stood near me expectantly. His half-
seeing eyes looked straight at me. I asked him when the Pasola
was. It was on Saturday, he said. Today was Thursday. We
would make it after all. 'Can we get transport to the west of the
island?' I asked. With a conspiratorial half-smile, he replied,
'Anything can be arranged. There is a Chinaman at the Losmen
Surabaya . . .'

The Losmen Surabaya was a squalid-looking guesthouse by
the bus station in Waingapu. It was hot and dusty, buses hooted,
and everyone stopped whatever they were doing and gawked at
us instead. A spaced-out, bearded, saronged Australian
wandered lethargically out of the Surabaya to see what was going
on. He had obviously been there for a long time and, like the
locals, was attracted by anything that strayed from the norm. We

told him that we were planning to take a bus over to the other side of the island for the Pasola. 'Oh right – yes, the Pasola,' he said vacantly and without enthusiasm.

'Aren't you going?'

'No, there's a boat on Saturday to Ende (in Flores) and I've got to get that.' The Ende boat was a weekly event – the Pasola an annual one. It seemed his priorities were confused, but he was adamant in his abstracted way, so we made no attempt to interfere with his obvious date with destiny.

The owner of the Surabaya had an incredibly long body and short legs, and was dressed in all-purpose Chinese garb – shorts and a sleeveless white vest. The bus standing outside was his, too, and we bartered over the price for the 137-kilometre journey to Waikabubak. Having started at Rp100,000, we finally agreed on Rp70,000 to be paid between the two of us and two businessmen who wanted to join us. As we sat and waited outside the Surabaya, three more young men piled in. By the time we left there were nine of us crammed in the eight-seater bus. So much for the comfort of only five passengers. As we pulled away from the Surabaya, the Chinaman was staring thoughtfully at the tyres. A few hundred yards up the road, he came running after us waving a tyre pump.

The bus whined along recently paved, narrow roads which twisted and turned through the hilly East Sumban landscape. The view was extraordinary; barren, treeless hills with the tops shorn off, as if someone had wielded a gargantuan *parang* and sliced them off in one stroke.

As there was very little other traffic to contend with (just as well, as the road was only wide enough for one vehicle at a time), our driver, Alosius, egged on by a Chinese businessman in the front seat who was clearly in a hurry to get to Waikabubak, drove like Alain Prost. The bus careered chaotically along the road, screeching around corners and sending us flying out of our seats whenever we hit a bump. 'Must be a graduate from the Missionary School of Driving,' said Donna, recalling Mad Father Bollen and gripping the seat in front with white knuckles.

An hour from Waingapu, the bus suddenly veered off the road and bumped to a halt, inches from a tree. Alosius and his three assistants leapt out and announced that the steering had broken. So the extra passengers we had taken on board were the maintenance crew. It started to rain. The men worked soggily on the bus. After half an hour we were back on the road and travelling faster than ever. Twenty minutes later one of the rear tyres burst. It was replaced by one which appeared to have decent tread on it – until Donna pointed out that the 'tread' was actually canvas showing through bald rubber. Again we accelerated. Now we had rain coming in through a leaking roof to contend with, too, which didn't ease the anxiety of hurtling along these narrow roads with broken steering and sixty-foot drops at either side.

The sun started to set, turning the grassy hills copper and gold. Soon the entire sky was lit with a metallic orange glow so extraordinary that it made us seriously wonder whether we were travelling just ahead of a giant forest fire.

Late that evening we arrived in Waikabubak and screeched to a halt outside the Rakuta Hotel. I had sent a telegram informing them that we would be on the Tambolaka flight and expected to be with them mid-morning. Nobody seemed to be bothered that we were over nine hours late. By the somewhat lax Indonesian standards of *jam karet* (rubber time), we were right on time.

From a huge front verandah, we stepped into a long reception room. Chairs lined walls which were covered with photographic montages of the local 'sights' and, at one end, lit up like a museum exhibit, was a glass case containing the owner's camera equipment. Beyond this there was a central corridor with bedrooms on each side and then the dining-room. Our room smelt musty and damp and contained two enormous double beds – each big enough to accommodate an extended Indonesian family – with ornate, padded maroon and gold bed-heads, edged with elaborate wooden carvings. They looked worthy of a former Sultan, and didn't go with the pokey room whose walls were mottled with damp. By the door stood a massive Victorian wardrobe whose doors had warped so much that they were unopenable.

For dinner, we had what we later remembered as our last decent meal in Waikabubak: clear soup, fried chicken and, as always, stacks of boiled rice. The dining-room could have come straight out of the '60s, with walls covered with faded psychedelic murals. One thing we were desperate for after our long and harrowing journey was a drink. However, as the cold beer was 'finished', we had to wait half an hour while more was fetched by motorbike. Mopi, the hotel dog, came and sat at our feet, hoping for a few scraps. We became very fond of Mopi. He was a sweet-natured, battle-scarred mutt of the first order, who never uttered a bark or a whimper, even when he was forcibly kicked out of the dining-room. We fell asleep that night to the sounds of giant frogs in the field outside, so big that they sounded like sea-lions.

Though it is the biggest town in West Sumba, Waikabubak was idyllically quiet and peaceful after Jakarta. Little houses with neat, pretty gardens lined the street. Hibiscus and bougainvillaea bloomed in abundance. There were pigs everywhere, snuffling about in the ditches, trotting along the road. This was a sure sign that we were back in non-Muslim country. A road led us out into the countryside and we were soon passing scenes of green rice-*padis*, leading to distant hills topped with clusters of the high thatched-roof houses that characterize Sumban traditional villages. Small Sumban horses were grazing or being ridden bareback along the roads and through rice-*padis*. People passed by, carrying coconuts and sheaves of cut rice balanced on poles on their shoulders.

We returned to the Rakuta, looking forward to a cold beer. 'Cold beer finished,' we were told. It was only towards the end of our stay at the Rakuta that we worked out that, despite knowing that we always wanted cold beer, Jon, whose job it was to fetch supplies on his motorbike, was insuring his job security by making sure the hotel was permanently out of everything.

'WHAT is this?' asked Donna, peering into the soup tureen and poking dubiously at the contents. Floating in the greasy water were pieces of what looked remarkably like astro-turf. We looked at each other.

'Carpet soup?' I suggested. After prodding it with the spoon, we decided that our soup consisted mainly of stomach. Green stomach. Not very appetizing. We set it aside and ate our rice and fried chicken. After lunch the owner's wife – whom we called *Ibu*

(Madam) – came to our table. She folded her arms across her chest in best seaside-landlady style, looked at us with piercing black eyes, took a big intake of breath and said, 'So, you no like my cooking?' This short, plump, daunting woman ruled the place with a rod of iron. All the staff – not to mention the guests – were frightened of her. 'So,' she thundered, 'tell me what you like and I cook.' She stood there bristling, waiting for an answer. Some of the staff drifted in, anxious to see this confrontation. Or maybe they were just pleased to see someone else getting the rough side of her tongue for a change.

'Er, perhaps some vegetables?' we ventured.

'Yes. Yes. We can do cats.'

'CATS??' Bearing in mind the stomach, anything was possible.

'Cats. Long, red vegetable.'

It took a few seconds before it dawned on us that she meant carrots. We burst out laughing and, though they couldn't have followed the conversation, so did the staff. Ibu looked like a thunder cloud. We agreed that cats would be lovely, as would spinach, chicken, potatoes; anything except carpet soup!

Visitors to the hotel came and went. Fathers-in-law, cousins, friends of friends of Ibu or her husband. Amid the activity, we sat down with Eddi, a swarthy young man who drove the hotel jeep, to negotiate hiring it to take us to Wanokaka for the Pasola the next morning. Here follows a typical Indonesian negotiation:

Annabel: 'How much to drive us to Wanokaka and back?'
Eddi: 'How much do you want to pay?'
Annabel: Pause. 'Rp20,000.'
Eddi: Laughter. 'Not enough. Rp60,000.'
Annabel: More laughter. 'Too much. Rp35,000.'
Eddi: 'Rp55,000.'
Annabel: Consultation with Donna. 'Rp45,000. Final price.
Eddi: 'Rp50,000. Final price.'

A stalemate appeared to have been reached. To preserve face – or, in our case, money! – neither side would back down. It was then that we called upon our secret negotiating weapon. The Imitation Lacoste T-Shirt. As if possessing some kind of sixth sense, Ibu appeared on the scene. She stood in her characteristically arrogant posture, arms folded across her chest, head cocked slightly to one side, her mouth set in a quizzical line. 'I like that one,' she said, pointing to the yellow shirt that Eddi had picked out. Considering the jeep belonged to her anyway, and Eddi was only hired as the driver, he clearly had very little say in the matter. The deal was done. Rp45,000 and a shirt for Ibu.

We were curious to see what she had concocted for dinner that night. The soup tureen appeared. No carpet. So far, so good. Donna ladled out the liquid, which looked harmless enough; until we tasted it. The soup wasn't merely flavoured with chillis, it comprised nothing else.

'I think she's trying to punish us for not eating the Axminster,' Donna spluttered.

'MORE BEER!' we yelled. Mopi raised one eyebrow and lay down to sleep under the table, as Jon revved up his bike and sped off into the night. We weren't sure what the rest of the meal consisted of; we were incapable of tasting anything else for hours!

After dinner, with glasses of strong, black, grainy coffee, we set out our scrabble board on the dining-room table. Within ten minutes we were surrounded by curious staff and guests, who leaned over us and pondered our letters seriously. A small boy called Kalindi, who was part of the massive family network and worked at the hotel instead of going to school, took a great interest in the game. Actually, after a while, Kalindi became rather a pest. He had an annoying habit of repeating *any* sound that one made. Even a sniff or a sigh or a cough. I put down the word 'armpit'. Kalindi pointed to it and looked quizzical. 'A-R-M-P-I-T,' I spelled out for him. 'ARMPIT! ARMPIT! ARMPIT!' he yelled, running round and round the table. I picked up five more letters, only to find that they were mostly vowels.

'Christ! What letters!' I exclaimed to nobody in particular. 'CHRIST LETTERS! ARMPIT! CHRIST LETTERS!' shouted Kalindi, jumping up and down.

It was totally dark when the alarm went off at 2.15 the next morning. Stumbling out to the hall, we discovered the prone figure of Eddi sleeping on one of the reception-room sofas, and within minutes we were bumping along the road to Wanokaka.

Sumba

It was a beautiful night; clear and fresh with a very bright moon and stars in the sky. We were alight with anticipation. We were heading off into the unknown to an ancient pagan ritual fraught with magic. Our adrenalin was pumping. We giggled hysterically as the track worsened and we were thrown around inside the jeep like dummies in a stunt car. An hour later, we neared Wanokaka and started to pass groups of people walking along the road in the dark. The nearer we got, the more people there were; some on horseback, many in ceremonial regalia. Shadows of houses, trees, people and horses passed us by silently like ghosts.

Finally, after one and a half hours, we came to the beach and Eddi parked the jeep. I leaped out, stepped aside to let a shadowy figure pass, and immediately fell thigh-deep into a rice-*padi*! A bad start. The moon and stars lit our path as we made our way along the beach to the sacred black rocks where the sea worms always appear.

There are various explanations as to why the *nyale* come to the surface at this time of year. Unromantic scientists tell us that the *nyale* are actually segmented sea worms of the Eunicid family, which usually live buried in sand in shallow water. At the same time each year, in response to the full moon, their tails swell with sperm and eggs, rise to the surface to mate and then get caught by the tide and washed ashore.

So much for the scientific explanation. The Sumbanese version is much more poetic. Many hundreds of years ago there lived a beautiful young girl called Nyale, who was the daughter of the moon. In an attempt to make his human subjects prosperous, the moon sacrificed his daughter. She was dismembered and thrown into the sea, whereupon her teeth changed into rice, vegetables and corn, her skin into cattle and goats, her ribs into turtles and her heart into bananas. Every year the many-coloured sea worms come from Nyale's body to make the land fertile again. The blue *nyale* are said to come from her hair, the red from her blood and the yellow from her lips.

Another Sumbanese legend tells of a woman called Bota, who travelled across the sea sitting on the back of a crocodile to search for food for her starving people. She found the *nyale* at the

116

seashore and brought them back, whereupon their own land became fertile.

The *nyale* ceremony heralds the start of the rice or fertile season and the end of the 'bitter months', during which many prohibitions are enforced. For example, in the months prior to the ceremony, the people of Wanokaka are not allowed to wear bright colours, make a lot of noise or exchange presents. During the Pasola the riders wear remarkably bright, colourful head-dresses, presumably to mark the end of the prohibition on such dress.

Throngs of people had already gathered on the beach. I searched for the village priests or magicians. I had read about these old men and was anxious to see them for myself. These *Ratos*, as they are called, act as the go-betweens between the everyday world and the spirit world. Each *Rato* represents a clan from the different districts of West Sumba, and has specific ritual duties to perform at certain times of the year.

The duties of the *Rato* priests had started long before the actual *nyale* ceremony. For weeks before, all the priests congregate on top of a sacred hill, which is a place charged with mysticism and taboos. The hill abounds with ever-powerful ancestral spirits, who guard holy paths which must not be crossed. Ghost dogs are said to roam free, inflicting insanity on anyone they bite. From there the *Ratos* watch the rising and setting of the moon and calculate the precise time of the Pasola. At two o'clock in the morning, eight days after the full moon, as moonlight illuminates the countryside, the priests begin to chant in unison; an eerie '*Huuuuuuuu. Huuuuuuuu*', their voices slowly dropping to silence before starting up again. Still chanting, they follow the ancient magic paths down from the hills to the seashore to await the arrival of the *nyale*.

The sky had begun to lighten to a luminous grey. Offshore, softly chanting in the shallows, stood the solitary figures of the *Ratos*. Each held a long staff, taller than himself, and they all held baskets for the *nyale*. Their dress was traditional, with *ikats* draped across their shoulders and turbans (held in place by long red or black cloths tied under the chin), from which stood tall head-dresses made of flowing horsehair. The thin, fragile figures soon became silhouetted against the sky, which began to glow

117

until deep orange flames licked the cool silver grey clouds. I could almost feel the magic in the air as suddenly, without warning, three horsemen charged down the beach in the half-light, hooves thundering on the sand, the bells on their bridles jingling. An old priest – a man with intense, fearsome dark eyes and high cheekbones – stalked towards us, sweeping us out of the way with his long stick, just as the horses skidded to a halt in front of us.

From around a bend at the far end of the beach, hundreds of people poured through the dawn mist. At last a haunting cry went up from the rock pools. '*Huuuuuuu. Huuuuuuu*'. The *nyale* had been sighted. The priests bent down to scoop up handfuls of the worms into their baskets. Excitement spread through the waiting crowds and, at a sign from one of the priests, they picked their way over slippery seaweed-strewn rocks, into the shallow water, to collect as many worms as they could. Not only do these creatures have magic properties, they are also a local delicacy – particularly fried!

As one of the younger, less frightening-looking priests walked back up the beach, he showed us some worms writhing uncertainly in a coconut shell of water. They ranged from one to six inches long; most were green, some red and some yellow. He explained some of the ways they can foretell the outcome of the rice harvest. For example, if the worms are shattered or broken, there will be too much rain and the harvest will be damaged, and if the worms bite the priests' fingers, the harvest will be infested with mice and rats!

It was beautifully cool and clear; cold, slate-blue breakers were rolling in gently over the reefs, while the clouds were turning soft rose and shades of peach. All along the steep, rocky coast as far as the eye could see, there were hundreds of people splashing about in the water. It was a fantastic scene.

The sun had fully risen by 6.00 and it was already becoming hot. 'Jesus,' said Donna, 'what's it gonna be like at midday?!' Suddenly, from around the bend in the beach, dozens of horses appeared. In ones and twos they galloped hell-for-leather along the sand, manes flowing, bells jangling, hooves pounding, sand flying. Their riders, dressed in stunning bright head-dresses and brandishing wooden lances, shouted and whooped as they swerved briefly to a halt, then gathered their mounts and galloped from a standstill back along the beach. The sturdy little horses were foaming at the mouth and glistening with sweat. The energy being generated was terrific. The horses snorted and puffed and cocked their heads, as if enjoying the occasion as much as their riders, each one beautifully decorated with head-dresses made from swatches of blond horse-hair, colourful ribbons and crêpe paper.

The horses and riders departed to cool off in the sea before the actual Pasola began, and our attention shifted back to the priests. They had congregated under a huge tree at the top of the beach and were exclaiming the results of their examination of the *nyale*. The consensus was that, as the worms were small, the harvest would be poor. Then, facing each other in two lines, each raised his spear in turn and proclaimed what his function would be during the coming year.

I was really taken with these old men. Their dark, wizened faces looked as though they had seen many weird and wonderful things over the years. They were intense, serious and wise. I was struck more than anything else by their great dignity. It was clear that this event really meant something to them, whereas its symbolic meaning was perhaps becoming less important to the younger people. The *nyale* is the true pagan ceremony. The Pasola is more like a sporting event, festive in nature – and obviously more popular with the general public. Only a handful of people stood watching the priests, compared with thousands of spectators who were gathering to watch the Pasola. Few people had travelled all those miles just to see a bunch of doddery old men chanting at each other and the sea. Sad.

We, too, eventually left the old men to their chants, as the first of the two Pasola events was already in progress along the beach. We could hear it long before we could see anything; the gasps and roars of the crowd, the whooping and shouting of the riders, the whinnying of the horses, the thud of wooden spears colliding in mid-air, and that faint, magic, jangling of bells.

On a large, flat, grassy area just up from the beach, scores of horses and riders stood waiting to plunge into battle. There were two distinct teams – warriors from the highland clans pitted against those from the lowlands. The warriors would ride into the centre of the field alone or in groups, trying to score a hit against one of the opposing team. Spears flew through the air like shooting stars. During a mass charge, the air was full of them. The priests say that the rain of spears symbolizes real rain, which is all connected with the fertility connotations surrounding the *nyale* ceremony.

Without a doubt, the most dangerous job of the day was that of the lance-boys, who rushed onto the field to pick up the fallen spears and return them to the riders. Not only did they have to duck flying lances, but horses' hooves and falling riders as well!

Several hundred people were already lining the steep hill of terraced *padis* overlooking the field below. Many had climbed into trees for a better view. I counted twenty-two men and boys in the branches of one tree alone. We picked our way cautiously around the side of the arena – not wanting to get too close to the charging horses – and along the narrow dykes between the *padis*. At 8.00 we were already soaked with sweat and my head was throbbing with the exertion of clambering up the hill. Hundreds of pairs of feet had already passed the same way and the path was extremely muddy and slippery, as well as being liberally sprayed with bright red splotches of betel-coloured spittle. Young and old seemed equally drawn to its narcotic effects. Most of the old people we met in Sumba had no teeth left at all, displaying only gnarled, red stumps when they grinned.

Hysterical shouts emanated from the excited crowd whenever hits were scored. If their man's spear struck its target, or if he executed a particularly skilful or daring manoeuvre, the women uttered weird, ululating cries sounding like a cross between an Indian war cry and someone yodelling. The breakers rolled in. A mist hung lightly over the water. The foam-flecked horses' head-dresses glistened in the sun, the riders' long scarves billowed behind them in the breeze as they galloped into the arena, the jangling bells sounded like crazy Christmas sleighs.

'Whomp that sucker! Go get him, you dumb kluck!' shouted Donna, getting into the action. One team had singled out a lone member of the opposite team – perhaps an old and hated enemy – and all went for him at once, heading him off from the others and from his escape route. In the heat, tempers were beginning to flare. The teams mocked and taunted each other, tempting them to make a false move. Soon we were as emotionally involved as everyone around us, gasping when someone came close to being hit, roaring approval of a skilful parry, shouting our concern when a rider came unseated.

Eventually, the Lowland Pasola wound down, and riders and horses retired to rest and lick their wounds. The spectators, meanwhile, slowly made their way single-file along the *padi* banks the four kilometres through rice-fields and woods, to the main field at Wanokaka; the Highlands.

Hundreds more horses and riders gathered to take part in the main jousting match. It was like a colourful medieval pageant, with the proud warriors in their striking fluorescent green, yellow, red, orange and blue head-dresses, and their perky horses. However, their numbers were nothing compared to the thousands of spectators who were arriving every few minutes by the bus load. There was a carnival atmosphere. Friends greeted one another and breakfasted on sticky rice, prawn crackers, fresh coconut, sweet biscuits, cold drinks and Bintang beer bought from food- and drinks-vendors under the trees.

One rider had been eliminated for having sharpened his lance, and was arguing noisily with the policeman who had discovered his misdemeanour. In days gone by, real spears were used and many more deaths and serious injuries occurred. Only recently has the government ruled that blunt-ended sticks must be used. This infuriates the Sumbanese, who believe that it is necessary for people to shed blood. If a person has offended the ancestral spirits, then his injury is the true way to atone for his sins. Only then can he and his family start the new year with a clean slate. Even today, it is quite common for a rider to fall 'accidentally' onto his lance and snap it in two in order to sharpen the end!

The feeling in the crowd was that this was expected to be a 'grudge match'. One man had been hit in the neck in the morning's Pasola and was badly injured, so his team would be out for revenge. When it began, the main Pasola was breathtaking. Hundreds of horses and riders plunged into the middle of the field at once, charging, ducking, parrying, hurling spears at the enemy. The crowd roared. The sun pounded. Our heads throbbed. The air was thick with spears. We had opted to be as close to the action as possible this time and stood right at the edge of the field. Horses thundered past us, spears flew within feet of us. It was wonderful! At this close range, one could really appreciate the horsemen's skill. Riding bareback, steering one-handed, the other hand full of spears, they seemed as one with their horse – almost like centaurs. As they galloped again and again into the arena, facing possible death every time, I realized how incredibly brave they were.

The priests had gathered on a mound under the shade of a large tree, to watch the match. They looked on intently, no doubt remembering when they were young and were out there risking death in the arena; days when real spears were used and much more blood was spilt. The scene was of another time, another world. Suddenly there was a great gasp from the crowd. A man had been struck from his horse and was lying motionless on the grass. Everything stopped. Riders leapt off their horses and ran, along with many of the spectators, towards the body.

The man was carried from the field covered in blood. 'He's been hit in the head,' we heard from the crowd. 'He will die soon.' Nothing stopped the Pasola, though. Within five minutes the riders had re-mounted and were charging at each other with renewed vigour. The wounded man's side were clearly out for vengeance and charged frenetically, hurling their lances indiscriminately. Several flew into the crowd, one hitting someone nearby.

'Jesus, this is dangerous,' yelled Donna, jumping back a few feet. It is some measure of how influenced we were by the general fever that even that didn't make us give up our prime position next to the action. There is no denying the enormous thrill of being in danger.

By the time the Highland Pasola was over, hours later, a total of six men had been injured. Soaked with nervous sweat, we finally left at midday and succumbed to exhaustion as Eddi drove us back to Waikabubak through countryside which previously had been obscured by night. The road wound through gently rolling hills covered with rippling green grass. To our left were sweeping views to the coast with deep blue sea beyond. Had it not been for the occasional palm tree and rice-*padi*, I could have sworn that I was driving over the Sussex Downs. Off the road a little way we stood on top of a large, domed hill, gazing out to sea. It was cool and quiet there, peaceful and unspoiled. Clusters of traditional houses nestled in the valleys, horses grazed in the lush grass, streams glistened in the sunshine. It was one of the most beautiful views I had seen in Indonesia.

By lunchtime we were back at the Rakuta. Everyone wanted to hear about the Pasola, or had further news for us. One of the injured men had been hit in the eye, apparently, but the priests had healed his wound with 'magic' water. 'Like that,' said Eddi, pointing to our bottle of Aqua mineral water. 'Like this?' we asked, astounded. Aqua was as good as any, he insisted, provided the right magic was involved.

Next morning we were woken by hideously jolly keyboard music emanating, at full volume, from the dining-room, so we made an early start for a traditional village called Tarung. Sprawling along the top of a hill, Tarung is famous for its size and for being the site of many important animist ceremonies. 'Hey! Killer dude – catch *this* wave!' shouted Donna. She had got to the top first and was gazing open-mouthed at the structures towering solidly around her.

Traditional Sumbanese houses are massive. They stand about twenty-five feet high, with a large proportion of their bulk consisting of a high, sweeping roof made from a special type of grass called *alang*. The main structure is made from huge tree-trunks with long, thick bamboo poles lashed together to make the walls and floor. The roof sweeps down to cover a large verandah where the family sits, works and socializes. Harvested rice is kept in the roof, and the space below the verandah is reserved for pigs, dogs and chickens.

Dozens of these tall, thatched houses formed a haphazard main street, with countless stone tombs standing higgledy-piggledy in the centre. The tombs consist of plain slabs of stone resting horizontally on four smaller rocks or pillars, like dolmens. Even though the tombs are sacred, the villagers were not averse to putting them to practical use; coffee and rice were spread out on woven mats, drying in the sun. They were a favourite spot for the mangy *kampung* dogs, too, who were sprawled out on the hot slabs – too lethargic even to bark at us. Most of the villagers were inside their houses sheltering from the heat, though one old woman stared out at us expressionlessly from her verandah, listlessly scratching a wrinkled breast from time to time, and a boy and a girl pounded rice with long wooden poles.

We came to the house of the *Kepala Kampung* (village chief), which overlooked spectacular views of green hills, *padis* and streams. He sat in the shade at one end of his verandah, carving a wooden sheath for his antique ivory-handled *parang*, and gestured for us to join him. The roof was so low that we had to bend double to get in, but it provided marvellous shade and made the house delightfully cool inside. His wife sat at the other end of the verandah, a small child asleep in her lap, dicing tapioca. On the wall behind them were hundreds of buffalo horns and pigs' jaws – remnants of past ceremonial sacrifices.

That afternoon there was a violent storm, after which the frogs' croaking rose to a deafening crescendo, sounding like church bells played through a cheap synthesizer! We spent the afternoon, with Mopi, on the dripping verandah of the Rakuta, reading and watching the soggy world go by. The road was quiet except for the occasional raucus horn from a passing bus or *bemo*, squealing of pigs, rustling of palm leaves and the sound of children singing hymns nearby. Horses clopped past. Children skipped by on their way home from school. Later on there was a small commotion when a pig strayed too far from home and its owners came running after it. Afterwards we laughed at ourselves as, like seasoned locals, we had leapt up to watch the ruckus. Such is the welcome diversion of a seemingly insignificant event when so little happens during the course of a normal day.

'Surely not!' I said, poking what looked suspiciously like boiled ferns which had been placed before us on the table.

'I fear so,' said Donna grimly.

'What's this?' we asked Olivia, the waitress.

'Vegetable,' Olivia replied in English, and rushed from the room.

Tentatively, we each took a forkful of the tiny green ferns and popped them into our mouths, but they were absolutely inedible. Ibu had done it again! We spat them out in unison, and got on resignedly with our other dull, repetitious fare of plain boiled white rice, fried chicken (an interesting pot pourri of beaks, feet, knee joints and other delicacies) and boiled spinach. There was no doubt that Waikabubak would be remembered, though not fondly, for its regional cookery!

On our last day in West Sumba, we caught a bus to Anakalang, twenty-two kilometres east of Waikabubak, where the most impressive tombs in Sumba can be found. Like every bus and *bemo* in Indonesia, this had a 'runner'; a young man who leant out of the open door drumming up business from passing pedestrians. This particular bus had two, who attracted passers-by and vastly entertained Donna and me by yelling our destination over and over without stopping for breath, sounding like a stereo recording with a stuck stylus: '. . . A-nak-alanganakalang-anakalang . . . !'

A few kilometres out of town, a deaf-mute got onto the bus. Grunting and gesticulating wildly at everyone, he made his way up to the front where we were sitting and shook our hands violently, wheezing and grinning like a lunatic.

The journey was pleasant; rattling along peaceful country roads with lovely views of green, grassy hills, banana trees, rustic huts and horses and cattle grazing in fields amongst crumbling stone tombs. Eventually, the bus stopped. Nobody got out. Everyone turned to look at us.

'Are we supposed to get out here?'

'I don't know. I don't see any tombs.'

'RRRHGGGHHH,' said the deaf-mute, pointing at the steps of the bus and then, forcibly, at us.

'We get out here?' Donna asked.

The deaf-mute pointed wildly to something behind us. There, standing unostentatiously in a field, were the tombs we had come to see.

'Oh, THERE they are!? We have to get out here!' we said. The deaf-mute disembarked and gestured for us to follow.

'He's not coming with us, is he?' I said.

'RRRHGGGH!' said Donna and grinned.

Offset from the road in a grassy area surrounded by palm trees, stood a grave called the *Pasunga*; one massive horizontal stone slab with another vertical slab behind it. This vertical slab is fabulously carved with two angular figures of a man and a woman. Below them, motifs of horses and ceremonial gongs are carved in relief. It is said that 150 buffaloes were sacrificed in the many ceremonies which were performed during its construction. Donna was especially taken by the 'textures' of this particular tomb and took many, many pictures of it. The deaf-mute was quite overcome with joy when I asked him to pose for a photograph, and stood erect, holding his head up proudly for the shot. A few minutes later, he disappeared, only to reappear very agitated. He grunted and whined and tugged at our sleeves.

'Yes, yes. OK. We'll come in a minute.'

'RRRHGGGH.' More tugging and pointing.

He led us down a small path to a house where several men had gathered. A young man in his thirties introduced himself as the *Kepala Kampung*. It didn't take us long to catch on that he was not pleased. We had had the gall to come to his village, take pictures and wander around without first seeing him and asking his permission. We had no idea that this was what was expected of us. It never had been before. He demanded to know where we were going, and when we replied that we wanted to go to a small hilltop village nearby called Lai Tarung, he informed us that this was a very dangerous place full of dishonest people and that he couldn't guarantee our safety. The only thing we could do to protect ourselves was to go and report to the *Kepala Desa*. From his attitude, we had assumed the *Kepala Kampung* was a fairly major local functionary, but despite his obvious illusions of grandeur he was a minor lackey compared with the rather more important *Kepala Desa*.

'Christ, what an officious little shit!' whispered Donna, as we walked away to find this alleged *Kepala Desa*.

'NNNGGGH,' agreed our friend.

I was beginning to find his constant grunts, grins and groans rather trying. We slogged from one house to another in our search for the *Kepala Desa*. In fact, we scared half the population to death, by turning up at their doors asking if we could 'report' ourselves! As we were trudging along the road in the heat towards Lai Tarung, our friend mimed how tiring it was going to be to get there. He made a series of steps upward with one hand and then wiped imaginary sweat exaggeratedly from his brow with the other. Despite our irritation, it made us both laugh.

Finally, we arrived in a small village called Resi Moni, which hugs the bottom of the hill where Lai Tarung is situated. Here we had to wait – again. It is amazing just how much of one's time is spent 'waiting' in Indonesia. We weren't allowed to go to Lai Tarung, we were told, until we had signed the guest-book. Where *was* the guest-book? The *Kepala Desa* has it. Where is he? In a meeting. When will he be back? (Silly question.) Oh, soon. We were hot, tired and, by now, extremely exasperated. We sat on the verandah of one of the houses and fumed. A young boy held out a gold ring he had for sale. It looked very old. We asked him where it came from. 'From one of the tombs,' he said casually. Donna and I looked at each other. What *were* we doing here in the middle of nowhere, surrounded by grave-robbers and deaf-mutes?

Just as we were about to leave, the guest-book arrived with two young men who claimed to have been appointed our 'guides' by the elusive *Kepala Desa*. We searched for a pen to sign the book, but were prevented from doing so. We should sign it once we were in Lai Tarung. Our deaf-mute friend was not coming with us. We shook hands and he beamed at us. As we walked away, I turned back and saw him mimicking how he had had his photograph taken. He looked so proud and held his head so high, I felt guilty that I had found him such a trial earlier. On balance, he was one of the nicest local inhabitants we met that day.

Lai Tarung is said to be one of the 'original' villages in West Sumba. Formerly the ancestral village of twelve clans, it is now almost abandoned. The view from the top was well worth the steep arduous climb. Standing on top of a stone tomb (we were assured that this wasn't offending some ancestral deity), we gazed out over mile upon mile of viridescent rice-fields, sparkling rivers and tree-clad hills. Three enamel plates were produced for us to put a donation to the 'gods of the village'. This seemed fair enough, and we dropped in some small change and a packet of cigarettes.

Sumba

Now we were allowed to look around. The 'Spirit House' for which Lai Tarung is famous was allegedly built over three hundred years ago around four huge carved stone pillars. It was mind-boggling to try and imagine how these pillars – let alone the massive slabs used for the tombs – were ever brought to such an inaccessible spot. According to our guides it had taken thousands of men months and months to haul one stone slab up the hill from quarries several miles away. Below were the dwellings of the few remaining inhabitants; they were quiet and reserved and had small, pinched, dwarf-like faces. An air of poverty and melancholy hung over them like a gibbet's shadow; their only outward hint of wealth being old silver bracelets worn by some of the men. One would have hoped that they would have benefited from the tourists that slogged up the hill to visit them, but we noticed that the 'gods' had opted to bestow our donation of the cigarettes onto our guides instead.

Now it was time to sign the guest-book. We had forgotten all about it. However, there was one small snag. In order to sign – and we *must* sign – we had to give a donation of Rp5,000 each. When you consider that the entry fee at Jakarta's National Museum is only Rp200, this sum was ludicrous. We were furious and berated our guides, but they were adamant. Who would get the money? Certainly not the people of Lai Tarung, who deserved it most. This was all taking place well out of their sight. Most likely, the Officious Little Shit who had told us he couldn't guarantee our safety if we didn't 'report in' to the – probably fictitious – *Kepala Desa*. Livid, we signed the wretched book, handed over our money and made our way back down the hill.

☆

We bought two tickets for the bus to Waingapu and I asked Jon how long it took to get there.

'Eight o'clock,' he said.

'What do you mean, eight o'clock? The bus passes *here* at eight o'clock?'

'Yes.'

'But on the ticket it says seven o'clock.'

'Yes.'

In a way Jon had been right. The bus left at seven o'clock. And eight o'clock. True, it passed the Rakuta at seven o'clock, which was when we got on. It also passed it at 7.15, 7.40 and 8.00! Each time Kalindi came rushing to the gate waving feverishly and shouting, 'ARMPIT! CHRIST! LETTERS!' The bus travelled here, there and everywhere, picking up passengers before it even got out of Waikabubak.

Another factor which we really should have foreseen was that we had failed to take into account the Indonesian physique. Two Indonesians could fit quite comfortably into a space for one Westerner. Thus, the two seats we had so cleverly (we thought) purchased the previous day, were sufficient only for one of us. I spent an hour moving from one empty seat to another, until their owners arrived and I would have to shift again. For some time I sat sprawled amongst various bags, boxes and pairs of feet on the floor at the front of the bus. The other passengers looked perplexed. What *was* this white woman up to, playing musical chairs and then – horror of horrors – sitting on the floor? I explained that I was simply too big to fit on the seats.

'*Aduh!* Too big,' they chuckled. The information was passed back down the bus to all the other passengers. The diagnosis was confirmed. I was, indeed, too big. When it became clear that all the seats were taken, I opted for the only viable alternative. I made my way to the back of the bus – the domain of the runners. One, Jani, had a shock of black curly hair around which he wore a brightly-coloured embroidered head-band. I found a relatively comfortable space for myself, sitting on one of the less ripped and damaged black vinyl seats with my feet up on a huge sack of onions. On the floor under my seat several chickens were lying mesmerized, with their feet tied together. As the bus stopped for the third time at the market in Waikabubak, a man approached the back door of the bus, carrying a swinging assortment of horrors. Impaled on one end of a stick, which he carried over his shoulder, was the severed head of a buffalo from which a length of dripping gullet and various entrails swung wildly as he walked. The only empty seat on the bus was next to me and I didn't savour the life-enriching experience of travelling five hours to Waingapu with a mobile abattoir. I breathed a sigh of relief when he merely stopped to talk to one of the passengers and went on his way.

Our bus boasted 'FULL MUSIC', and as we bounced along we were assaulted by appalling medleys of chart toppers played at full volume. 'Diana', 'One Way Ticket' and 'Love Potion Number Nine' belted out from speakers above our heads, all with an identical monotonous disco beat. The scenery flashed past; people on horseback, water buffaloes in the fields, women carrying stacks of firewood on their heads to their thatched huts. Plinkety-thump-plink went the music; 'I've Got Rhythm', 'Fernando', 'Quantalamera'. The driver – who had a cold – would meanwhile point his nose towards the window, close one nostril with his index finger and blow hard through the other, periodically covering the front passengers with a fine spray of watery snot. Maybe my seat at the back wasn't so bad after all.

During the five-hour journey there was plenty of opportunity to observe the changing landscape. As it receives over twice the rainfall, the west of the island is much lusher and more fertile than the east. Gradually the rolling hills, covered with lush green grass, the banana trees and crystalline rivers were replaced by a drier, more barren, steppe-like landscape. Crops changed from wet rice to maize and cotton. The hills became flat-topped and were strewn about with jagged white coralline rocks and boulders.

By the time we reached Waingapu we were exhausted. Jani had developed a fierce headache and asked me to tie his head-band as tight as possible to relieve the pain. We stumbled off the bus dishevelled, crumpled and tired, and found ourselves thrown into the midst of the chaos and noise of the bus station.

It took exactly twenty-three minutes for word to spread amongst the *tukangs* (*ikat* salesmen) that we had arrived. These characters hang around the few hotels and restaurants in town, hoping to interest the meagre numbers of tourists in their wares. We made every attempt to ignore them, but within minutes every available inch of railing around our hotel balcony was festooned with samples. We wanted to visit the weaving villages and buy directly from the source, so we stalled them by telling them to come back the following Friday. This seemed to do the trick; they bundled up their cloths and shambled off down the stairs, chuckling and wheezing amongst themselves.

Draped with voluminous white mosquito nets, our beds looked like those in a fairy tale where a princess might sleep for a hundred years. This was exactly what we felt like doing. Sadly, it wasn't a handsome prince that woke us, but hunger. We hadn't eaten all day, except for a few *jambu* fruit we had bought on the journey, and we were starving. Avoiding the inevitable cluster of *tukangs* at the entrance, we walked into the restaurant of 'the best hotel in town' – the Sandalwood – ordered some beers and scanned the menu, which featured:

Chicken in Eeg	Fried fawn with seat corn
Corn on the Crib	Child in Saus
Bitter Fruit in soap	Stomak fish in soap

As we did so, a shower of dead flies dropped on us from the ceiling. We could only surmise that the flies had perished on the ceiling fan and that when someone came into the restaurant the fans were turned on, thereby launching the corpses into the air.

We found Waingapu a sleepy, peaceful town, if hot and dusty. Everyone was extraordinarily friendly. We kept bumping into people who seemed to know all about us. 'You're the people who rented the bus to Waikabubak,' or 'We saw you at the Pasola.' It was a nice feeling.

We stopped at the bank to change some traveller's cheques. A transaction which would have taken a couple of minutes at a Western bank can easily take nearly an hour in Indonesia. The banks are a mass of worn carbons, yellowed papers and weary clerks fluttering about amidst a sea of cigarette smoke. There are no computers, no photocopying machines. No electric typewriters even; only ancient manual ones. Everything is done painstakingly slowly by hand, in quadruplicate. Our transaction was made even longer by the usual friendly questions. What were we doing in Sumba? Where were we from? How long would we stay? Forty-five minutes later we still sat waiting for our money amidst the constant clatter of typewriters and whirring of ceiling fans, while

Sumba

glasses of half-drunk sweet tea stood abandoned on desks, and pages of wall calendars curled in the heat.

We met 'The Spy' at the Sandalwood. He had been in Waingapu for a few days looking for *ikats* and regaled us with extraordinary tales of his near arrest and of complex 'mafia-esque weaving syndicates', which he was convinced were operating in East Sumba and out of Bail. It was nearly impossible to find good pieces in the villages, he said, as they are all snapped up by the big-time dealers. The Spy was in his fifties and had the unnerving habit of speaking in a conspiratorial manner; leaning forward, his eyes darting furtively from side to side as if what he was saying was deadly secret and vastly important. Unfortunately, he spoke so softly that it was almost impossible to hear what he was saying! As time wore on, and we met him a few more times, it became clear that the things he was saying were neither secret nor important, or even particularly interesting!

He did have one interesting legend to tell us, though, which explained why only certain areas in Indonesia produce weavings. It concerned a golden tree with massive branches and many golden leaves. The legend relates that only in those places which were sheltered by its leaves (i.e. certain parts of Flores, Sumba and Timor), were the people allowed to weave.

☆

We ordered *nasi goreng* (fried rice), bread and coffee at the Surabaya, before taking off on our trip to the weaving villages. The Chinaman was racing around the place like an overwound clockwork toy. '*Ada roti?*' (Do you have bread?)

'*Belum.*' (Not yet.)

'*Oohhh, belum ada roti!*' and he scampered out, waving his arms and literally crashed into the kitchen to see what had happened to it. We had chartered his jeep for the trip and, ever since, he had become noticeably attentive. Seeing us in the dining-room the previous night, he had rushed to turn on the airconditioner and position it so that we received the maximum effect. This was great for us, but left the poor Spy, who was sitting at another table, with no cool air at all. It was exactly the opposite of being left in the cold!

Benjamin, our driver, was dark and thick-set, with a face that was completely expressionless. It was quite unnerving. Nothing we said or did – at least at this stage – evoked even a glimmer of a smile or a response.

Away from Waingapu, the landscape opened out to grassy savannah, with horses and herds of grazing cows, reminiscent of the American Midwest. Our first stop was the village of Pao, which contained a cluster of sturdy traditional houses, some with wooden pillars carved with reliefs of horsemen. Opposite were several impressive stone tombs – one embellished with stone carvings of a horse and rider on one end and a dog riding a pig on the other – behind which were steep, craggy, green hills, which looked as if they had been plucked straight out of a fifteenth-century Italian painting.

Before looking round the village, we sat and exchanged pleasantries with the *Kepala Kampung*, an old man with grey hair and very few teeth, whose son insisted that if I was English I must have met Maradonna the soccer player. The old man made a comment about the colour of our skin compared with his – 'black and white' – something that Indonesians often alluded to. He was staring in particular at Donna's freckles. 'Freckles,' said Donna, trying to teach him the word for something he had probably never seen before: 'F-r-e-c-k-l-e-s.' Seeing she was getting nowhere, I looked up the word for freckle in the dictionary.

Tahi lalat,' I announced. The old man looked shocked.

'Jesus, Annabel, what have you said?' hissed Donna through her teeth. 'He doesn't look very pleased.'

'I don't know. I'll look up each word and see what they mean.' Pause. I chuckled. 'Sorry Donna, it looks as if I've told him that you're covered with fly shit!'

We were taken to the indigo dyeing enclosure and watched a young woman (her hands permanently stained blue by her work) immersing some bound threads first into one pot of stinking, fermenting indigo dye, squeezing them out and then plunging them into a second and a third pot. This continued until she was satisfied that she had achieved just the right colour.

The brightly-patterned weavings of Sumba are the best known of all Indonesian *ikat* cloths. They are characterized by bold naturalistic designs depicting such objects as horses and riders, deer, lions, dragons, chickens, lizards, turtles, sea horses and skull trees – the tree in a village where skulls taken from enemies would be hung.

Unfortunately, there were no *ikats* for sale. Everything was still being worked on the looms. We stopped at several more weaving villages – Rende, Kaliuda and Melolo – but everywhere we went we got the same impression; nobody had cloths for sale to tourists, and as a result they seemed bored and uninterested in us. It was very disappointing, but confirmed the Spy's story that all the good cloths were being saved for the big dealers from Bali.

By lunchtime we were hot and thirsty. A quick swim in the sea – or at least a paddle – sounded refreshing. Benjamin's face unexpectedly lit up. 'Swim? You want to swim? I can take you to river near here. Very good place for swim, especially for ladies.'

'Well, I don't think we'll actually *swim*, Benjamin. We don't have swimming costumes,' said Donna, still taken aback that we had managed to elicit some kind of human response from our companion.

'No problem,' he urged with a nasty glint in his eye, 'no need for costume!'

As there were no passable roads to the coast, we opted for the river. Surrounded by tall pampas grass swaying in the light breeze and washing down from the hills to the sea, the water was almost too hot to be refreshing. There was little shade, and it was hotter than hell. Benjamin settled himself down on the sandy river bank, expectantly. 'Now ladies swim?' he asked rather too eagerly, and was visibly disappointed when we merely rolled up our trousers and waded about in the water. He stalked off in a huff, reappearing an hour later as we sat by the water attempting to combat impending dehydration with hot Aqua water.

Still aggrieved, Benjamin drove back to Waingapu like a man possessed, whizzing through villages and hurtling past cattle, goats and buffaloes, which were being herded home. We caught fleeting glimpses of old, bare-breasted women sitting on the verandahs of low-roofed thatched houses, of children peeking out from under the roofs, and of men mending vast, shimmering fishing nets in the late afternoon sun.

The governing party, Golkar, was in town for a big rally. As the Sandalwood was the best hotel that Waingapu had to offer, that was where they were staying – or trying to. We watched, vastly entertained, flicking dead flies off the table, as dozens of tough-looking men in bright yellow shirts and berets swarmed all over the place in total confusion. They had arrived en masse from Jakarta to find that nobody had pre-booked them at the hotel.

Friday dawned bright and clear. Our last day in Sumba and 'The Day of the *Tukangs*'! As we sat out on our balcony, deeply engrossed in a game of scrabble, they started to appear like termites out of woodwork. While we pretended to be absorbed in our game, one carefully unwrapped his *ikats* from the shabby piece of cloth he carried them around in, and hung them out over the balustrade. Most were of very inferior quality; poorly bound so that the pattern was blurred, and hastily dyed so that the colours were pallid, or mixed with chemical dyes which resulted in a harsh synthetic hue. Two, however, caught our eye.

'How much for these?' asked Donna.

The *tukang* paused, as if making complicated calculations in his head.

'Rp200,000,' he eventually replied.

'Uh-uh,' said Donna, shaking her head. 'No way!'

Eventually, one and half scrabble games later, after the *tukang* had left in mock disgust, twice, then returned to continue the bargaining, amidst much amiable laughter and hand shaking, a deal was struck.

After this initial assault, the rest of the *tukangs* appeared. Our small balcony literally came under siege, with as many as fifteen tenacious, obstinate hawkers all thrusting their cloths under our noses at once. Some of the *ikats* were quite nice, but we never got a chance to look at them properly without several others being pushed at us at the same time. It was frenetic. '*Berapa Mrs?*' (How much?) '*Kasih harga!*' (Give me your price!) they yelled. The situation became so baffling and exhausting that it was physically impossible for us to see any more. We fled to our room and locked the door!

The *tukangs* weren't easily got rid of. They knew full well that we were leaving on the only flight the next day and we heard

135

them massing like vultures on our balcony well before dawn. Getting from our room to the hotel lobby was like a military manoeuvre. I quietly unlocked the door and we charged downstairs, closely pursued by a bevy of hawkers shouting, 'Look at this, Mrs.' 'Give you good price.' 'How much you want to spend?' and so on. We had heard it all before and we weren't interested. Before leaving for the airport, we indulged in a final cup of coffee at the Sandalwood. The Spy had gone, leaving only us and the flies in the restaurant.

A Red Cross collection box greeted us as we entered the waiting room at Mau Hau airport with the legend: 'Your small chang will support a grat caus!' A pleasant-looking airport official approached and excused his intrusion. 'I think I saw you at Pasola,' he said. 'How did you like it?'

We told him we thought it was marvellous.

'It not too violence for you? It's only a game and many games are violence are they not – like soccer or boxing? And you know, we have to do this or maybe the rice will not grow next year.'

While he was speaking, our flight to Bali was called. 'So when are you coming back?' he said, smiling. 'Soon,' I said. Already, the memory of the Hell Ride to Waikabubak, the Carpet Soup and our grilling by the Officious Little Shit in Anakalang were starting to fade. Instead, as I walked across the tarmac towards the plane, I could almost hear the thunder of hooves, the jangling of bells and the chanting of the *Ratos*.

7. Super Bloody Bali Bagus

Bali

'No worries, Narlene. Let's face it, if you can't get laid in Bali either you don't want to or you're dead.'

Donna and I were waiting for our bags at Denpasar airport as this sentence wafted past on the lips of the taller of two Australian girls. Sadly, this is what Bali has become for thousands of tourists these days; especially for Australians who flock there as frequently as the British to Benidorm or Californians to Hawaii. A book on Bali – or more specifically one small part of Bali, the legendary tourist enclave of Kuta – could well be titled *Sex and the Single Sheila*, for it seems to be for single women what Bangkok is for their male counterparts. Many an entertaining hour can be spent at the beach or in a bar in Kuta, watching tanned women with sun-bleached hair being chatted up by one of the droves of good-looking Balinese Toy Boys, who earn a living by offering their company to unattached ladies.

Kuta Beach – which is in the southern part of the island – exudes hedonism. Everyone at Kuta is tanned and beautiful. Even ugly people are beautiful, or at least beautifully dressed. Everyone wears bright, frivolous clothes that are sold ridiculously cheap in the shops; people on motorbikes ride leisurely along in the surf, being seen or looking for a pick-up. The air reeks of coconut oil and beer. Nobody sweats in Kuta. They are all too hip. Droves of conical-hatted Balinese women ply the beach with bottles of exotic oils on their backs, and offer half an hour's worth of gritty massage for next to nothing. 'You want company?' they will inevitably ask if you are alone, 'I know nice boy for you.'

At night Kuta comes alive. A myriad cheap restaurants tempt one's palate with everything from fresh lobster to egg and chips.

Boutiques and souvenir shops stay open until the early hours. Loud music pulsates from brightly lit tape stores where cassettes are on offer for a couple of dollars each. And then there are the Pubs. Wandering along the Kuta streets, one is constantly entertained by a chaos of signs such as 'Bloody cold Aussie beer', or 'Come in for shit hot meat pies', while others invite you to partake in the dubious delights of an All-Nite Pub Crawl. At bars with names like the Bali Billabong one is spoilt for choice between a 'Super Bloody Bali Bagus', an 'Arak Attack' or a 'Rocket Fiel' cocktail.

But is that all that is left of the Bali of Walter Spies and Covarrubias? Of course not. Kuta has about as much to do with the 'real' Bali as the Ginza has to do with the 'real' Japan, though even in Kuta the true spirit of Bali is alive and well. For an island which has been written off as corrupted by tourism for at least fifty years, it is relatively easy to get away from it all and blissfully lose yourself in a world of calmly swaying coconut palms, immaculate emerald green rice-terraces and decaying Hindu temples.

Bali is remarkable for its stubborn resistance to change. In the 1930s, Walter Spies and Beryl de Zoote were quoted as saying that the Balinese people have 'a suppleness of mind which has enabled them to take what they want of alien civilizations and to leave the rest.' It is still true today. Over the years, Bali has been assaulted by the Dutch and Japanese troops, traders bringing with them the teachings of the Muslim religion and – finally – tourists. In a country that is over ninety per cent Muslim, Bali is the only island in Indonesia that has retained its ancient Hindu religion. It was one of the last islands to yield to Dutch rule, submitting only after – in a type of ritual suicide – an entire Balinese court walked straight into Dutch gunfire in 1908, rather than face the humiliation of outright defeat.

Even in Kuta, which has changed so much outwardly with the onslaught of tourism, the spirit of Bali – the religion and the culture – remains doggedly intact, mainly due to the strength and resilience of the *banjar*, a sort of community association of which everyone is a member. *Banjar* buildings are distinguishable by their tall towers, which house the *kul-kul* (wooden drum). In the days before the telephone, the *kul-kul* was used to summon *banjar* members in times of trouble or when they were needed to perform some function for their community. Spiritually, the *banjar* exists in order to support the needs, and maintain the harmony, of the community.

The Balinese believe that the gods dwell in an upper world. As the highest mountain on the island, the volcano Gunung Agung is said to be the holiest place in Bali. Demons and bad spirits live in the sea and underground, and humans occupy a sort of spiritual 'middle ground'. Preserving the harmony of this middle ground, keeping it free from evil spirits and at the same time acceptable to the gods, is the basis of Balinese religion. The offering is a fundamental part of this belief. Whether it is a massive occasion such as a cremation, where weeks are spent preparing sumptuous and elaborate offerings, or just a simple daily ritual outside a house or a shop, offerings are presented to the gods to win favour for the worshipper and his community and to help the gods in their ceaseless battle against evil. The most basic offering consists of flowers and rice and perhaps some banana or payaya, over which a little holy water is flicked with the fingertips. An incense stick is lit and left with the offering. Each house, shop, restaurant, hotel or *losmen* (guesthouse) has its own temple; some so tiny and unostentatious that passers-by rarely notice them.

☆

Donna and I found ourselves in a Kuta which was temporarily transformed; its emphasis switching from rank tourism to joyful religious celebration. It was the day before *Nyepi*, Balinese New Year. A huge procession had amassed on Kuta beach for a spectacular ceremony, where offerings were being made to the sea and to the spirits. The sand was strewn with fragrant white and yellow frangipani and red hibiscus flowers; tall, brightly coloured parasols had been stuck firmly in the sand, their tasselled fringes fluttering in the breeze; under a canopy of palm leaves a large gamelan orchestra was playing; women in their finest and most colourful sarongs and *kebayas* (long-sleeved, tight-fitting blouses) danced elegantly in front of simple bamboo 'altars', which were festooned with offerings of flowers, fruit, ducks and chickens.

Bali

Beneath a grove of parasols, dozens of white-robed Hindu priests
with scarves tied around their heads, sat cross-legged on the
sand, chanting, ringing bells and flicking holy water. *Tjili* – long
tasselled ornaments made from palm fronds which look rather
like corn dollies – dangled and danced in the breeze from long
pieces of bamboo twenty feet tall. In the background one could
detect the gentle lapping sounds of the sea and, on this occasion,
the smell of incense drowned out the coconut oil.

Everyone looked happy. The atmosphere was one of a fête or
carnival. Everywhere I looked there were starbursts of light and
colour; purples, deep reds, oranges, pinks and yellows and whites
of the fluttering parasols; brightly woven baskets containing
precious offerings that were being carried on women's heads;
orange, red, yellow and white flowers; even the sarongs and
kebayas that people were wearing that day had particularly
vibrant colours and patterns. Some were even embroidered with
gold thread. The tourists looked ridiculous next to this joyful and
dignified ceremony. Two Japanese men lay nearby in G-strings
looking utterly absurd and, I thought, slightly embarrassed.

Later in the afternoon the procession moved along the beach to
Legian, the next village up the coast. Huge gongs hanging from
sturdy bamboo poles were struck rhythmically as the procession
moved onwards; parasols glinted and fluttered. A massive circle
of women formed, all of whom were carrying intricately carved
and painted wooden images of dogs, birds and dragons on their
heads. Within the sanctity of this circle, priests performed
religious rituals amidst clouds of incense smoke.

After the circle disbanded, several groups formed at the water's
edge to be blessed by priests with holy water. Under a watery
pink sky, they knelt with their hands raised in prayer, their bodies
reflected in small pools at the water's edge. Standing nearby,
I overheard a conversation between two men with beaded hair and
thick Australian accents:

'Christ, this is bloody amazing, isn't it?'

'Yeah. Is this what Bali's really about then?'

'Shit, I don't know. I guess it must be.' Pause. 'Fancy a beer?'

That night we asked Tomi, the manager of the guesthouse we
were staying at, more about *Nyepi*. 'Well,' he told us, 'tomorrow is

what we call the Noisy Day. This is the day when everyone in Bali they make a *lot* of noise, with fire cracker, gong, shouting and general silly din.'

'Why?'

'Actually very bloody simple. If we are very noisy and loud and crazy, then the bad spirits will be so frighten, they will all disperse and go aways.'

OK. That made sense. But what then was the significance of the Quiet Day the day afterwards. 'Well,' said Tomi, 'after all the crazy noise and the bad spirits fly away, the next day maybe some of the naughty ones come creeping back. But they are so confuse by the absolute quietness that they will disappear and not bloody well trouble us again for the whole year!'

True to Tomi's word, the next day people started letting off fire crackers from the early hours and all day there was a definite sense of expectancy and excitement in the air. However, this was nothing compared with what was to come once the sun had gone down. Once it was dark the *kul-kul* could be heard being beaten in the tall towers of the *banjars*, young men cavorted in the streets beating pieces of bamboo together in a fevered rhythm, fire crackers popped and exploded all around. Some tourists – having somehow managed to remain oblivious to *Nyepi* – were wandering about looking utterly perplexed, obviously having no idea what they had stumbled into but half-fearing some kind of native uprising was afoot.

Later that night, a mammoth procession took place starting at Kuta and making its way up to Legian. The street was lined with spectators. Away in the distance we could see and hear the crowd approach. The excitement and energy of it was tangible. Dozens of children holding long bamboo tapers stuffed with flaming coconut fibres led the procession, singing at the tops of their voices. Behind them came the 'floats'. These were a succession of grotesques – some eight feet high – made out of fibreglass, papier-mâché, chicken wire, odd bits of cloth, or whatever the members of the particular *banjar* had managed to get their inventive hands on. Each figure was attached to a bamboo frame and carried by up to twenty men. Not only did each creature seem to be more outrageous than the last, but its bearers were ever more creative in making it appear to come alive; propelling it around and around in circles, bucking and dipping it and even at times careering into the crowds. This was accompanied by yells, shouts and shrieks from both the participants and the excited spectators.

Hundreds more people walked between each float, brandishing bright tapers, shouting, and beating gongs or hitting pieces of bamboo together. Cheers greeted a huge, green dragon which spat fire, then a vast, red-eyed hippopotamus, a talking frog, two fighting cocks and, most popular of all a male and female pig complete with sexual organs, who would copulate – frequently – at the whim of their bearers.

The chaos and noise continued until midnight. And then it was quiet. After the previous night's assault on the senses, the next day was probably the most extraordinary we experienced on our trip – especially in Kuta of all places. For the normal Kuta day, which is continually punctuated with sounds of people talking, dishes clattering, motorbikes, bicycle bells and general everyday din, was replaced by total silence. Even the dogs stopped barking. Everyone, we were told – not only in Kuta, but over the entire island – was at home observing the Quiet Day. Nobody was out on the roads, in the streets, on the beach, in the bars. Everything was closed and silent. There were no taxis, buses, *bemos*. Nothing. During the day we heard a hushed telephone conversation between Tomi and an incoming guest, who was calling from the airport. From what Tomi told us later, the conversation went something like this:

> Guest: 'I'm at the airport. What the hell is happening? There are no taxis here. How do I get to Kuta?'
> Tomi: 'Very sorry. Today there are no taxis. It is religious holiday.'
> Guest: 'What the hell? So how am I supposed to get there? I've got all my luggage and everything here.'
> Tomi: 'Very very sorry. You have to walk.' (It is about five miles from the airport to Kuta!)

And so the conversation continued, until the wretched guest gave up and told Tomi he was starting walking. We never did see him arrive!

After *Nyepi*, we left Kuta and caught a crowded *bemo* to Ubud. Particular villages in Bali are renowned for certain crafts. Mas is where wood carvers live and work, Batubulan is known for its stone carvings, Celuk for its silverwork. Ubud is the painters' colony. It is the village where the unfortunate artist Walter Spies lived and worked in the 1930s, until he was imprisoned by the Dutch for being homosexual. As there were no prisons for white men, he was kept under house arrest and later transferred to a prison in Surabaya. As a German national, he was interned by the Dutch during the war and died when the prison ship he was on was sunk by the Japanese.

Although it attracts many tourists, the pace in Ubud is markedly more relaxed. We found a delightful *losmen* set amidst the rice-fields, and were shown to a spacious and airy upstairs room. The feeling of airiness probably had something to do with the fact that the top half of one side of the room was completely open to the elements, with only a bamboo blind to let down at night if necessary! Nearby, a Baya Weaver bird was building a nest shaped like a set of bagpipes in a coconut palm. Looking out over the trees towards the *padi*-fields in the near distance, one had the feeling of hardly being indoors at all.

'I think I've died and gone to heaven!' exclaimed Donna. Just a few minutes away from Ubud's tourist-oriented main drag, we were strolling through rice-fields, past small stone temples covered in offerings of flowers. Cows munched at the side of the road, bicycles rattled by, the sun was comfortably hot. In the near distance a small boy was herding an unruly line of ducks along the edges of the *padis* with a feather on the end of a long stick. The sun was setting as we walked back to the *losmen*. A flock of herons was flying home in a 'V' shape across the hazy purple sky. In a courtyard nearby, gamelan music was being played. Coconut palms rustled dry fronds in the breeze. The smell of burning coconut husks from a *saté* burner wafted in the air. This was magic. This was Bali.

One of the most popular tourist dishes in Bali is the Mexican avocado dip, guacamole. Walking along Ubud's Monkey Forest Road (so named for the small patch of forest at its end, which is inhabited by a thieving band of greedy macaque monkeys), one small restaurant had a blackboard outside on which was written: 'Special Today – GOATAMOLE'. Unable to resist such a challenge, we went in and sat at a table near a small fishpond. While we were waiting somewhat apprehensively for our goatamole, a little boy came out of the kitchen carrying a long stick with a spike on the end. Carefully he prodded and turned over the large lily leaves that were growing on the surface of the pond. On and on he prodded and poked, until suddenly he thrust the stick into the water. When he withdrew it, there was a tiny frog impaled on the end. He ran excitedly into the kitchen with it and returned a few minutes later to begin again.

'If someone's ordered frogs' legs for dinner, they're going to have to wait a bloody long time for it!' commented Donna.

☆

The next morning, after a breakfast of tasty banana pancakes and utterly tasteless toast with the consistency of cotton wool, we hired some bicycles to explore Ubud and its environs. They were ancient, battered machines and extremely uncomfortable. Weaving our way uncertainly down Monkey Forest Road, we put our trust in the Balinese gods that the brakes would last and the tyres wouldn't burst. We clunked and rattled past a large open *banjar* barn, where people were busy preparing for a massive cremation ceremony. It was a hive of activity; priests were chanting, and women preparing dozens of offerings of rice coloured with pinches of turmeric, which they placed in round baskets of woven palm leaves. Others were cooking *saté* in shrouds of smoke. A colourful row of wooden bulls, brightly painted and decorated with beads and silver paper, stood sentry. A little further back, the bodies – scores of them – lay in specially built shelters, silently waiting their passage to the spirit world.

We pedalled on, past people winnowing rice in the *padi*-fields. The sky was a brilliant blue, the *padis* stunningly verdant. Every now and again the gentle sounds of bamboo wind-chimes or the evocative sounds of Balinese gamelan music would waft along on the breeze. Buses careered past on their 'see Bali in five hours' tour route. The jaded faces of people who appeared to be in the terminal stages of sensory overload stared dully out of the windows.

A little further on, we came upon a large, crumbling, moss-covered temple. Peering inside the small doorway, we saw that the usually bare stone temple complex was brightly festooned and adorned for a ceremony of some kind. Tables had been erected and covered with white cloths on top of which elaborate offerings had been placed. Tier upon tier of oranges, apples, pink *jambu* fruit, eggs and rice-cakes had been painstakingly arranged in colourful pyramids on pedestalled dishes. There were flowers and incense on top, and slender golden strips of palm frond hung down over the sides. All around the temple, bright parasols fluttered.

'Where is everyone?' we asked some women who were still busy preparing offerings. They exchanged glances, lowered their eyes and said nothing. At that moment, a man walked in. 'You want to know where all the people are?' We nodded. 'Then come with me.'

He took us along a small path leading away from the road, through a copse of trees and then down a steeply winding path into a clearing. Here, obscured by clumps of tall bamboo, an enormous crowd was gathered. Cock fighting, and the gambling that goes with it, is illegal in Indonesia, but often takes place anyway, always in an inconspicuous spot – such as this one – in a token gesture of compliance with the law. It is a sport for men. The sole function for women at such gatherings is to stand at the periphery and serve food, drinks and cigarettes to the menfolk. We strained our necks to see what was going on inside a circle of a hundred or more people. Two men were showing what fine specimens of fighting cock they each had; holding them aloft for the crowd to see, ruffling their feathers proudly and extending the legs, to which lethally sharp spurs had been attached. More would-be champions were clutched protectively to their owners' chests, or rested on the ground or hung from the branches of trees in bell-shaped cane baskets.

'What are they doing?' shouted Donna, who was less able to see than I was.

'They're showing off their cocks!' I yelled back. 'Just like Torajaland!'

The crowd became agitated, shouting for attention and waving their money frantically at the two men who walked round the circle taking wagers. There was feverish noise and excitement. Once all the bets were placed, the birds were set down on the dirt and flew and struck at each other repeatedly. Every man in the crowd strained to see, their faces tense and animated. Eventually, one bird was victorious. Money was doled out to the winners' grasping hands, the bleeding corpse was removed and it started all over again. We stayed and watched for some time, enjoying the excitement and rarity of the occasion far more than the cock fighting itself, which was cruel and bloody.

That night, back in Ubud, tiny, darting fireflies lit our way through the *padi*-fields and thousands of frogs joined in a croaking chorus as we walked home. Back at the *losmen*, one recalcitrate firefly got itself stuck behind a picture and was drawing dizzy light circles behind the canvas, until we relented and set it free to the night air.

It was hard to leave Ubud. The sun speckled through banana leaves and sprinkled us with light, as we ate our last breakfast of banana pancakes and cotton-wool toast. Tiny birds fluttered about after the rice offerings on the *losmen* temple. Lizards scuttled crustily on the stones, the palm leaves rustled in the breeze and the watery rice-*padis* glistened in the distance.

We had heard that there was a village on the east coast called Candi Dasa, which was like Kuta used to be before it was 'discovered' – quiet and unspoiled. We found a bungalow right on the beach. It was fairly spartan – there was no bed linen or pillow, for example, but there *was* electricity. It came on only between the hours of 6.00pm and midnight, and even then our bulbs were only fifteen watts, so it made very little difference!

A few miles on, the road just tapers out, so there was no through traffic, A few simple shops, *losmens* and small restaurants were scattered haphazardly along the main street, and we stopped at one of these for a quick lunch. We ordered fried chicken and *mie goreng* (fried noodles). Half an hour later our food had yet to arrive. People came and went. A *bemo* stopped outside and disgorged chattering school-children clutching text-books. Eventually the fried chicken appeared and the restaurant cat meandered over and sat optimistically under our table. We waited for the rest of our order. Nothing. I went to ask what had happened to the *mie goreng*. The man at the counter look puzzled. '*Mie goreng?*' Oh, *MIE GORENG.*' He shouted back into the kitchen, '*Mie goreng.* Quickly quickly.'

Fifteen minutes passed. No food. Exasperated, I returned to the counter.

'*Mie goreng??* You want *mie goreng?* Ah YES, *MIE GORENG!*'

Eventually, he brought the *mie* and placed it, with infuriating slowness, in the centre of the table. He then produced two cracked plates, a bottle of hot chilli sauce and one knife.

'How are we supposed to eat a bowl of noodles with one knife between us?' cried Donna. He turned his face up to the ceiling, clamped his eyes shut with a tortured expression and wrung his hands, as if desperately hoping that by some miracle we wouldn't have noticed. There was a huge fuss and several kitchen boys were dispatched to find us two forks!

We sat on the verandah of our bungalow and watched as the tide turned in the late afternoon, exposing a massive coral reef. Throngs of saronged women appeared with baskets to collect crabs and other creatures. At sunset a young girl brought flower petals, incense and holy water, which she presented with dainty flicks of her graceful fingers as an offering at the little temples outside each bungalow. These were the things that made Bali such an enchanted place; the small, intricately beautiful rituals which went on all over the island as a natural part of each day.

There was no noise except the crashing of the waves, as we sat out on our verandah, straining to play cards under the gloom of the fifteen-watt bulb. Later, as we walked along the main street away from the beach to find somewhere to eat, the quiet was absolute. There were no cars, no bikes, no electric lights; only the twinkling of paraffin lamps in the restaurants.

Wandering back to our bungalow we paused to gaze at the round, ripe, full moon, which was casting its cold silver light on the waves. As they broke, they caught the moon's rays and gleamed and glistened like thousands of tiny diamonds.

☆

Behind the bungalow was a pig pen. The next morning we awoke to the sounds of frenzied squealing and, looking out of the window, caught sight of eight little piglets steaming past at full possible speed; corkscrew tails waggling frantically with excitement. They had managed to break out of the pen and were scampering beachwards along the path. I could almost hear the screech of trotters as they wheeled around the corner of the last bungalow. Sadly, their taste of liberty was short-lived. They were back in the pen that evening – no doubt plotting their next bid for freedom!

The day was idyllic; brilliant blue skies, warm sunshine and a light breeze ruffling the red hibiscus flowers and bright yellow iris in the garden. Some of the other occupants of the *losmen* were out and about in the surf. One of the most visible – or perhaps noticeable! – was an outrageously handsome man we called 'Mr Chippendales'. He was obviously well aware of his appealing physique and wore little other than a G-string, in which he swaggered around the beach and up and down in front of the bungalow or – even more provocatively – sunbathed on his stomach on a picnic table in the garden, displaying his muscular, bronzed arse.

Washing was done at an old pump. I had soaped my clothes and was filling a tin bucket with water from the pump to rinse them, when a Dutch woman came over to talk to me. Her name was Margot. In Dutch the 'g' is not pronounced hard the way it is in English, but is, rather, replaced by a sound similar to someone clearing their throat of phlegm! Donna was keen to go to the nearby walled village of Tenganan, as it was the only place not just in Bali, but in the whole of Indonesia, where double *ikat* weaving (*geringsing*) was done. Margot had already been there.

'Oh ya. I haf been there,' said Mar-ghhh-oh. 'De weafings are fery fery expensife.'

'You didn't buy one then?' I asked, smiling.

'Oh what a joke! Of course not. But really, the people there are fery interesting. They are the *Bali Aga* – the original peoples of Bali – and Tenganan is a fery old, traditional village. I heard a nice story of how the people of Tenganan came by all their land. Long long ago, the King of this area lost his favourite horse. The fillagers of Tenganan found its body and as a reward the King promised to gif them all the land where the horse's carcass could still be smelt. The King sent one of his men, who had – how you say – a keen sense of smelling, out with the fillage chief and together they covered many many miles without efer managing to get away from the terrible smell of the dead horse. Efentually, weary from all the walking, the two men agreed on a fery large amount of land and the official returned to the King's palace. As soon as he had gone, the fillagers gathered around and, to great clappings, the chief pulled a piece of the horse's carcass from under his shirt!'

'Talk about flogging a dead horse!' said Donna, who had joined us at the pump.

Later that day, I spotted Donna down on the beach with Mr Chippendales, and made a mental note to give her a hard time about it later. That evening, as we sat in our sarongs sipping beers on the verandah feeling like something out of a Somerset Maugham short story, we spotted a ferry sailing lethargically across the horizon.

'I wonder where that boat goes?' I said.

'Margot said it was the ferry to Lombok.' Pause.

'What happens in Lombok?'

'I don't know. It means "chilli pepper" in Indonesian.' Another pause.

'Well, perhaps we need somewhere hot and spicy . . .'

'Yes, Bali's too easy . . .'

We sipped our beers and watched the ferry slowly disappear. A decision appeared to have been made.

Next day, though, we went to Tenganan. It was a short walk along the main road to the turn-off. After that it was a long hike uphill to the village. Two enterprising youths were waiting at the turn-off with small motorbikes. They smiled as we approached.

'You want ride? Rp500 usual price, but as you such big ladies, special price Rp1,000.'

Nestling amongst dense palm covered hills, Tenganan was charming. A series of stone steps led us through the village, which is built on the gentle grassy slope of a hill. Humble, whitewashed stone houses contrasted with the deep orange-coloured, ornamented brick wall, which defies entry to the village at any point other than the single entrance gate. Venerable frangipani trees stretched their limbs protectively over the village and scattered their fragrant blossoms over the grass. Everything was so neat and ordered it looked as if the village had been preparing for inspection in a 'Most Beautiful Village' contest. Even the trees were surrounded by neat stone walls. Along the centre of the village stood several communal buildings where families were preparing and consuming their midday meals. Even a village as tidy as Tenganan had its quota of mangy dogs, who positioned themselves around the edge of the building, snarling and fighting for scraps.

We found a house where a middle-aged couple were weaving the *geringsing ikats*. The process of tie-dyeing the pattern onto both the lengthways and the widthways threads and then weaving them together by hand is incredibly complicated and time-consuming. One cloth allegedly can take up to *fifteen years* from start to finish! As a result, double *ikat* weavings cost the earth. Around $1,000 and up. 'Do you know about the *kamben geringsing* we weave in Tenganan?' they asked. 'Very special cloth. If someone is wearing it, they are protected against black magic.'

'At those prices I should hope so,' said Donna.

While cradling cold beers at a small café near the village gate, we noticed large amounts of food being taken outside; bowls of rice, fruit and vegetables piled high on women's heads, children carrying coconuts at either end of a piece of bamboo and even a massive pig – still alive – which was being carried upside down with its trotters tied over a pole and was eventually loaded unceremoniously into a waiting *bemo*.

We walked back down to Candi Dasa in the relative cool of the late afternoon. The road wound steeply downwards through dense groves of coconut and banana palms. Three women were walking along the road in front of us. Dressed in festive sarongs and *kebayas* with sashes around their waists, they each carried plates on their heads, piled high with fruit. With absolutely straight backs, their movements were as graceful as those of a prima ballerina. The sun breaking through the trees overhead dappled the road like marble, and lit the women as if with thousands of tiny spotlights.

After a while we passed three strange constructions made out of palm leaves which looked like Indian 'teepees'. We found two men inside with their sons, busily decorating some figures which, they explained, were for a forthcoming cremation. Carved and painted by hand, they were now being decorated with coloured ribbons, paper and gold tinsel. A great deal of money is spent on cremations and the amount of decoration possible varies with the wealth of the family. As with the Torajans, a funeral usually takes place months and sometimes years after death, by which time the family will have saved enough money to pay for the decorations, priests, offerings, holy water, cremating coffin, not to mention adequate refreshment for all the guests.

To the Balinese, the impure material body is only a temporary frame for the pure soul. After death, it is vital that the body be dissolved completely and given back to the demonic material elements. Well, that is the theory; in practice, many bodies are buried 'to await cremation' for twenty or thirty years and then conveniently forgotten to avoid the cost of a cremation.

Walking back along the beach to Candi Dasa, we discovered where all the food from Tenganan had been going. In front of a rather haphazard gamelan orchestra, stood thirty or more men and women and, before them on the sand, offerings of food and flowers had been arranged on a carpet of palm leaves. As this was a ceremony to the spirits of the sea, two harridans shouted at anyone who tried to walk between them and the water, so we sat well to the side to watch. Several women danced with slow, measured movements on the sand, each holding a small *tjili*, while a small boat appeared and came in closer and closer to the shore. Inside was the village priest of Tenganan, who performed special religious rites from the boat and eventually sank all the offerings. 'I don't know about the sea gods, but it's certainly a bonus for the fish!' Donna said, as we splashed back through the surf.

☆

To get to Lombok, we had to catch the ferry from the small port of Padangbai, a few miles along the coast. We were standing with our bags on the road just outside the *losmen*, when a *bemo* screeched to a halt. The driver was short and stocky and had either had one too many cups of coffee that morning or was naturally hyperactive.

'Where you going?' he asked, skipping from foot to foot, his hair sticking straight up and out at all angles, so that he resembled a sea urchin.

'Padangbai. How much?'

'Rp1,000.'

We laughed. 'No. Too much.'

'How much?' He gesticulated wildly.

'Rp300 each. Rp600 total.'

'Rp800.'

'No, still too much!'

He tossed his head melodramatically and marched defiantly back to his driver's cab. This was most unexpected. Donna and I stood there blankly, not sure whether to throw out another price or just let him go. After all, an empty *bemo* going all the way to Padangbai with just us in it was very tempting. However, instead of getting into the driver's seat, he scampered around the side and, to our complete surprise, reappeared beaming broadly and displaying a mouth full of gold teeth. 'OK. OK. Rp600!' he roared and, shaking with laughter, grabbed our bags and started tossing them vigorously into the back. Donna and I looked at each other, dissolved into giggles and clambered in.

The practice of queueing just doesn't exist in Indonesia. In order to buy our ferry tickets in Padangbai, I reluctantly joined a frenetic, seething mob about forty strong, who were all hell-bent on getting to the one small ticket window at the same time. I was ill-prepared for this. The tranquillity of Candi Dasa could not have made a greater contrast – a foretaste of Lombok, had we but known it. There were no rules. Being a woman and being a foreigner had no positive effect whatsoever. I was jostled and shoved, my toes stamped on, arms and elbows were thrust in front in an attempt to push me to the back of the crowd. Nobody was prepared to give up a millimetre of fought-for space. An Australian was trying to maintain his position near the window. Obviously feeling sorry for me, he turned and yelled, 'Here, take my place when I'm done. There's no way you'll get through if you don't.'

Eventually I got to the window. 'Two tickets, please,' I shouted, trying to make myself heard above the ruckus, and thrust my fare – Rp8,000 – through the window. 'Not enough,' said the mustachioed official on the other side. I was being shoved from both sides, making it difficult to keep my place at all. It was hot. It was dusty. I was feeling the beginnings of claustrophobia.

'What do you mean, not enough?' I cried. 'It says on the notice up there, "One person, Rp4,000".' I could feel the sweat running down my back. 'Very old notice,' he replied nonchalantly. 'Now Rp6,000 each.'

I had only Rp8,000 on me. Surely I wasn't going to lose my place and have to go through all this again? I couldn't bear it. I looked round frantically to find Donna and attract her attention. She was standing some distance away deep in conversation with none other than Mr Chippendales, who was there to see off one of his recent female conquests. I did a double-take. Good grief, not now, Donna! My head was beginning to pound from the accumulating aggravation. Suddenly the Australian pushed his way over through the sea of heads and hands, waving crumpled rupiah notes. He had Rp4,000 in his hand, which he passed to me. I took it gratefully and handed it to the official, who was still apparently oblivious to the mayhem on the other side of his window. The exchange over, I pushed my way wearily out of the crowd and thanked the kindly Australian. Donna wandered over. 'Any problems?' she asked innocently. I could have garrotted her!

The ferry took a good number of cars and trucks as well as a couple of hundred passengers. We settled ourselves down on the top deck, where one could wander outside for some fresh air when the smells of *kretek* smoke and the food people had brought with them became too much. There was no escape, however, from the boat's PA system, and throughout the four-hour journey to Lombok, we were assaulted by blaring 60s music.

'. . . *If you're going to San Francisco, be sure to wear some flowers in your hair . . .*'

A businessman in his thirties, wearing a light grey safari suit and carrying a tatty briefcase, asked permission to sit next to us. He introduced himself as Mr Hartono. He worked for some public information bureau in Lombok and often travelled to and from Bali on business. Donna seized the chance to add to our zero knowledge of the island we were about to visit, and pelted the poor little man with questions.

'All across the nation, there's a strange vibration, uhuh, people in motion. People in motion . . .'

How appropriate, I thought, as I felt the ferry lurch to port-side and concentrated more on the sensation of my stomach going with it, than on Mr Hartono pouring out useful information about Lombok.

'. . .island is only 4700 square kilometres in size and is eight kilometres from east to west and north to south – roughly. We grow very good rice in Lombok, but only one crop per year, not like in Bali. This is because the climate is drier and less fertile than in Bali. Do you hear of Mr Alfred Wallace?' We nodded. 'You may know, then, that the Strait of Lombok which we are travelling at this moment is where that famous man drew his very famous Wallace Line which separates east from west in the world of flora and fauna. I have yet to see the tigers that Famous Mr Wallace says should be in Bali!'

'I don't suppose you see many kangaroos in Lombok, either,' said Donna.

'. . . There is a house in New Orleans, they call the Rising Sun . . .'

'What else do the people of Lombok do?' I asked. The boat started to lurch to starboard, while my stomach was still moving to port.

'Many of the people are fishermen. Also there are plantations where we grow such things as coffee, coconuts, kapok, tobacco, cotton and cloves. Recently we start to grow vanilla and pepper too. We have a famous volcano called Mount Rinjani, which is much revered by the people of Lombok and Bali. There is a legend which tells that long ago, some monkeys were playing with the moon and broke a bit off. They dropped this piece in three chunks. One fell in Java and became the volcano Semeru, one fell in Bali and became Gunung Agung, and the other descended in Lombok and became the volcano Rinjani. These three volcanoes are therefore sisters and are regarded as sacred by the Balinese. In 1963, when the volcano in Bali erupted, priests were sent hastily to Java and Lombok to make offerings to the volcanoes in an attempt to pacify Gunung Agung. Funnily enough, after Agung had calmed down, Semeru started erupting. They say that Rinjani did also.'

Mr Hartono ground to a halt. Nervously, he fished a crumpled packet of cigarettes out of his chest pocket, took one out and lit it, using several matches to do so. We asked him about the history and religion of Lombok.

'Lombok was ruled by the Balinese until 1894, when the Dutch took over. Because of this bit of history, there are still many Balinese Hindus in Lombok. They live on the south-west of the island and have some temples there. Otherwise, most of the poplation are Muslim – the further east you travel the more devout they become.'

By now we were getting near to land. We went out onto the deck to watch our approach. It seemed incongruous, to say the least, to sail into Lombok to the sounds of 'Tell Laura I Love Her', but so we did. From the sea, Lombok did indeed look very dry and its barren hills rather forbidding. As they loomed closer and closer, so the peaceful paradise of Bali slipped away from us. At this stage neither of us could have foreseen what mixed delights Lombok was to offer us. If we had, we would probably have stayed on the boat and gone straight back again . . .

8. Getting stoned

Lombok

'DON'T MOVE!' I screamed, as the huge truck underneath which I was crawling suddenly began to roll forward. My words were lost as it fired up its engines with a roar. This was the stuff of nightmares. All I could think of was 'I don't want to die under this truck . . . At least let me see the bloody island first . . .!' Managing to avoid the massive tyres only by dropping my bag and diving between the wheels, I scrambled out and collapsed against the wall, my heart racing. As soon as we had docked at Lembar, there had been a horrendous scrum to get off the boat; as if there had been an announcement informing the passengers that they had exactly two minutes to disembark before a bomb exploded on board! 'Hey, let's get a head start and get over to the other side,' Donna had said, already squeezing between and under the cars and trucks on the vehicle deck.

Immediately we emerged from the boat, we were surrounded by youths hassling to take us into town. It was hot, dusty and hellish. We lost Mr Hartono in the crush, and were eventually swept up in a tidal wave of people and bags, and deposited in a mini-bus with fifteen others and only the vaguest notion of where it was going.

Over an hour later we were dropped at the small, dusty bus station in Ampenan, which used to be the main port before Lembar superseded it. Nowadays it is an unimportant fishing town and little more than an extension of its neighbour, Cakranegara. Hot, weary and dispirited, we made an effort to get our bearings. The bus station stood near what was clearly the main square; a grandiose term for where several small roads converged. Dull, grey concrete buildings housing shops and small restaurants stretched into the distance, and nearby a garish banner advertised 'Sex, Love and Money' at the local cinema. '*Hey! Touris!*' shouted a young man on a passing motorbike, turning back to grin at us, then spitting copiously at the side of the road. 'Now what?' asked Donna, kicking disconsolately at the small stone wall that surrounded the bus station. 'This place is terrible.'

Mr Hartono had mentioned a hotel up the coast called Sasaka Beach Cottages. Despite the late hour, we decided to try it.

In Lombok the most common mode of transport for short journeys is the *dokar*, a simple horse-drawn cart with narrow benches on each side for passengers. The driver sits up front. Each *dokar* is colourfully painted and decorated with bells and ribbons, tassels and pom-poms, which reminded me of the *becaks* in Ketapang. How long ago that seemed. As we hauled our bags out of the bus station, a *dokar* appeared, bells tinkling merrily, the horse's tired hooves clopping along the road, and the driver agreed to take us to Sasaka for Rp500, which seemed very reasonable. The cart sagged unnervingly under our weight, but with a flick of the driver's whip we were off, and in seconds were out of Ampenan and clipping along quiet country lanes. If I had thought that our *dokar* was overloaded, it was nothing compared with some of those we passed, which were so full they almost scraped the road. I counted fourteen people in one (and those were just the visible ones!), as well as huge baskets of vegetables and fruit that they had bought from a nearby market.

We had begun to relax a little and enjoy the mood of the late afternoon – the sinking sun casting a thick warm light onto the pastoral landscape, people making their way home from the fields or from the market with sacks or baskets on their heads, chattering children running back from school – when the *dokar* pulled up abruptly at the bank of a wide river. Donna and I looked at each other suspiciously. 'Sasaka?'

'No, Miningting. You get down here.'

'But we agreed you would take us to Sasaka.' He ignored this.

'From here you must get boat over the river and then another *dokar* to Sasaka.'

We had been ripped off. The *dokar* driver never had any

intention of taking us all the way – only as far as this bloody river. I was hot. I was tired. My head was throbbing. I had no idea how far we still had to go. In fact, neither of us really knew where we were going at all. Despite a wealth of experience telling me it was a waste of time in such circumstances, I lost my cool, and ranted and railed at the driver. He remained, of course, entirely unruffled, merely shrugging his shoulders or shaking his head while I cursed, complained and snivelled. The crowd – other *dokar* drivers and passengers waiting for boats across the river – were highly entertained by the spectacle of the huge white woman making a fool of herself. Eventually Donna intervened. 'Come on. We have to get there so let's just get a boat and get on with it.' By this time it was getting dark. She took my arm and pulled me, still fuming, over to the river bank. As I suspected, the *dokar* driver's prestige had risen in the eyes of the other passengers as a result of my railing at him. He drove away clearly pleased with his new role as our victim – and Rp500 richer.

It was obvious from the appearance of the road, which just stopped on one side and carried on over the other, that there used to be a bridge over the river. It had been washed away in a flood two years before, but nobody had got around to rebuilding it yet! Probably attempts to rebuild it had been thwarted by resistance from the 'Confederation of Boatmen', who were making a very nice living from ferrying people across. We climbed tentatively into a sturdy canoe, which already contained several other passengers, two goats, a large pile of coconuts and a Suzuki motorbike. The canoe had bamboo outriggers at each side for stability and was guided by a boatman with a long bamboo pole. The journey took only a couple of minutes. On the other side we negotiated with another *dokar* for the continuation of the journey to Sasaka.

The moon was shining by the time we arrived outside the gates of the Sasaka Beach Cottages. It looked fairly smart, with individual bungalows set in well-tended gardens; there was a central bar and restaurant and a swimming pool, and all this was only yards from the beach which we could hear but not see. But it was completely deserted. If the place hid some dark secret, we were far too tired to find out what it was, and we checked into one of the bungalows for a good night's sleep. Minutes later, as I was trying to flush a huge poisonous centipede down the plughole of our washbasin, the electricity failed. The centipede escaped, but I was too tired to care.

'You have not tried our swimming pool!' cried our waiter at the restaurant the next morning. 'But we have the most very famous pool in Lombok.'

'Yes, I can see why!' commented Donna acidly, staring at the pool full of stagnant, pea-green water. 'No amount of money or free beer would induce me to consider even dipping a finger in that water!'

We left the pool to its thriving population of algae and hitched a ride to Cakranegara, where we had learned there was a weaving factory that was worth a visit. Entering the massive barn where the weaving was done, we were assaulted by a momentous cacophony; dozens of wooden looms click-clacked, as women worked with amazing speed and dexterity, controlling the loom with foot pedals. *Click* – up went the heddle rod to raise the warp threads, *whhssht!* – through shot the shuttle; *clack* – up went another row of threads, *whhssht!* – through shot the shuttle. Shards of sunlight streaked through holes in the roof and onto the richly colourful fabrics on the looms; bright purples, yellows, greens, golds and reds flashed and shone. Decades of dust whirled and danced in the sunlight. Old, broken looms lay stacked up chaotically in a corner covered in the cobwebs of years.

It is impossible to spend any length of time in Lombok and *not* go to Sweta – at least once. No matter where you want to travel on the island, you invariably have to get there via Sweta. Sweta's *raison d'être* is its frenetic bustling, noisy, dusty bus terminal. All the accoutrements of a transport terminal are there; small boys circle decrepit, rusting buses packed with waiting passengers like sharks around a shipwreck, hawking peanuts, drinks, cigarettes, sweets or hard-boiled eggs for the journey. When you walk in you are instantly surrounded by a crowd of runners demanding your destination and then trying to drag you off to their bus. A dilapidated mini-bus was just about to leave for Sukarara – a village in the south with a small weaving community – so we squeezed in. Everyone seemed delighted by our presence and there was much giggling and joking. The runner even proposed marriage to Donna at one stage of the journey. When I had room to turn my head and look out of the cracked and rather greasy windows, I could see that the countryside was becoming quite pretty; vegetables were growing in the fields, women working in rice-*padis*, and the hills in the distance were shrouded in a hazy mist which bestowed on them a magical aura. Or maybe it was the hair grease on the windows!

Beside me, next to the window, sat an old woman with the bright red lips of a betel-nut user. After a while, she took an old tin out of her basket. From the tin she took a small green leaf and smeared it with a little lime paste. Then she broke off a small piece from a nut and put this, along with a bite from a dark red cube, into her mouth. She chewed this concoction for a few moments before adding the paste-smeared leaf. To finish off, she took out a wad of raw tobacco, wiped it around the outside of her gums a few times and poked that in as well. This ritual was performed slowly and with great precision. When she had finished, she carefully put all the ingredients back in the tin, closed the lid with a snap and tucked it down into her basket. Only then did she turn towards me, gave a little half-smile and returned her gaze to the window.

Finally we arrived in Sukarara and found the Kios Subahnale, which had a type of hand-woven sarong called *kain songket* hanging outside. Inside, the room was bare except for a cupboard and table and chairs. The business was family-run, and we were greeted warmly by an elderly couple – Pak and Ibu. We asked if we could look at their *songkets*, and they both gestured graciously for us to go ahead. When it was clear that Donna and I were not very interested in the 'run-of-the-mill' sarongs hanging outside, the wife took a small key out of her pocket and walked over to the locked cupboard. The pieces she brought out were really beautiful; all woven by hand, many with the silver and gold threads which are characteristic of Lombok textiles. Pak held one up for us to see. It was the most beautiful deep purple colour and had unusual dragon motifs woven into it with silver thread. 'I *have* to have that piece,' Donna whispered.

Now the bargaining began. The old couple stated their price. We, in turn, gestured that we were unhappy with it and spun a yarn – so to speak – to the effect that as we had missed the banks, we didn't have much money on us. They nodded under-standingly. Much to-ing and fro-ing and many hushed consultations ensued. It was like some kind of elaborate mating ritual; Pak and Ibu sitting patiently on the sofa, while Donna and I sat, then rose and walked pensively around the shop, wandered over to inspect the quality of the weaving, sat again, consulted our wallets and each other.

Interestingly, it was Ibu who had the final word. She finally agreed on a price somewhere – as it should be in any satisfactory bargaining session – between her original one and ours. That, and four packets of cigarettes thrown in for good measure. The official business over, we settled down to eat a bowl of *jambu* fruit together in an atmosphere of great warmth and conviviality. We took a photograph of them and their shop, they gave us all the *jambu* fruit that was left over. When we left hours later, it felt like saying goodbye to one's family.

As we clip-clopped back along the narrow country roads from Sukarara – bells jangling on the horse's harness, red tassels and pom-poms dancing with the movement of the *dokar* – the late afternoon sun swathed the fields in the most beautiful golden light. On the leg of the journey from Mininting to Sasaka, we shared our *dokar* with four local women, all of whom were laden with huge baskets of fruit and vegetables. Far from being irritated by the cramped conditions, it seemed to them to be an excellent joke that we were all women travelling together. 'No men. Just us girls!' they said, chortling with infectious laughter. Even though they spoke in a dialect that we found hard to understand, we were still somehow able to communicate. As usual, the conversation turned to children. They, it seemed, had between twelve and fifteen each! I felt genuinely sad when the *dokar* stopped at Sasaka Beach and we had to part company. There was such warmth, generosity and openness in those women. The *dokar* clopped off into the sunset, taking the women, their chattels and their chuckles with it.

On the beach, hundreds upon hundreds of fishing boats, as far as we could see, had been dragged in and laid to rest for the night on the dark volcanic sand. Simple canoes with an outrigger on each side for balance and a single mast, each was colourfully painted and had gaily patterned sails. They would have looked bright at any time, but the effect of the golden rays of the setting sun, picking out the oranges and reds in a luminescent glow, was dazzling.

☆

We had almost finished our duck cooked in banana leaves when an enormous tour group was shepherded into the restaurant by a fraught-looking guide. So, we were alone no longer. The tour consisted entirely of elderly Germans, Swiss and Americans. The five Swiss sat at the table next to ours and raised their glasses of beer to us in an amiable greeting. The guide was not so relaxed. He was darting from table to table in an agitated manner, conferring anxiously with each group. He scurried over to the Swiss table. 'Very very sorry everyone,' he started, smiling too broadly. 'There is big problem for tomorrow. Because you are so many big people, we have to splits you up into two buses.'

The Swiss frowned and rumbled between themselves in Switzerdeutsch.

'What would be very very nice for me,' continued the guide, 'is if you will please to join the German-speaking group tomorrow.'

The reply was immediate,

'No, ve are very sorry, but ve vill not join ze Chermans.'

'But, you speak German can't you?'

'Of course. But ve vill absolutely not spend ze tour with zem,' was the adamant reply.

'But why?' asked the tour guide, by now close to hysteria.

'Because ve hate ze Chermans.'

☆

'Jesus, Annabel, I thought this was supposed to be a leisurely stroll!' Donna complained, as we slogged wearily up the beach.

The hot sand seared our feet, and the beach sloped steeply, making our progress awkward and hard work. We had decided to walk to a small Hindu temple up the coast called Batu Bolong. The fishing boats had all disappeared. It was almost as if their presence on the beach the previous night had been a figment (or possibly a pigment) of our imagination. Some were visible far out to sea, the sun catching their colourful sails. Every few yards we passed rows of men and boys sitting on the sand gripping fishing nets which they had cast out into the surf. When it felt as though they had a sizable catch, they would laboriously haul the massive nets in. The majority of their catch seemed to consist of jellyfish, among which they would search hopefully for something edible as well. What painstaking work for just a few fish; the discarded jellyfish lay in sad heaps on the sand. At least I assumed they were jellyfish. They were completely transparent and looked rather like plastic bags filled with water. In fact they looked so much like plastic bags filled with water, that I put my foot on one just to see what it felt like. It didn't help. It even felt like a plastic bag filled with water!

I was still pondering this when we ran out of beach. We had reached a headland, which was cut off by the incoming tide. A gaggle of curious, giggling children had been following us.

'Where is Batu Bolong?' we asked them in Indonesian.

They giggled. Two pointed in one direction, three in another and the smallest directly upwards. This was not helpful.

'Is it far?' we asked, going for basic information only this time. They shook their heads. By now it was nearing midday and most people were, intelligently, inside sheltering from the heat. We carried on along the coast road, passed only by the odd *dokar* and panting dog. As we reached the brow of a steep hill, we stopped to ingest the view. Through frangipani blossoms we gazed out across the deep blue sea, which was framed by a sickle-shaped coastline. Fishing boats glided across the horizon, their sails glinting in the sun, and in the far distance smouldered Mount Rinjani, its apex obscured by thin cloud.

The view was stunning. So, unfortunately, was the heat, and we were both extremely thirsty. A little further along the coast, an oasis appeared in the form of a tiny roadside *warung* (foodstall), inside which we thought we spied some coke and sprite bottles. It wasn't a mirage, but it might just as well have been; their original contents had been consumed long ago and they were now filled with hot chilli paste! The only beverage on offer was hot coffee, which didn't sound particularly refreshing, but was better than nothing. We squeezed in at the small wooden table next to a man who was devouring a plate of rice and fish. The woman who ran the *warung* took two half-pint glasses and put one heaped spoonful of coffee in each. Then she added three enormous spoonfuls of sugar and poured on boiled water from an aluminium kettle. The result was so sweet it set my teeth on edge.

We told her we were looking for Batu Bolong. 'Is it far?'

'No, not far,' replied the man. We looked at each other doubtfully. That was what the children had told us three quarters of an hour ago! 'Just along the road a little way. *Tidak jauh,*' he repeated reassuringly (not far).

The woman had five children. We asked how old she was. Twenty-four, she said. I looked at the two small children playing in the dirt at the back of the kitchen; at their filthy old clothes, their mucus-strewn faces and their little arms and legs covered in sores and rashes. And I thought about the Indonesian government's rather desperate attempts at stemming the country's population explosion by trying to enforce birth control. In towns throughout Indonesia, large, faded billboards and posters depict the 'ideal family' – mother, father, two children and a washing machine! – with the accompanying slogan: *'Dua anak cukup!'* (Two children enough). Obviously the campaign hadn't reached Lombok – or, if it had, it wasn't sufficiently convincing. This coastal area of West Lombok was one of the few places we had been in Indonesia where poverty reached up and slapped us in the face, and in the light of that it was disturbing that people should have so many children, when they were so ill-equipped to clothe and feed them. Ironically, the woman pitied us; older than her and yet no children! Who was going to look after us when we were old?

When we finally arrived at Batu Bolong, we were exhausted! The tiny temple, which faces towards Bali, is built into the black rocks at a point in the coastline where the waves crash against them, sending spray high into the air and over the temple.

According to local legend, beautiful virgins used to be sacrificed
to the sea from these rocks, which is supposed to explain why
there are often sharks in the nearby waters. We were looking
forward to enjoying the scenic beauty of the temple in relative
peace and quiet. Neither of us had anticipated the crowds. They
weren't Hindu worshippers, either. They were day-trippers;
families dressed in their 'Sunday best', who had come to visit one
of the few sights on Lombok. Worst of all were the prowling packs
of lustful teenage boys, sporting Western-style baggies and cool
shades. God knows what they were doing there, unless they were
hoping for a glimpse of the odd beautiful virgin! In their absence,
however, we were clearly an adequate substitute, and they were
drawn to us like wasps to a jam pot. No matter how many times we
walked away from them, they refused to take the hint, but pestered
us even more. I was determined not to lose my temper this time.
Finally, when one youth sat down next to me and edged closer
and closer, I said, very calmly, 'Do you understand English?'

'Oh yes,' he replied, grinning foolishly, his thigh now pressing
against mine.

'Then FUCK OFF!' I said and walked off down the beach.

Accumulated stress and heat exhaustion left us shattered by
the time we got back. A simple jaunt that was to have taken a
couple of hours had taken almost all day. We retired to the beach
to watch the shapes of the resting outriggers turn to silhouette as
the sky turned a dusky orange behind them. As it became dark,
scores of little boats began casting out to sea, complete with
paraffin lamps for night fishing. Saronged figures walked home
along the beach and, in nearby huts, fires were lit and oil lamps
twinkled. And so life continued.

It was time to move on. We decided to head for a cool
mountain retreat at the foot of Mount Rinjani in eastern Lombok
called Tete Batu. Our route there was fairly complicated; a *dokar*
to Mininting, a boat over the river, another *dokar* to Ampenan,
then a *bemo* to Sweta. (All roads lead to Sweta!) Having got that
far, we would then have to take a bus to Pomotong, another *bemo*
to Kotaraja and yet another *dokar* up to Tete Batu. It was a
daunting prospect; if it had taken us all day to get to Batu Bolong,
which was only a few kilometres up the coast, how long could we

expect this trip to last? We were, by now, well known to the *dokar* drivers and boatmen in and around Sasaka, so we swept through that part of the journey with ease. We were lucky, too, to arrive in Sweta just as a bus was about to leave for Pomotong. 'Yes. Yes. Here is bus to Pomotong,' cried the runner, hoisting our bags up onto the roof. 'But surely this one is full,' I said, looking at all the people crushed inside the twelve-seater mini-bus.

'No, not full. Plenty of room,' he replied, tying our bags tightly onto the roof-rack. Well, our bags were going on this bus. If we wanted to go with them, it looked as if we would have to get onto it too. Sighing and raising our eyebrows, we squeezed our way in, eliciting several pained but amicable '*Aduh's!*' from our fellow passengers.

'Are there really twenty-seven people on this bus?' shouted Donna as we rattled along towards Pomotong.

'No, you haven't counted yourself,' I replied. 'That's twenty-eight!'

The penultimate stage of the journey, the road from Pomotong to Kotaraja, was exceedingly bumpy. Our rusty old *bemo* was full of people from eastern Lombok, who regarded us with suspicion. There was none of the open friendliness that we had experienced on the western side of the island. Two women sat opposite us clutching baskets full of *saté* ingredients – small chunks of goat meat, peanuts, chillis and thin wooden sticks. Next to them sat a miserable looking man with a towel tied around his neck, which was horribly swollen. I searched in my pack for some aspirin and handed him one. '*Obat*,' I assured him. 'Medicine. Very good.' He took the aspirin and frowned at it and then at me. We bumped along. Silence. Everyone was watching, riveted. They looked from him to the aspirin to me. I became rather uncomfortable. Finally, he dropped the pill on the floor, tied the towel tighter and scowled at his feet.

At Kotaraja, we took a *dokar* up to Tete Batu. We were at a much higher elevation than we had been at the coast and it was much cooler and more temperate. We wound steadily uphill, passing enormous fields where cabbages, corn and potatoes were growing. Children ran beside the *dokar* and screamed at us. There was definitely a different feeling about this place. We had come

here to get away from the heat, but here the people were colder
and less friendly, too.

At Tete Batu, the road runs out at the gate of a large estate.
Inside the grounds, surrounded by shady trees, stood a large old
house with white-washed walls and shuttered windows, which
looked like a relic from colonial times. On the driveway, cloves,
tobacco and coffee had been laid out to dry on large palm mats. A
dog barked. There was nobody about. We walked around to the
back of the house, where a young man was cutting up coconut
with a *parang*. 'Yes, we have a room. Follow me.' Instead of being
shown into the house, he led us to one of six extraordinary buildings.
Built on four sturdy stilts and with rounded, tall palm-roofs, which
swept almost to the ground, they looked rather like wagon trains.

'This is a traditional Sasak house,' said the young man, whose
name was Benni. The Sasaks are the original inhabitants of
Lombok. Previously animist, most have converted to Islam.
Things seemed to be looking up. Benni was friendly. Perhaps we
had been imagining things. With renewed optimism, we set off on
a walk to a mahogany forest that Benni had recommended. Our
path took us along charming lanes, where hibiscus and
poinsettias bloomed in abundance and where properties were
delineated by neat bamboo fences. After a while, three boys
latched onto us. They seemed very friendly and asked if they
could accompany us to the forest. We agreed and walked on.

The forest was marvellous. Immensely tall, dark mahogany
trees towered up to the sky and every now and again we caught a
glimpse of a jet black monkey way up in the branches. They were
shy though, and never dared to come very close to us. 'So, do you
want to go further?' the boys asked, 'we will come with you.' We
shrugged; we could hardly stop them. We set off along a very
narrow path, which wound through a thick forest of vast trees
covered in dangling vines, orchids and tree ferns, but eventually
opened up, offering sweeping vistas of vast rice-terraces leading
up to Mount Rinjani in the distance. One of the boys spoke quite
good English. He said, 'You can see volcano from here. It is very
beautiful. Also very powerful. Many people climb the volcano
many times a year because they want to please the gods of the
mountain. The Sasak people go at big moon.'

167

'You mean full moon?'

'Yes, yes, big moon. The people from Bali come here also and throw in gold and give offerings to the spirit of Rinjani. It is a magic place.'

'Have you been up there?'

'Yes, many times. The best thing about the mountain is the hot springs. People say they have magic healing powers. I like them because they are good place to meet girl.' He chortled at the thought. His friends chortled too. Though they probably had no idea what he was talking about most of the time, they evidently knew the word 'girl'.

After this, the mood changed. As if by pre-design, the boys paired off with us. The one who spoke good English walked in front with Donna. The youngest one walked alone in the middle and the third, about whose mental capacity I was beginning to have serious doubts, walked with me some way behind. He was a gangly, awkward youth. One minute he was grinning insanely, the next staring up at me moronically. I began to feel distinctly uncomfortable. If I walked faster, or hung behind, he was there right by my side, leering and frequently leaning and pressing against me. Donna was oblivious. The other was holding his ground and keeping the two of us apart. The scenery was stunning, but I was far too nervous to enjoy it. Here we were in the middle of nowhere with no idea what these youths' intentions really were. Eventually we approached a river, and I heard my 'escort' say to the boy in front – in Indonesian, so that he thought I didn't understand – 'One for you and one for me.' They laughed. That was it. I had had enough. I shouted to Donna up in front that I thought we should go back.

'But Leon here was just telling me about this beautiful waterfall a little further on where . . .'

'We are going back.'

I was sure now that they would demand payment for their services. I was right. Leon looked embarrassed, but the other two became quite nasty. We tried to argue with them, saying that we hadn't asked for their help, they had offered it and we thought they were being friendly and hospitable. It was no use. We had some packs of Marlboro cigarettes for emergencies such as these.

We held them out to the boys. They scowled and said that they didn't want cigarettes. They wanted money. To hell with it. We thrust the packs at them and walked off as they shouted abuse after us from their house.

It had been a tense and unpleasant experience. Had they automatically expected payment when we agreed to their company? The ridiculous thing was that we would probably have given them something at the end of the walk anyway. A clash of cultures. We drowned our frustrations with lots of Bintang beer.

Next morning, sunny, bright weather replaced the gloomy, overcast skies that had seemed so appropriate for the previous day. As we sipped tangy ginger coffee and demolished banana pancakes, we felt our optimism return. The restaurant overlooked a fabulous view of rice-terraces and a river; the kind of view that does wonders for the digestion – and the spirits. Benni was serving our breakfast.

'Who owns this place, Benni?' I asked.

'Very rich lawyer in town,' replied Benni, putting plates of banana pancakes on the table.

'Doesn't he live here?'

'No. That would be not suitable for his purpose.'

'What do you mean his "purpose"?'

'He comes here every morning for some, er, business and then goes back to town.' Benni paused and smiled. 'If you wait for a while, maybe you will see what kind of business.'

As if on cue, a car pulled up. The doors slammed and a fat, greasy-haired, middle-aged man with a pockmarked face walked over to the barn next to ours, his hand placed solicitously on the back of a pretty young girl, who was giggling beside him. They went into the barn, closed the door and the giggling continued. Donna and I looked at each other and raised our eyebrows. Was that the boss?

'That's the boss!' confirmed Benni, 'but don't tell anyone or I lose my job!'

From Kotaraja, we set off on foot in search of Loyok, a small village a few kilometres away, where traditional baskets are woven. The road narrowed and led us away from Kotaraja and into the countryside. We passed a school just as the children were coming out, and in seconds we were surrounded by dozens of literally screaming children, some of whom even shook their fists at us. This was not the normal, friendly, curious crowd of youngsters that we were used to. This was weird. And it felt hostile. Out they poured, masses of them. Old and young, they all stood around us and screamed and shouted, '*Hey Belanda! Hey Belanda!*' (Hey, Dutch). The noise was so piercing that I had to put my hands over my ears to block it out. We tried to walk on down the path, but had taken only a few steps when something stung the back of my leg. Then again. I looked round and saw one of the older boys bend down to pick up a stone. Others were doing the same.

'My God, Donna. They're stoning us!' I cried, alarmed.

'Don't be ridiculous. Come on, let's just walk on.'

We continued along the path. Several more stones struck us. I cried out in pain as a large one cut my arm. The mob behind us was still growing and working itself into a frenzy. I was beginning to wonder whether we really were in trouble; there were more than enough of them to overwhelm us. I turned round, drew myself up to my full six feet and one inch – desperately hoping this would terrify them into submission – and yelled at them at the top of my voice to stop and go away. To be honest, I can't remember whether it was in Indonesian or English, but it felt good! We turned once again and marched purposefully down the path. Dozens more stones hit us. By now I was frightened, and looking for ways of escape, when an elderly man walking home from the fields stopped and shouted angrily at the children. The mob froze, some with stones held aloft. They stared at the old man and then at us. We held our breath. Finally, they threw down their ammunition sulkily and slowly dispersed, shooting menacing looks back at us as they went. The old man said nothing, picked up his basket and walked on.

Donna and I sat, stunned, on the path and examined our injuries. We were both cut, bleeding and disgusted. 'But why?' was the question we kept asking. Mr Hartono had warned us that the eastern side of Lombok was predominantly Muslim and, because of that, we had been careful to dress conservatively in skirts over the knees and unprovocative T-shirts. That couldn't have been it. 'They kept calling us '*Belanda*', perhaps they had just come out of a history class where they were being taught about "the atrocities of the evil Dutch and Indonesia's brave fight for independence", and they just decided to take it out on us,' suggested Donnna. 'After all, being white and fair is often synonymous with being Dutch.' She paused. 'Plus, they're little shits.'

This was the only explanation we could come up with for such a totally unprovoked show of agression. Dejected and saddened, we returned to Tete Batu. The hassles weren't over, however. At the crossroads in Kotaraja, we waited for ages for a *dokar*. When one finally arrived, its ill-tempered driver refused to take us for anything less than twice the normal fare. As a foreigner, one is naturally prepared to pay a little over the odds, but not twice as much; at least we weren't. Even some of the locals were arguing with him. In the end he agreed, but the journey was terrible. Whatever it was that was bugging him, he took it out on his malnourished horse, hitting it cruelly with his whip if it slowed down at all. Each time, the horse went beserk, bucking and swerving all over the road. We held on for grim death, dreading each flick of the whip.

'The only nice thing about this place is the dogs!' Donna exclaimed, looking affectionately at a group of mongrels who sat patiently at our feet as we sought solace in the Bintang bottle once again. 'Let's get the hell out of here.'

☆

Off the north-west coast, there are three small islands. Of the two we had heard of, Gili Trawangan was the larger and better known, but Gili Meno had also been recommended and had some 'rustic' accommodation, which sounded appealing. To get there, naturally, one had to go to Sweta first. Our runner on the bus from Pomotong was an extraordinarily aggressive little man, who scowled constantly and cursed and argued with passengers whom he considered had underpaid. His temper was not improved by the fact that we were followed all the way to Sweta by another bus. Whenever there were people waiting at the side of the road, the two buses would screech to a halt simultaneously, and the two runners would leap out and argue over the passengers. One encounter became so heated that our runner actually raised his fists at the other and would probably have knocked him down if the drivers hadn't intervened. We watched, aghast, as one baffled prospective passenger was pulled this way and that by the two men like a favourite toy between two spoilt children. We were quite nervous by the time we got to Sweta. We were pretty confident we had got the right fare, but what if we hadn't? Were we going to incur the wrath of our petulant runner? Get our teeth knocked out, or at least our knees bitten? In the event, he took the fares sullenly, but didn't question them.

When we boarded the bus to Pemenang, we were still undecided which island to go to. As we sat waiting in the beaten-up old bus, three American girls approached, sagging visibly under large rucksacks. Two were tall and fair, and the way they bulged out of their shorts indicated that they had had a few *nasi gorengs* too many! The third was a complete contrast. She was remarkably short and slight, with long dark curly hair.

'Hey! Is this the (pause) "transport" to the islands?' asked one of the Hefties to nobody in particular. Everyone in the bus, and all the snack sellers around it, stared at them uncomprehendingly.

'Where you want go?' asked the runner, using up in one fell sentence the sum total of his English language proficiency.

'Gili Trawangan,' she replied.

He started explaining in Indonesian that they would have to take this bus to Pemenang and then get a *dokar* to where the boats left for the island. The girls looked mystified.

I leaned out of the bus and repeated the explanation. Before I had spoken more than three sentences, the girls gaped at me and one of them said in that slow deliberate tone one uses for non-English speakers, 'Do you speak English?'

'For Christ's sake, what do you think I was speaking?'

'Gee. Sorry. It didn't sound like English!'

I pursed my lips. 'Why don't you just get in and we'll show you what to do when we get there.'

'But, like, this does go to Gili Trawangan, right?'

'Yes and no.' They looked baffled, but got in anyway.

The bus was so packed that the runner set about re-arranging us, putting Donna and I in the front seat with the tiny American. The Hefties sat in the back. They had already caused a fracas by refusing to have their backpacks put onto the roof, and were sitting soggily with them on their laps, complaining bitterly about the heat.

'Y'know,' said the Tiny One in a strong Brooklyn accent, 'those two're driving me craaazy. I'm gonna ditch them and go owf on my own as soon as I can.'

'Aren't you all travelling together?' asked Donna.

'Are you kidding? We just met up on the ferry over here from Bali. They're driving me nuts. They complain awl the time. First the hotel's not good enough, then the food. Then they can't get cold enough beer. So it kinda wears me down after a while, y'know? (She hardly paused for breath.) And I'm pretty weak as it is right now. I've been so sick since I got to Indonesia, y'know? Some kinda stomach bug. Some guy I met in Bali said he thawt it was frawm the fruit there. What do you think? Do you think it could be the fruit? That sounds kinda nuts to me. I brawt some pills with me for this kinda thing, but they don't seem to be working too good. Do you have any medication for stomach troubles? Hey, you speak the language pretty good, don'cha? Have you two been here in Indonesia long?'

And so she went on for the entire two-hour journey. It was like getting into conversation with someone who has been in solitary confinement for several months. We were passing fabulous mountain scenery, families of monkeys at the roadside, occasional glimpses out to a brilliant sea from between the trees, but the Tiny One seemed oblivious to it all. She could just as easily have been on the New York subway, as she babbled on and on about her health problems, her problems with the Hefties, who complained steadily on behind us, her problems with her boyfriend back home, her family, her apartment, her hairdresser, everything. As the bus neared Pemenang, she asked, 'So anyway, we're going to Gili Trawangan. Which island are you two gowing to?'

Donna and I looked at each other and replied without hesitation, 'Gili Meno.'

Lombok

An old man with a flowing white beard on the boat to Gili
Meno took a massive, lethal-looking knife out of his bag and
began very slowly, very precisely, to cut his fingernails with it. I
watched mesmerized. It was like peeling an apple with an axe.
He made as neat a job of it as I would have done with a pair of
scissors. The journey only took forty-five minutes. The turquoise
water was so clear that, near to shore, one could clearly see fish
swimming amongst the coral reefs below the surface.

Gili Meno is tiny. It takes less than an hour to walk all the way
round. It has forty-five inhabitants, no electricity, no fresh water.
Built right on the beach are several bungalows and a large
communal hut, where guests congregate for meals. The first
person we spoke to was a tall, blond Norwegian with a great
name. 'Did you jost arrive?' he asked.

'Yes. I'm Annabel and this is Donna.'

'Hello. I'm Odd. Follow me, please – I will show you to your
room.'

Donna and I shared a bungalow built out of bamboo and palm.
Behind was a separate hut, where you could take a salt-water
mandi and wash clothes. Donna went off to get some water for
washing. 'Do you know what?' she said, returning with an old tin
bucket of salt water. 'I just found three fish in the well!'

The food left a lot to be desired, but stuck out on an island
where nothing grew except skin cancer and coconuts, one could
hardly expect a gourmet spread. That night, ten people sat
around a long table, paraffin lamps providing our only light.
There were Germans, Swiss, Australians, British – and Odd! We
were served some kind of meat curry. When all you have in front
of you are various bits of tube and gristle, it is hard to distinguish
what animal they originated from! As I peered rather
disconsolately at my plate, Odd offered to mix me a 'Meno
Mesmerizer'. He took an old beer bottle, which had a wad of
material stuck into the top as a stopper, poured out half a glass of
the murky, lethal-looking contents, then topped it up with 7-Up.
'Voila! This is – how do you put it – the cocktail of the week. Or,
rather the cocktail of every week! It's *brem*, local rice wine, and 7-
Up. Maybe after a few glasses you will forget about the food!'

At 5.30 the next morning our room was lit by a rich red glow.

Disentangling myself from my mosquito net, I walked down onto the beach to watch the dawn. Very slowly the sky turned from murky orange, to shining red, until finally a brilliant red sun emerged from behind the silhouetted shape of Mount Rinjani. As slender wisps of gold crept out from behind the volcano, a solitary fishing boat sailed across my vision, two fishermen reaching to raise the sail, and then it was gone; leaving the steel grey sea empty except for flecks of gold like rivers of molten lava.

'Beaut, isn't it.' A statement rather than a question. Liz, an Australian, sat down on the sand, next to me.

'Yes, it is.'

'This place is like paradise. We can't bear to leave.'

'How long have you been here then?'

'Well, I'm not exactly sure. The days tend to meld into one another after a while,' she chuckled, 'but I'd give a guess at nearly nine weeks now.'

'Nine weeks!' I wondered how they could stomach the tubes for so long, if not the boredom. After all, there wasn't much to do on Gili Meno except eat, drink *brem*, and sleep it off!

'Seems like a long time I guess, but we love it – especially the snorkelling. The island's surrounded by amazing red coral reefs, you know. You have to be a bit careful, though. If you cut yourself on the coral, it can be a bugger. Something in the water here seems to stop cuts healing and they get infected. Have you met Fabienne, the Swiss girl? She cut her foot a week ago and now it's so bad she can't even walk on it. Ought to leave and get it seen to I reckon.' And as if this wasn't bad enough: 'You have to watch the currents a bit round here too. Strong as anything, they are. They seem to sort of flow round the island. So if you did get caught, no worries – you'll come round again eventually!' I didn't find this information particularly encouraging.

By now the sun was up and I returned to the bungalow. Walking up the steps, I heard a loud scream from the wash-house. 'What is it, Donna?' I shouted, fearing that she might have trodden on a scorpion or found another mega-spider. 'My damn toothbrush is full of ants!'

Ants were, indeed, a problem. I had left a half-finished can of 7-Up at the bungalow before lunch. When we returned later in the afternoon, I settled in one of the bamboo chairs, put my feet up on the balcony and picked up my book. Absent-mindedly, I reached for the can and put it to my lips. It only took a micro-second for me to realize with horror that it, my hand and my mouth, were swarming with ants!

Gili Meno was relaxing, and a good place to nurse our bruised bodies and spirits after Tete Batu. We read, sunbathed until it became too hot, had long siestas. Every now and again schools of dolphins would pass by just off-shore, some flipping right out of the water as we watched. According to Liz, they saw them every day; perhaps they were just going round and round on the current as well! Later, we walked round to the other side of the island with Odd to watch the sunset. Sitting on the cooling sand with glasses of *brem*, we could see the soft purple grey shape of another volcano in the distance.

'That can't be Rinjani, can it?' I asked.

'No indeed,' he replied, 'that is Mount Batur.'

'You mean Bali's Mount Batur?' Donna gasped incredulously, with a discernible hint of homesickness as she pronounced 'Bali'.

'Could there be more than one?' Odd chuckled. 'Yes, we cen often see clearly ofer to Bali from here.'

After another evening of assorted internal organs for dinner, we decided to quit while we were still ahead – or at least before malnutrition, coral poisoning or Gili Meno lassitude set in – and leave the next morning. At 8.30, a small boat arrived to transport departing guests and to take the cook over to the mainland for supplies. The boatman had his small son with him. He was dressed in just a dirty, worn pair of underpants and a torn shirt. Deep depression is an emotion normally associated with adults, not children. But this child looked clinically miserable. I rummaged in my pack and found two ballpoint pens and an old notebook, which still had some unused pages in it, and held them out to him. His face transformed instantly into the biggest beaming smile I have seen.

On our last night in Lombok, we stayed at a hotel in Cakranegara. Our room was tiny and dingy, so we sat outside – which would have been most pleasant except that our next-door neighbours, two oily businessmen from Sumbawa, were unable to keep their eyes off us, or to leave us alone. All we wanted was to sit and read in peace, but every few minutes they would ask us another leading question. Eventually, to shut them out, we both took out our Walkmans and clamped the headphones firmly over our ears.

Next morning we were woken at 4.30 by the muezzin wailing from the nearby mosque. Wearily, we packed our bags and headed back to Lembar to catch the ferry back to Bali. *'Think I'm going back to Massachussetts . . .'* warbled Robin Gibb from the ferry's speaker system as we stood watching Lombok recede into the hazy blue distance.

'Well, where next?' I asked Donna. There was no answer. Her attention was focused on the iron stairwell that led to the deck below. Ascending the staircase was the unmistakably muscular shape of Mr Chippendales. It seemed obvious that it was going to take all my powers of persuasion to separate Donna and the island of Bali.

9. Mud, sweat and tears

Timor and Savu

Timor is the largest island in Nusa Tenggara and owes much of its distinctive rugged character to its position between Australia to the south-east, and Flores to the north-west. Geologically speaking, Timor exists because the Australian continent is moving north and bumping up against Indonesia, which has given rise to Timor's jagged mountain scenery and bubbling mud volcanoes.

As I had rather expected after Lombok, Donna was more than a little reluctant to give up the varied delights of Bali just to see some 'damned mud'. It took me some days to convince her that there was more to Timor than mud. There was a fairly turbulent history, for example. Like the Moluccas, Timor was caught in the middle of wrangling between the Portuguese and the Dutch for control of its precious natural resource; in this case the sandalwood trees which grew plentifully on the island and were highly prized in Europe for their fragrance and a medicine made from their oil.

In the mid-nineteenth century, the Portuguese moved to the eastern half of the island, leaving the Dutch to maintain control over most of the west. The Dutch left West Timor after Indonesian independence was realized in 1949, but the Portuguese stayed on in the east until a military coup overthrew the dictatorship of Marcello Caetano in 1974 and Portugal's new leaders attempted to abolish all the untidy remnants of the Portuguese Empire.

Following the coup, several political groups formed in East Timor, including Fretilin (The Revolutionary Front for an Independent East Timor), who advocated total independence for

178

East Timor. On December 7th, 1975, the Indonesian army invaded East Timor starting with an assault on Dili, its capital, but met fierce resistance from the Fretilin group. Although East Timor was officially declared Indonesia's twenty-seventh province in 1976, resistance to Indonesia's rule presumably continues today, as we were refused travel permits to go to the eastern part of the island.

Although East Timor was closed to us, West Timor had recently opened its doors to visitors and was alluring not least because few tourists went there. However, in Bali we had read in the *Jakarta Post* that a severe drought was plaguing Timor and threatening its population with food shortages, so on the strength of this we decided to go straight to a tiny *ikat*-producing island to the west of Timor called Savu. According to our venerable Merpati timetable, there was a flight to Savu on the Friday afternoon that we were due to arrive in Kupang. Unfortunately, travel in Indonesia – as we had so often discovered – doesn't always go according to plan.

As we stepped off the plane at Kupang, we were greeted by the incongruous sight of three tall, blond, bronzed men carrying surf-boards in carry bags emblazoned with large maple leaves. Neither of us had associated drought-stricken Timor with a surfers' paradise.

'Canadian surfers?' said Donna. 'This is Timor, not Bali – what the hell are they doing here?'

The Merpati counter was deserted. A sign on the wall listed an impressive number of destinations served by Merpati from Kupang, all of which it read, left at 8.30am on Mondays! We stopped an airport official and inquired about the 2.30 flight to Savu. He looked puzzled. We repeated the question.

'You want to go to Savu?' he asked, looking uncomfortable.

'Yes. When does the plane go?' A pause.

'Already gone.'

'What?' shouted Donna, 'but our timetable says it leaves at 2.30. It's only 2.00 now.' She showed the man our battered Merpati schedule. 'See? So where is it?'

'Schedule is change. Now plane to Savu leave at 1.30.' Good old Merpati!

'So it's gone?'

'Yes, it's gone.'

'And when's the next one?'

'Sunday.'

'SUNDAY?!'

'I think we're destined to discover the untapped joys of Kupang after all,' I said, sensing Donna's frustration. 'There's nothing we can do about it. This is Indonesia, remember.'

'Shit! Maybe I've just been here too long,' she said with a deep sigh. 'All of a sudden, these little irritations are really getting me down.'

A man with a face set into a perpetual frown ushered us to his car. It would be 'No problem!' he said, 'absolutely no problem!' to convey us into town.

'We need somewhere to stay,' said Donna, getting into the front seat.

'Yes, yes, no problem. Absolutely no problem!'

The taxi, which was the kind of dilapidated vehicle we had now come to expect, whined through flat green savannah, dotted here and there with rocks and lontar palms. Lontar palms always reminded me of a child's drawing of a tree, with their long thin trunks topped with a haphazard mass of leaves. They exist in the drier parts of Eastern Indonesia and are infinitely versatile. Not only are they used extensively for building materials; wine and sweet syrup are made from the fruit and sap, and the large, concertina-shaped leaves are used to make just about everything else: baskets, water carriers, sleeping mats, cups, umbrellas and hats.

Craggy mountains loomed in the distance. Herds of goats grazed in the fields and we had to stop several times for cows crossing the road. Our horn made a ridiculous quacking noise; it was so realistic, the first time our driver used it, I thought we had run over a duck! It was a beautiful morning; clear, bright and sunny. It was the last decent bit of weather we would see during our stay in Timor.

'Sure doesn't look like there's been a serious drought here,' Donna remarked. Our driver, assuming that she had addressed him, replied, 'Absolutely no problem!'

180

'What is this,' she snapped, 'a person or a wind-up doll?'

We stayed at a *losmen* on the sea front. We settled ourselves on the verandah and ordered tea. Within minutes we were being pestered in equal measure by flies and *tukangs*. It was like Sumba, but with one difference. In Waingapu the *tukangs* were lively and raucous. Here, in the humidity of Kupang, they approached deferentially, one shoulder lowered meekly, as they offered us sandalwood oil, silver bracelets and Timorese *ikats*. The flies were less polite and clustered around the brim of the inadequately washed teacups, rooting for vestigial sugar left by the previous users.

One *tukang* reached into his shoulder bag and brought out some genuine French perfume. We could tell it was genuine because it had 'genuin Franch parfum' printed on the label.

'No thanks!' said Donna, brightly, clearly irritated with these unwelcome intrusions just as she had sat down to rest. But he wasn't to be deflected.

'Where you from?' he asked.

'Nicaragua,' said Donna. Quite unruffled by this answer, he continued, 'Neeagwah *bagus*,' (Nicaragua good), and he put down his bag to make an exaggerated thumbs-up sign.

'No, Nicaragua really isn't *bagus*,' I said, 'and we really don't want any French perfume, though I'm sure it's the most *bagus* in town. Thank you.'

He stood looking at us for a few seconds and then gathered his bag, put on his sandals and walked away with a wry smile.

Timor is a real mixed bag of peoples; Chinese and Arab migrants have mixed with those from Flores, Savu, Java and the neighbouring island of Roti, though the Atoni (the original people of Timor who inhabit the central highlands) make up the predominant population in the west. East Timor is even more diverse with the added confusion of Portuguese influences, and Africans who were brought there by the Portuguese as slaves.

Owning one's own vehicle in Kupang is rare, and most people get around town in one of the hundreds of available *bemos*. We watched dozens whizzing by, brightly painted and with names on the outside in large decorative letters. MICK JAGGER seemed to be one of the most popular; others included BODY ROCK,

CHELSY, COMMANDO, AMERICANA, MADONA, MELODI, MICK BRAVO, DAYA TIMOR (the power of Timor) and SINDY LORPER. Over the driver's cab was often an impressive array of space-age coloured lights and 'heraldic devices' such as butterflies and anchors. Anywhere in Indonesia, one hears a *bemo* before one sees it – they approach with horns blaring; but the Kupang *bemos* were different, for their ploy was to play disco music tapes *so* loudly and with the bass turned up *so* high, that you could hear the throbbing bass approaching like some appalling giant heart-beat. The noise was bad enough outside the vehicle, inside it was absolutely deafening. The giant speakers responsible were invariably placed underneath the passenger benches, so that even the seats reverberated with the pulsating rhythms. Every ride, no matter how short, was guaranteed to make our heads throb.

We needed to change our Savu tickets to the Sunday flight, so we took a BONANSA *bemo* to the terminal, near which, so we were told, was the Merpati office. At the terminal we met an English-speaking local, who insisted very gallantly on showing us to the very door. 'What an incredible office!' said Donna as we approached. She was right. This wasn't the standard shop-sized Merpati affair – they seemed to own the entire building. I was impressed. We were escorted by a security guard to a large office festooned with Indonesian flags. A secretary asked us to wait as the 'Bupati' was in a meeting with the governor. A dim light started to flicker. I reached for our much-thumbed Indonesian dictionary and looked up the word 'Bupati'. It appeared we were about to ask the Regent (the modern equivalent of a Sultan) if he would mind changing our air tickets! We toyed with the idea of brazening it out – after all, neither of us had ever met a Regent before – but chickened out and left before the great man's meeting ended.

We drifted into a restaurant called Karang Mas, which had an inviting view out across the ocean. Wherever we had been in Indonesia and however low we felt, a good meal was usually guaranteed to cheer us up. Conversely, whenever we had to deal with dull, unappetizing fare, our hearts tended to sink. We left the Karang Mas feeling even more despondent than when we went in.

As we waited at the *bemo* terminal, we noticed a woman walking by with two lontar palm baskets swinging from a yoke across her shoulders. She was wearing a strange straw hat with a spike shaped like a rhino horn sticking out from the top, which distinguished her as a native of nearby Roti. Inside the baskets swished a gallon or more of frothing liquid, which looked like used washing-up water. It was only after we observed a customer handing over a few rupiahs and being given a cup (also made from lontar) full of the liquid, that we realized it wasn't washing-up water, but *tuak*.

The next morning clouds hung low over the mountains. We caught a *bemo* to Pasar Inpres, on the outskirts of Kupang, from where we squeezed into a crowded bus to travel the twenty-four kilometres to the weaving-village of Baun. The only seats left were right at the back of the bus, which was crammed with the usual assortment of humans, chickens, pigs, baskets of produce and, in this particular case, six goats lashed helplessly onto the roof. I was wedged between Donna on one side and a goat on the other, which occasionally peered myopically into my face and snorted. In the seat in front, a family of five was piled on top of one another. I could see nothing clearly except for the goat and a faded Sonny and Cher sticker on the roof. Only occasionally did I catch glimpses out of the cracked windows at a strange landscape criss-crossed with stone fences made of lumps of coral, in which casuarina trees – and of course lontar palms – predominated. Halfway to Baun, the bus stopped and body after body after body, that I hadn't been able to see from the back, tumbled out. I had had no idea the bus was so full.

Baun consisted of a single street lined with massive, dignified banyan trees. The banyan tree has a special place in Indonesian culture; for centuries its branches traditionally provided the shade under which village members would meet to discuss matters of importance. It is a symbol of consensus and harmony, and for this reason it has been adopted by Golkar as the symbol of their party.

Walking past the trees and a few small shops, we came unexpectedly upon a beautifully preserved Dutch colonial house with a large glass conservatory at the front full of old European furniture. A middle-aged woman in a flowery print dress called out to us. Introducing herself as Ibu Loeci, she showed us into a dark inner reception room. It was like walking into a downmarket antique shop. There were beautiful marble-topped tables riddled with termite holes, heavy ebony chests, delicate chairs. On the walls were several ancient clocks, all of which had stopped at different times. Chests, sideboards and tables were covered with bright cloths and knick-knacks; old woven bamboo *sirih* (betel nut) boxes, a chipped Delft tray with a picture of windmills on it, small framed oval photographs of her family, plastic flower arrangements, a tea service. In pride of place, pinned to a wooden screen, was a tea-cloth with a picture of an Aussie swagman crouched over a fire and copious instructions on 'HOW TO MAKE BILLY TEA'.

Ibu Loeci was the widow of one of the *radjas*, whose ancestors had ruled the various Atoni kingdoms since before the arrival of the Europeans. She was a voluble old lady and was obviously thrilled to have some visitors who were not only interested in her house but could also speak a little of the language so that she didn't have to struggle to speak English. I asked her how old the house was.

'Oh, it dates from pre-war days. The Japanese lived in it during the war and made a terrible mess of it. Luckily they didn't destroy the furniture as well. After they left, we repaired the house and restored it to how it is now, but, as you can see, it is falling into disrepair once again.' She indicated a large hole in the roof, which let in the rain.

'Do you know if we can find any weavings in Baun?' Donna asked.

'Weavings? *Aduh!* You've come to the right place. We do weaving here, but as this is the wet season still, we don't do very much now. The blue dyeing we can do, but if you try and do the red dyeing in the wet season it doesn't work so well; the colour will come out a nasty brown. You know, to get really good colours, really deep red, you have to dip the threads forty to sixty times. It takes such a long time and it is so expensive that most people don't want the real textiles any more. The shops in Kupang, they all sell cheap sarongs made from commercial

threads. They don't want traditional cloths in Kupang any more
– only the modern designs. Nobody wants them except tourists
and we don't get very many of them. So, the traditional methods
and the traditional motifs are dying out. I think it's very sad.
Very sad.'

Donna had brought a photocopy from an expensive American
coffee-table book about Indonesian textiles. There was a long
chapter on Timor, which she showed to Ibu Loeci. Loeci
searched in a drawer for her glasses, perched them on the end of
her nose and began turning the pages. '*Aduh!*' she exclaimed,
shaking her head. 'No, no, these are wrong – they don't come
from there . . . no, this is not traditional, this is a modern design
. . .' Finally she took off her glasses and, handing back the
photocopy, said, 'These people didn't ask Loeci!'

By the time we got back to Pasar Inpres, the weather had
broken and we stepped off the bus into torrential rain which
soaked us to the skin in seconds. Timor is infamous for its
extremely heavy and continuous rains during the Rainy Season,
though by our calculations – not to mention the testimony of the
Jakarta Post! – it should have been well into the Dry Season. The
roads were already flooded and the rainwater streamed down the
hills in sheets. The rain seemed to bring out a strange kind of
collective hysteria in the inhabitants, which we hadn't seen in the
western part of Indonesia where rain is not restricted to a few
months of the year. On the way back in a *bemo* belting out a disco
version of Mozart's *Eine Kleine Nachtmusik*, we passed countless
games of soccer going on in the middle of the road, as well as
children running around screaming in the rain and one boy lying
ecstatically spread-eagled in our path. The *bemo* only just avoided
him.

After the rain, the air was languid and thick without a flicker of
a breeze. We sat out on the verandah vacantly waving away the
flies from our teacups and feeling as if we were sitting in a bowl of
tepid custard.

'I can't believe this place,' exclaimed Donna, shifting
lethargically in her chair. 'This heat is unbearable. It's worse
than in the middle of the Borneo rainforest!'

'I wonder if it will be any better on Savu?' I pondered.

'It can't possibly be any worse.'

Donna had cheered up considerably at the prospect of leaving Kupang. On Sunday, we held out our tickets to the man behind the Merpati counter. 'You want to go to Savu today?' he asked brightly.

'Damn right we do, buddy! said Donna, grinning.

'I am very sorry. The plane is brok and it will not now go to Savu until Wednesday.'

He smiled cheerfully and turned back to his companions, leaving Donna and I with tickets in hand and frozen smiles on our faces. Donna recovered first. 'I can't believe this,' she said between clenched teeth, 'I can't believe this is happening – NOT AGAIN.' She slammed her ticket down on the counter and repeated, loudly, 'I can't believe this is happening. Bloody Merpati – you're all absolutely useless. I refuse to stay in Kupang with the flies and the heat and the godawful food . . .' Everyone looked acutely embarrassed. I tried desperately to suggest ways to resolve our – admittedly somewhat wretched – situation.

'Look, we've got two days. Now we have a chance to go to Roti!' She pursed her lips doubtfully. I carried on, 'There must be a boat to Roti two or three times a week. Maybe we could get that.' Donna sighed and flicked a fly from her arm. Did the Merpati man know if there was a boat to Roti?

'Oh yes, there is ferry. Three hours. It goes on Monday, Wednesday and Saturday. Very cheap. It's a very *big* ferry.' This sounded encouraging. I envisaged a large boat, the size of the one that took us to Lombok. 'Yes' he continued, 'very big ferry. It can take *five* car!'

The ferry office was way across town. The girl sitting behind the desk was called Merry and she spoke good English. She was from Roti, she said, so we asked her what it was like.

'Everything to see in Roti, you can see in Kupang.'

'But there's nothing to see in Kupang.'

'Exactly.'

Seeing the expression on Donna's face, I hurriedly pressed on, asking her about accommodation and transport on the island.

'The ferry takes three hours and then you must take a truck for three more hours from the harbour to Ba'a where there is a *losmen*.

186

That's the only one there.' Donna interjected, 'A truck? You mean there are no taxis or buses?'

'No, no buses. But who knows, maybe now it's changed. I left as soon as I could. When do you want to go?'

We told her we *had* wanted to go the next day.

'But there is no ferry tomorrow. The schedule just changed. But there is one on Wednesday.'

It was touch and go whether Donna was simply going to curl up and die on the spot or take someone with her first. She winced visibly, sank down onto her much-travelled bag and went very quiet.

On the way back to the *losmen*, I noticed that the *bemo* had pictures, cut out from magazines, of provocatively dressed Western women giving blatant 'come on' looks to the camera. If these were the only impressions consistently available of Western women, then it was no wonder we got hassled so often by young Indonesian men (older men very rarely did such things). Obviously all white women are 'easy' and so they could sidle up and try to touch us in a way that they would never dream of doing to an Indonesian woman of the same age. I was startled out of my reverie by a touch on my arm. I looked up angrily, expecting to see a grinning youth, but instead saw a young mother with a child on her lap who was sitting opposite. Too shy to touch my white skin herself, she had taken her child's hand and used that instead. The child was clearly unimpressed and had already been distracted by something else, but the woman smiled shyly. It had been an act of curiosity, not one of aggression.

The rain modified to a steady, protracted drizzle, but there was still no breeze and we felt that we would suffocate in the heavy, dull atmosphere. *Tukangs* came and went hawking *ikats*, silver bracelets and, of course, perfumes. Our Floresian room-boys brought us cups of tea, which were immediately descended upon by flies. A few other guests walked past, some uttering, '*Aduh! Panas sekali!*' (My God, it's hot!) We could only agree and smile gloomily.

At least that night we found a decent restaurant, the Lima Jaya, which was bright, cheerful, clean and served excellent Chinese food – it became our place of solace during the remainder of our time in Kupang. The owner, an old Chinaman with dyed black hair called Rao Kie Yung, was always in attendance and could sometimes be persuaded to give spontaneous renditions of traditional Chinese ballads on a two-stringed Chinese cello which he played on his lap. Once he got going, though, it was hard to get him to stop. A group of customers had asked him to play for them and had shown much polite enthusiasm for the first twenty minutes, at which point Mr Rao clearly felt he had just warmed up. By the time we left, forty-five minutes later, he was still going strong and even starting to get a little moist-eyed, thinking of the old country, while the party were beginning to look distinctly jaded. It was going to be a long night!

Despite the fine meal and entertaining evening at the Lima Jaya, I was beginning to feel as if an invisible and indefinable weight was pressing on my shoulders and was slowly dragging me down. I put it down to the deleterious effects of months of travelling, of being stuck in a place where our endless stash of good luck seemed to have run out, and of finding myself having to cope with a normally good-natured, easy-going travelling companion who seemed to be going over the edge. Donna, who had always been game to try anything and was full of ideas and suggestions, had undergone a strange Jekyll and Hyde transformation and had become silent and gloomy. On top of everything else, she was convinced she was coming down with some kind of infection and was not feeling well. Scraping the bottom of the barrel of my own dwindling reserves of good humour and enthusiasm, I tried to chivvy her out of her melancholia, but to no avail. She started talking longingly about Bali; didn't we have a wonderful time there, think of the great meals at Kuta compared with the muck served in Kupang . . . and so on.

As she seemed unwilling – or psychologically unable – to suggest ways of resolving our unfortunate situation, I insisted that we hire a car and go to Kefamennanu in Central Timor to look for traditional weaving villages. At first she seemed reluctant, but eventually – with the assurance from a travel agent that there was a 'very good hotel' at Kefa – she agreed.

It was impossible to find a taxi driver anywhere that morning.

The 'big fight' between heavy-weight boxers Mike Tyson and Tony Tubbs was being televised on Monday morning and every man in Kupang within two day's walk of a television set was glued to it. Indonesians love boxing. They excel at playing badminton and volleyball, which rely on nimbleness rather than huge physiques, but they love to watch boxing. Whether this is something in-bred – a national characteristic – or a result of their unrelenting diet of sadistic action movies, I don't know.

When the match was over, the hotel taxi driver appeared wearing a black T-shirt with 'I love you honey – don't tell it!' on the front, and an old-fashioned knitted tartan golfer's hat. 'Who won?' I asked.

'Mik Teeson!' he said, 'Champion!' and bobbed up and down like a miniature Mohammed Ali.

Donna's normal good humour appeared to be returning. It was still raining as we left Kupang and nosed into rural Timor. Near Kupang the terrain was flat and littered with rice-fields, but the spine of large mountains that runs through the centre of Timor was visible way in the distance. Several houses had huge, gaudily painted reliefs of Jesus Christ holding a lamb on their front walls. Perhaps it was these that gave added confidence to the livestock who would stare down the car until the very last moment before moving lethargically out of the way. Considering our experiences on other islands, the roads in Timor were outstanding; wide and very well maintained. There were obviously some advantages to the military presence on the island.

Our driver was called Isak. He was a Protestant. Indonesian Christians always tell you they are Christian as if it is a bond with foreigners, who are – by definition – Christian, too (religion is compulsory in Indonesia). Muslims, on the other hand, seem more self-confident, and rarely mention their religion. Always interested in original religions, we asked Isak what the animist religion of Timor was.

'Christianity,' he answered.

And before that?

Isak said, 'You mean before Protestant?'

We said yes.

He thought for a while then said, 'Catholic.'

Not letting him off the hook, we asked what religion there was before the Dutch were here.

We didn't understand, he said. The Dutch had now left. And before that, the Dutch were here. That was all the history he knew!

Isak was a nervous fidget. He turned the wheel not just with his hands, but with his entire upper torso. The energy he expended in one hour's driving was probably comparable to a week's worth of aerobics. He also had the disconcerting habit of turning round 180 degrees to talk to us in the back. Thank God for the military presence and wide roads! We were both suffering not only from being cramped with our accumulated goods and chattels in the small car, but from the heat and humidity, which wasn't helped by an overheating transmission under the back seat.

In an attempt to forestall any more tricky historical questions, Isak snapped a cassette into his tape-player. It was a hideous medley of jolly songs about East Nusa Tenggara backed by tinny synthesizer. By this time it was really pelting with rain, and I had to strain to see the landscape clearly. Once we were in the mountains, the crops changed from rice to corn. Fields and houses were surrounded by fences of coral or criss-crossed lontar branches. The landscape seemed lush yet empty; it was hard to believe the stories we had heard that in the Dry Season this same landscape would be parched and yellow. The palm-frond roofs of tiny roadside stalls dripped onto the piles of mandarin oranges and avocados for sale. Others sold wild honey in beer bottles; insects and beeswax floated on the top and the honey had a sweet, slightly fermented taste reminiscent of mead. Swollen by the rains, wide furious rivers, the colour of milky coffee, rushed by in angry torrents and people scuttled by using huge banana or lontar palm leaves as umbrellas.

It was so wet, and our windscreen wipers were so inefficient, that Isak compensated for his lack of forward vision by hooting wildly at everything we passed. The ensuing 'bips' from our tinny little car, and the 'honks' from the buses and trucks we overtook, sounded like a conversation in morse code. 'Bip, bip, b-bip, bip.' 'Honk, honk.' 'Bip, bip, bip, b-bip, b-bip.' 'Honk, honk.' Later he extended this technique to 'bipping' at fallen trees which had been washed down onto the road by landslides, and seemed disappointed at their lack of response. On and on we drove, through Soe, Niki-Niki, and eventually arrived at Kefa.

The 'very good hotel' at Kefa, wasn't. It wasn't so much that the hotel itself was bad, it had just – like so many things in Indonesia – been allowed to slide into decay. It was run by a scowling hunchback, who showed us to a room which was dank and depressing. We searched for ages for a light switch, only to discover that to turn the lightbulb on – though the difference was minimal – one simply screwed it into the wall. I encountered a long, aquatic leech in the bathroom. Donna tried to sit outside and read and was attacked by clouds of mosquitoes.

Once again, we endeavoured to cheer ourselves up with food, but the dining-room did nothing to ease our despondency. Resisting the temptation of ordering what we assumed was a regional speciality, *mata sapi* (literally cow's eyes – actually fried eggs!), we felt moderately safe ordering chicken *saté* and fried vegetables, and had ample time while waiting for our food to study the decor. The walls had been painted a sickly green colour and on one of them hung a garish painting of 'The Last Supper' next to a poster advertising cigarettes, which seemed appropriate, as the restaurant was full of cigarette smoke and the service was diabolical. When our food did finally arrive, the hunchback put the dishes down on the table with a grunt and promptly disappeared. 'He's probably gone to find a bell-rope to swing on,' Donna suggested irritably. We were left in a deserted dining-room with cold food, no plates, no cutlery, no napkins and, by that time, no appetite.

If it isn't actually raining, Central Timor, at the end of the Wet Season, is extremely beautiful. Grassland dotted with rocks and interspersed with corn fields shimmered green and fresh in the morning; light and smoke from cooking fires filtered up through thick lontar palm roofs into the sky. Close to the road were rain-eroded stone walls covered in columbine, while in the far distance Mount Fafi Nisum stood with its apex disappearing in the clouds.

On the way to the Atoni village of Oelolok, there is a natural limestone cave called Gua Bitaumi. Once the sole domain of swifts and bats, the dripping cave has been transformed into a

religious shrine. A statue of the Virgin Mary looks down
benevolently at rusting paint tins full of dusty plastic flowers, a
maze of cobwebs and assorted church candelabra. A sign on the
wall – over the collection box – reads, 'Let's pray; Happy are
those who are merciful to others as Mary!' Everything, including
the Virgin, is covered in bird-shit. A set of extremely deep stone
steps takes you back to the road over a field of red, sticky mud,
which should make even the most devout think twice about
making the pilgrimage.

At Oelolok we saw several women setting up their looms in a
large, round, open-sided hut. Each village in Central Timor has a
similar hut (*lopo*), which serves a plethora of functions, from the
venue for religious ceremonies, to the place where villagers
simply meet and talk over the events of the day. This *lopo* had a
tall, thickly thatched palm roof, in which harvested corn, family
heirlooms, tools and ceremonial pieces were kept. The roof was
supported on four stout palm-trunk pillars, at the top of which
were round shelves. Donna and I evolved a romantic theory that
these must have some special ceremonial or religious significance,
but were informed that they were there to keep mice and rats out
of the storage area, and as a handy place to keep tools!

Word spread fast that we were on the lookout for weavings,
and soon the *lopo* was teeming with locals wanting to show us
their cloths. Although many of the villagers were dressed in
modern clothes, some of the men still wore the traditional striped
Timorese sarongs or *selimuts* (man's cloth). Even though, as Ibu
Loeci had lamented, traditional textiles may be dying out, people
still frequently wear a scarf – or *selendang* – over their shoulder, or
around their neck or head, to identify them with the region of
their birth.

Donna's battered photocopy provoked much interest and was,
once again, proven wrong. A round-faced, jovial woman with a
quick smile dismissed almost all of the descriptions of the textiles.
Oh no! That's not from Atambua, that's from such and such a
village; or, my goodness no – we make this kind right here – it's
not from West Timor at all. So much for the expensive book.

In rapid Indonesian, the woman explained that all the 'real'
ikats were snapped up by Chinese traders, who then sold them in

Bali. When I asked why they didn't sell them direct to tourists, and probably make more money, she explained – with much gesticulation and to loud laughter – that the problem was that most tourists don't speak Indonesian and so in the end it was easier to sell to the traders. She painted a hilarious picture of groups of bemused tourists standing amidst an unruly crowd of jibbering, gesticulating villagers who were just trying to make a sale!

We offered round cigarettes. To our surprise, most of the villagers refused and those who did venture to take one out of the packet laughed and giggled embarrassedly. As non-smokers, they must be unique in Indonesia. To repay the compliment – or perhaps to turn the joke onto us – they offered us *sirih*, their nicotine substitute. We laughed and declined the offer, suggesting that Isak take it for us. He was only too happy to do so. As a result, the discomforts of our long journey back were compounded by a driver who was so stoned on *sirih* that his driving was little better than that of a performing bear on a tricycle.

Back in Kupang, the simple fact that our flight to Savu – already delayed five days – was to be further delayed by several hours was enough to send Donna over the edge. She took a sharp intake of breath, pursed her lips and announced that she had had enough and was catching the flight to Bali, which was leaving in half an hour. I was sorely tempted to go with her, but the draw of going on into the absolute unknown was too strong and I decided to go to Savu alone. I watched Donna walking towards the large, safe Garuda jet en route to a comfortable, pleasant destination with a mixture of envy and excitement. She had left me in the lurch, and even though her desertion should automatically have endowed me with a measure of intrepidity, I didn't feel at all brave as I scanned the overcast sky for a sign of the little Merpati Twin Otter that was – if it ever arrived – to convey me to Savu.

☆

We landed in a field. It was drizzling. There were more cows and

193

goats standing inquisitively around the small plane than there were people. From the air, Savu had looked like a giant ornamental garden. Maize fields surrounded by closely planted trees had the look – from afar – of carefully planted flower-beds complete with decorative borders.

I suddenly felt very lost. Everyone seemed to be being met by someone, or knew where they were going, whereas I had no idea where to start. The only vehicle in sight was a truck parked beside the field, which, I was told, would take me to one of the two unofficial *losmen* in Seba, the only town on Savu. My bag was hoisted into the back, and I sat in the driver's cab next to a man called Dafid Kido, who, it turned out, was the owner of the *losmen*.

The *losmen* was in fact his house, which had a few extra rooms that he rented out to visitors. Owing to a past business deal which had misfired, Kido had over-estimated the amount of paint needed for the local mosque and the entire house was painted in Islamic green and white. It was a maze of rooms and corridors. The concrete floors were always wet and dank and the lavatory (which was next to the kitchen) stank. Bright green mould thrived on the walls. Building materials – planks of wood, corrugated iron, sacking – were stacked up outside my room and piles of coconut shells and sacks lay abandoned and rotting.

I sat in the reception room drinking tea politely with Dafid Kido, who was plucking wisps of straggling hair from his chin with a pair of tweezers. Kido was almost inscrutable; he never smiled and when he spoke his words were tinged with pessimism. Was I still in Indonesia, I wondered? This wasn't the normal hospitable Indonesian mentality I was used to . . .

'*Ada banyak hujan,*' (We've had much rain) he commented tersely. '*Tidak bisa jalan . . .*' (Can't go anywhere.)

I asked him if there were any weaving villages nearby.

'*Ja, tapi tidak bisa – banyak hujan.*' (Yes, but you can't go there. Much rain.)

I tried again. Maybe I could go by truck?

He shook his head, '*Tidak. Hujan.*'

Perhaps I can walk?

'*Tidak. Hujan.*'

This was getting nowhere. I retired to my room to unpack. The room obviously belonged to some unfortunate adolescent member of the Kido clan who had been evicted in the interests of commerce. The walls were festooned with soft-porn magazine pictures of large-breasted blondes. I sighed and thumbed through the guest-book while waiting for the rain to stop. There were only a couple of foreigners' names in the book – both Australians. One had put his reason for coming to Savu – rather optimistically, I thought – as ski-ing!

The 'town' consisted of a few streets with a scattering of shops and stalls selling *sirih*, dried and fresh fish, peanuts, papayas, bananas, chillis, eggs, tobacco and ginger. It was a sleepy place and seemed to be inhabited more by pigs and poultry than by people. The people were friendly, but reserved. There were no excited children running after me yelling 'Hello Mister', just one or two smiles and nods of acknowledgement from adults, and nervous giggles from the children as I walked by.

I met Aba by accident. Looking around at the shops rather than at where I was going, I stepped into a pothole, lost my balance and fell over. Feeling stupid and embarrassed, I started to get up and found myself looking into a pair of incredibly dark eyes, a winning smile and a mass of corkscrew hair tumbling out from a black, John Lennon cap. 'Please. Helping you. Upwards,' said Aba in awful English, and invited me inside for a glass of tea.

The walls of his guestroom were adorned with posters of Western heavy-metal bands. Unhealthy white bodies squeezed into tight black leather trousers struck lewd, macho poses, while sullen eyes accentuated with ludicrous black make-up stared out menacingly into the simple, quiet room with its rickety table and plastic chairs. Not for the first time, I felt ashamed of Western values. No doubt the members of the bands would be gratified to know that their silly posturing had actually managed to find some people in the world still simple and naive enough to corrupt. I was never quite sure whether Aba's dark-rimmed eyes were natural or if he was mimicking the posters and using eye-liner. I hoped it was the former. He proudly showed me his book in which he had collected the addresses of other foreigners he had met. In the back, he had made a valiant attempt at his own English-Indonesian dictionary:

jangan ambil (don't take) was translated 'don yu taiks'
mahal sekali (very expensive) was translated 'es veru ekspensif'.
Aba was exhausting company. He never stopped talking and,
as he had by now given up trying to speak English, had lapsed
into rapid Indonesian. I would understand only about three out
of ten words in a sentence and found it impossible to keep up.
Even worse, he would never let me off the hook, but would always
ask if I had understood. Did I agree? What did I think?

I returned to Dafid Kido's to rest. It really was a very strange
place. It was as if Kido's personality had affected each member of
the family, all of whom were silent and subdued. I never heard
any laughter in the house – I hardly ever heard any conversation
other than Kido calling to one of his daughters to fetch him
some tea, or food, or to go out on some errand. I felt very uncomfortable; not a guest (for this was not a hotel) and not a
family friend either. There were no attempts to make me feel
welcome. I was ignored, except for being summoned to the table
at meal-times. I always hurried, hoping to catch one of the family
for some conversation, but the room was always empty, my food
laid out ready and a candle burning, but no sign of any people. It
was almost as if I had wandered into their home in error and they
were merely tolerating me, not wanting to tell me to go away.
Nevertheless, despite the lack of hospitality, Kido was charging
me steeply.

I didn't think it possible, but the weather was actually worse in
Savu than it had been in Kupang. The air hung over me like a
shroud. All I felt like doing was lying under my mosquito net and
reading. However, in the end, even the minimal effort required to
lift my book became too much and I gave up and slept. Electricity
came on only from 6pm to 6am, during which time an ancient
electric fan whirred in an attempt to beat the heat, but it was
useless; like trying to cool a pitcher of warm water by blowing on
it.

During the night, Aba's wife had a baby son, and when I went
to the house next morning Aba asked me if I could think of a good
name for him. The first name that came into my head was
William. I told Aba that William was the name of the future King
of England. He looked very serious and nodded thoughtfully. He

Timor and Savu

knew about 'Sharless' and 'Princess Dian', he said. He thought
Dian was very beautiful; he had seen her in magazines. Aba
thought the name William perfect for his second son and so did
his wife. So now there is a little boy in Savu called William.
Aba had agreed to take me on a lightning tour of the island on
his motorbike and, before we even started, I made a spectacle of
myself by sitting astride it. Indonesian women usually sit side-
saddle, as to do otherwise is considered immodest. Foreigners'
eccentricities are generally tolerated, however, and besides I was
certain I would fall off within minutes if I tried to sit side-saddle.
The paved roads gave way to dirt tracks as soon as we left the
town. The flat, grassy landscape was dotted with boulders and
rocks. The closely-planted trees I had seen from the air provided
incredibly efficient fences around corn fields. Several piglets
trotted by with sticks tied to their necks like miniature handlebars
to prevent them poking their snouts through the gaps in the fence.
Tall coconut trees and lontar palms swayed in the light breeze as
we passed. Rags had been tied around the trunks of the lontar
palms at regular intervals to make it easier to climb and gather
the multi-functional leaves, fruit and sap.
Men wearing Savunese *ikats* over their shoulders rode bareback
on prancing little horses along the road. Women worked in the
rice-fields, planting fresh young green shoots, while others
washed clothes in a nearby stream, and a young man was
'ploughing' a rice-field by letting a family of untethered water
buffaloes stampede round and round it!
Our first stop was an ancient, ceremonial village called
Namata, which contained a strange circle of megaliths.
'I hope you are strong,' said Aba, as we waded through a river
to get there, 'many many steps to get to the magic stones.'
'Many?'
'Many, many!' he laughed. 'I think you are strong so no
problem. Japanese are not strong for climbing steps. After only a
few they are already like this . . .' he imitated someone panting
and gasping for breath. 'No strong for climbing steps, but very
strong for eating fish! *Aduh!*'
As usual, we reported at the *Kepala Kampung*'s house. He wasn't
there, but his wife and a very old woman were. The house had

been extremely solidly constructed out of aged lontar wood. The roof, made up from layer upon layer of lontar leaves, was so thick it looked as if it could stand the most torrential rain storm without letting in a drop. Inside the house was dark and cool. Even sitting on the verandah under the overhanging roof, it was several degrees cooler than outside in the sun. A curious selection of pictures adorned the outer wall; a deodorant advertisement, a Stray Cats poster, a faded newspaper article about boxer Larry Holmes, and – incongruously – a picture torn from a magazine of an 'ideal kitchen'. The gleaming formica counters, fitted kitchen units, food processor, electric toaster, microwave oven and all the other accoutrements of Western hi-tech screamed out as a mockery of their simple lifestyle. By contrast, they had a palm-roofed cooking hut and a couple of blackened pots, in which they cooked over an open fire. 'Would you like a kitchen like this?' I asked.

'A what?'

'A kitchen – like this,' I said, pointing to the picture. They looked blank. Suddenly it occurred to me they didn't even associate the gleaming plastic palace with a place where food was prepared.

The old lady – whom the two younger ones called *nenek* (grandmother) – was marvellous. Wearing a traditional sarong, her grey hair tied back in a bun, her hands were blackened with tattoos, though the designs had long since faded. When she spoke, it was in the Savunese language, which was full of diphthongs and odd-sounding words like *nga'a* (food) and *kemang'ukoo'ko* (thirsty – you would die of thirst before you got the word out!) or *nginu nginu* (drink). The old lady accepted my gift of *sirih* with a delighted smile and immediately retrieved a well-chewed wad from her mouth and threw it against a small wall, where it splattered, leaving a large red stain.

Carved into the limestone behind the house was a rough line-drawing of an ancient sailing ship. As one can see the sea clearly from Namata, it was probably drawn from life. The artist also carved his name (which is now so eroded that it is impossible to decipher) and a date, 1864. Beyond the house, on top of a small hill, was the circle of round, black megaliths. This was the *tempat adat* (ceremonial place) and it was taboo to enter; the ceremonial season had begun and normal mortals like me could enter only during religious rituals. Apparently I had just missed a ceremonial dance called the *Pado'a*. I cursed Merpati; if I had been a few days earlier I would have seen it.

Aba was insistent on showing me the ruins of an old Dutch fort next, and led me over several fences and through fields of giant maize plants to get there. Unfortunately, this fort was *so* ruined that Aba had a very hard time finding any remains at all. Eventually we located five crumbling flights of steps, a water-tower and a fish-pond, but trees and vegetation had overgrown the entire site and, as the view to the sea is now completely blocked, it was difficult to understand why the Dutch had bothered to build a fort there at all.

'What are those plants, Aba?' I asked, pointing to a small bush which I had noticed growing in profusion on the island.

'That is a very important plant for the Savunese people; for the *obat asli* (traditional medicine). If you put the sap on a cut, it will stop the bleeding.'

He pointed out an aloe vera plant, which the Savunese also use for treating burns. In Savu it is known – endearingly and most descriptively – as *lidah buaya*, or crocodile tongue.

In the afternoon we stopped at a weaving village called Bora, where, again, all the houses were built exclusively from lontar palms. We watched a young woman sitting on the earth under the house and working at a back loom attached to one of the house supports. Around her gambolled three tiny kittens and two puppies. A large pig grunted contentedly in a hole it had made in the shade under the house. Ibu Loeci's complaint that traditional designs and methods were dying out appeared to be accurate here, too. Traditionally, Savunese *ikats* had geometric or rose designs and were fashioned from hand-spun cotton threads, coloured with natural dyes – usually blacks, blues and yellows. Here, too, they were being replaced by garish commercial threads and modern motifs. An older woman showed me some of her family's traditional *ikat* textiles, which are now worn only for ceremonial purposes. The motifs were handed down on the mother's side of the family, she said. I asked her what the different patterns on the textiles meant, but she didn't really know.

'The villagers want to know if you like fresh coconut milk,' said Aba. A large green coconut was produced. The top had been sliced off with a *parang* and a small hole cut in the skin for drinking. It was hard to see how to drink the liquid without spilling it; I lifted the coconut awkwardly to my mouth and twisted my head this way and that trying to find the best way to make contact. It suddenly reminded me of the awkwardness of a first kiss and I giggled at the recollection. The villagers – who had been watching intently – laughed too. Aba explained to the village that the reason I was having such difficulty was because my nose was the wrong shape. It was too long. The Savunese have small noses, which makes it easy to drink coconut milk without spilling it.

'So, my nose is too big?' I said, and put my hand up to feel it. The villagers were shaking in mirth by now.

'Yes, but the Savunese love big noses,' said Aba, tactfully. 'The bigger the better! If William grows up and has a big nose, all the girls will be after him!'

Amid the general mirth, a little girl asked Aba how people in England drank coconut milk if all their noses were too long. Aba thought for a while, then explained that in England people poured their coconut milk into lontar cups first. This explanation seemed to satisfy everyone.

The milk tasted slightly fermented, but was very refreshing. I was then handed a tin plate of *gula merah* – the thick, red molasses-like sugar made from lontar sap – which tasted like caramel. The way to eat it, apparently, was to cut off some coconut flesh, dunk it in the sugar, then top it off with a swig of milk. The combination was wonderful.

While I was delighting in the intricacies of Savunese regional cuisine, a young man took a lontar leaf and in a flurry of swift movements – cutting, bending, twisting, shaving, tying – fashioned it into an intricately made drinking vessel. I watched this demonstration of dexterity with a horrible feeling that I was going to be asked to try and, like a participant in a family TV game show, would make a complete fool of myself. I was; and I did. Even though my destruction of a perfectly good lontar leaf was going to involve someone in a fifty-foot climb to replace it, the entertainment and hilarity my feeble efforts caused were obviously well worth it.

On the way back to Seba we passed the 'airstrip', which was now almost entirely covered in grazing animals. The rest of the field was being used as a soccer pitch; I noticed that both goal posts had sprouted leaves on the top!

Aba insisted that I go to his house that evening to drink some *tuak*. 'It's OK,' he had assured me, 'you don't get drunk on *tuak*.'
'Never?'
'Never.'
'Really?'
'Well, sometimes!'

It tasted sour, fermented and fizzy. Aba's many brothers and friends were there, too, including Pak Umat, who was a man in his fifties, with greying hair and strong, kind features. He had heard that I was interested in *adat* (traditional life) and had gone to the priest – the *Dai'oh'rai* – to find out when the next ceremonies would take place. I asked him if there were many animists on Savu. 'Oh no, no,' he said, 'no more than fifty per cent. But on Raijua (a small island to the west) it is seventy per cent.'

There were five *radjas* on Savu, he said, but as far as the ancient religion (*Jingitiu*) was concerned, they were just 'ordinary people'. The *Dai'oh'rai* was the only person who could decide when the ceremonies could take place. Like Sumba, these were fixed not by calendar date, but by the full moon. It isn't possible to predict this in advance simply by adding twenty-eight days to the last one. You actually have to *see* the full moon!

A small bat flew into the room and crashed round the roof as I tried to concentrate on what Pak Umat was telling me. Six days after the 'moon's death', there is the *Pehere'jara* ceremony, where men and women dress in their traditional sarongs and ride round in a circle on horseback. This, he told me, rids the soil of pests, as well as offering a very good opportunity for boys to meet girls!

With great enthusiasm, he went on to describe another ceremony where dogs, pigs, goats and chickens are wrapped up in special cloths and thrown alive into the sea. Yet another sounded remarkably like the Pasola, but instead of hurling spears, the protagonists threw stones at each other from slings. I asked if people got hurt. 'Of course,' Pak Umat replied, 'it's good for the ground if blood flows.'

Pak Umat looked set – especially with a large lontar cup of *tuak* in his hand – to talk about *Jingitiu* all night, but a long hot day, combined with the effects of the alcohol, was making my eyelids droop. The bat followed me out of Aba's house as I headed back to Dafid Kido's for what I hoped would be a good night's sleep. I might as well have stayed at Aba's. I was kept awake for hours by a noisy, violent, exploitative film on TV. Screams and gunfire, interspersed with loud, oppressive music, cut through the night like a blunt scalpel. All night I was woken by barking dogs, yowling cats, a cricket with a chirp like a dentist's drill, engines revving up and even someone hammering at four in the morning. At dawn, as I lay awake fighting the heat and listening to rain pounding on the corrugated-iron roof like sustained applause, I decided to leave. Savu was a beautiful and fascinating island, but I really couldn't cope with the climate and the squalor of Dafid Kido's for another week or so, just in the hope of witnessing a ceremony.

Aba seemed disappointed that I was leaving. Even little William cried. But I was struck with delayed 'Donna syndrome' and determined to depart. In fact, I became obsessed with the need to leave and was almost panic-stricken at the thought that the plane might not come. It had started raining heavily, which often meant that the Twin Otter couldn't land. Carefully avoiding the goat-shit on the floor, I sat in the open-sided departure terminal, willing the clouds to clear. Like Donna in Kupang, I was beginning to salivate at the thought of a tasty meal and a cocktail at a Kuta restaurant. What did this mean? Did it mean that my urge to travel and explore was evaporating? That our time in Indonesia was drawing to an end? I wasn't sure.

Finally, to my immense relief, the little plane landed and, only three hours later, I was in Bali. I located Donna in Fat Yogi's, cradling a Super Bloody Bagus cocktail and talking to a craggy Australian called Pete. She was clearly back to her old self. 'Hey, welcome!' she shouted. 'Pete's just come from Kalimantan, and he's been telling me about this Dayak funeral taking place next week – fancy going?' Our travels, apparently, were not quite over yet!

10. Room service at the Headhunter Hotel

The Mahakam River – the Dayaks

The more Pete told us about the funeral, the more intrigued we became. The festivities had already been going on for about two weeks, he said, and we would be arriving in time to witness the climax – the slaughter of a buffalo. Donna grimaced. Neither of us had particularly relished the last bovine massacre we had watched. The village where the funeral was taking place was called Mantar and was one of the few places left with a living and working longhouse. It was approximately five hundred kilometres up-river and would take about three days to reach.

Mantar was the home of the Benuaq Dayaks. The word 'Dayak' is a collective name for hundreds of tribal peoples – the famous 'Headhunters of Borneo' – who differ widely in language, art forms, dress, architecture and social organization. All Dayak groups, though, have some fundamental features in common; they live along rivers and practise dry rice 'shifting' agriculture. One of the most distinguishing features of many Dayak tribes is their stretched ear-lobes. Men and – more commonly – women wear heavy brass rings in their ears, which stretch as more rings are added. (We were to see one old woman with lobes dangling to her breasts.) Nowadays young girls tend not to want to follow in the footsteps of their elders and ancestors. It isn't considered 'modern' to have stretched ears, and many of those who began wearing the brass rings at an early age have made the long journey down-river to Samarinda to have them cut and sewn up again.

According to Pete, the Dayaks of Mantar had been saving for this burial ceremony (the *Kwangkai*) for over thirty years, during which time sixty-one people had died. Although they had been 'buried', some for many years, this period is considered by the Benuaqs as an interim one, where the bodies lie 'in limbo'. They believe that after people die their spirit resides in their skull, while the soul inhabits their bones, and they can only be happily reunited to travel on safely to the Upper World if their living relatives organize a special ceremony – the *Kwangkai* – on their behalf.

We were hooked. It sounded too good to be true; an authentic ceremony and not just a tourist photo-opportunity. 'God knows what you'll be going into up there,' said Pete. 'It's a hell of a long way up-river. I certainly didn't have the inclination to go. I don't know if they've even seen white people before, let alone two white women.'

'I don't think anything can faze us after ten months travelling in this country,' said Donna.

'Well, rather you than me!' Pete gave us the name of a fellow Australian called David Boyce who worked at Kota Bangun – a town about two hundred kilometres up-river – and who supposedly knew the area better than anyone. 'At least you can split your trip and have a decent meal and a shower on the way!' he said. 'He might even be able to help you get to Mantar. It's pretty isolated up there, so if anything goes wrong just don't lose your heads.'

'So to speak,' said Donna.

So it was that Donna and I found ourselves standing on the river bank near Samarinda (the capital of East Kalimantan), gazing at the watery highway before us. With its source at the Schwaner mountain range deep in the interior of the island, the Mahakam River twists and turns like a figure skater through eastern Borneo and ends up, almost a thousand kilometres later, in the Makassar Strait. It is an immense and impressive river – over a kilometre wide in some parts – and its waters give rise to constant motion. Fast currents carry along a continual array of flotsam and jetsam, from huge logs dislodged from rafts of trees en route to plywood factories, to the odd coke-can tossed from a river taxi. Enormous numbers of boats ply its waters day and night; public taxis, fishing boats, logging boats, long motorized canoes (aptly called *ketingtings* because of the noise they make) and tiny dugout canoes, and thousands of people live and work along its banks.

'When is the boat to Kota Bangun?' we asked the man at the ticket office.

'*Sudah habis*.' (Already finished.)

'You mean it's already gone?'

'Yes.'

'So we've missed it?'

'Yes.'

'When's the next one?'

'Tomorrow.' We didn't savour the prospect of a night in Samarinda, but it seemed there was little alternative. As an afterthought, I asked: 'So there are no other boats to Kota Bangun?'

'Oh yes, there's one at one o'clock.'

'One o'clock? Today?'

'Yes.'

'But you said the boat to Kota Bangun had left already?'

'That was the boat *just* to Kota Bangun. This boat stops at Kota Bangun on the way to Melak.' Not for the first time in Indonesia I had the strange feeling that I was teetering on the edge of insanity.

'So it leaves at one o'clock?'

'Yes.'

'And you have tickets to Kota Bangun?'

'Of course.'

'Why didn't you *tell* us the Melak boat stopped at Kota Bangun?'

'You didn't ask!'

We bought two tickets. As we left, Donna turned, just to make sure. 'Are you sure it leaves at one o'clock?'

'Yes, sure.'

The boat arrived at 2.30 and left almost an hour later. It was similar in design to Pak Baso's *klotok*, but a lot bigger. The roof was crammed with paraphernalia: sacks of rice, gargantuan hands of bananas, ironwood, evil-smelling dried fish, jackfruit, baskets of vegetables, several goats and two motorbikes.

We quickly claimed a small area of linoleum for ourselves on the floor, and scrutinized our fellow passengers. Though it was to fill up quickly, at this stage the boat was relatively empty; two young women travelling with children, several men (one with a set of flashing gold teeth), two young couples and three old harridans with toothless grins, who were travelling with an entire shop. They occupied at least one-third of the floor space with their huge baskets containing everything from ladies' shoes to bright red chillis.

Close to Samarinda, the river was densely populated. Towns of wooden houses, shops, schools and mosques straggled along the banks. We chugged past several coal-mines and the numerous timber-mills for which Samarinda is famous – or infamous. Night and day, boats made their way down-river, pulling flotillas of logs which had been felled hundred of kilometres up-river. Each time one passed, I thought of disposable chopsticks and felt depressed.

The passengers seemed unused to the presence of foreigners, and our every move was scrutinized. I came across some photographs and showed them to Donna, never anticipating the havoc this would cause. Indonesians can't resist photographs. Everyone wanted to look and to know exactly who was who, and their relationship to me. They were passed from one eager pair of hands to another, along with an explanation: 'That's her father, and there's her brother . . .', and even made their way up to the captain, who perused them while he steered the boat. Their curiosity was warm and friendly and not in the least obtrusive.

After a few hours, having wearied of the unchanging riverscape, I took out our battered map of the region and tried to locate where we were. Whenever I glanced up, I found someone staring at me, but instead of hastily looking away as a Westerner would, he or she would smile shyly and break into a satisfied chuckle when I smiled back.

The journey was excruciatingly slow. The boat seemed to stop at every other town to pick up cargo and passengers. Each place was a hive of activity. Children splashed about in the river, women squatted washing clothes on small floating jetties which served as lavatory, bathroom and laundry. Men paddled past with fishtraps in small, dugout canoes and *ketingtings* puttered by. Large boats like ours passed, loaded to the gunwales with bananas or pineapples or barrels of oil. After the head-pounding

207

rhythms of Kupang's *bemos*, this was a very relaxing way to travel, chugging lazily along, watching the world go by. There was no way that you could be in a hurry, though. If the captain felt like stopping for two or three hours to visit a relative, or if it took nearly an hour to load tons of coconuts onto the boat, then so be it. The boat would arrive at its final destination at its appointed hour. It was just that nobody wanted to hazard a guess as to when that would be!

There were 'toilet facilities' on the boat, though it was some time before we worked out how to utilize them. Some of the larger taxis had a recognizable roofed, enclosed area at the end of the boat where you could shit in privacy. Ours seemed to be fitted with the ultra-basic model – a three-foot-high wooden box with a hole inside, over which one squatted as discreetly as possible. No doubt Indonesians could use this system with success. If your legs are more than three feet long (as mine are), it is impossible to disrobe and squat over the hole discreetly without the whole world seeing. From the numbers of young men who got up and followed me when I made my way to the back of the boat, you would have thought they had got on for no other purpose. They stood around watching unabashedly, some even positioned themselves on the roof for a better view! How would the giant white woman manage in the ablutions? I shouted for Donna, who stood giggling, holding up a sarong to shield me from the disappointed spectators.

At one town, the boat stopped long enough for us to disembark and take a stroll. The town itself was unremarkable; the usual straggle of dwellings, shops and mosques at either side of a central street. What *was* remarkable was a crocodile that one family kept in an old wooden bedframe full of water in their living room! The wretched creature had been captured when it was a baby and now, at the ripe old age of six, it was over six feet long. It lay, half submerged in its wooden prison, looking doleful. According to the family it had magical properties and was considered to be the 'sister' of one of their daughters, as they were exactly the same age. We watched nervously as the small girl climbed into the bedframe beside the huge croc and put her little arms around its neck. The crocodile appeared absolutely disinterested and didn't move a muscle, but then if I had spent all my life living in the confines of a bedframe, I suppose I would have been lethargic, too.

In the late afternoon there was a rainstorm, followed by a tranquil sunset; a washed-out watercolour painting with the merest hint of red wash in the sky. As the natural light faded, so the other lights of the river appeared; oil lamps twinkled from tiny fishing boats; harsher lights from river taxis and villages shimmered and danced on the water. Lightning flashed incessantly across the wide sky, but there was no thunder. Later, we pulled in to a town called Senoni. With its bright oil lamps shining in the dark and a general sense of hubbub and movement, it was like a riverine oasis after miles of black nothingness.

There is a floating market in Senoni. Dozens of stalls are built out over the water on a wooden boardwalk, and sell food for the hungry traveller: peanuts, sweet biscuits, *krupuk* (a prawn-flavoured, deep-fried, tapioca wafer), fruit, hard-boiled eggs and even fried vegetables or chicken and rice wrapped in banana leaves. No utensils are supplied for these 'take-aways'; they are scooped from their wrappings with one's fingers. Stepping onto the floating boardwalk, we were immediately enveloped in the aroma of cooking *saté* – and surrounded by a group of curious children who we persuaded to sing an Indonesian song for us. They all started confidently enough, but as the song continued, fewer seemed to know the words. Eventually there was just one tiny little girl who was singing the verses all alone with the others joining in with gusto as soon as it was time for the chorus!

It was after this that I began to feel ill. The combined effects of the boat's throbbing engine, diesel fumes and some very strongly flavoured deer *saté* from Senoni had given me simultaneous aches in both head and stomach, and I was feeling very much the worse for wear when we finally arrived at Kota Bangun at 1.30 in the morning. David Boyce lived at a guesthouse run by TAD, a German aid organization. Unfortunately, the boat dropped us off at the wrong end of town, which meant that we had to stagger with our bags the kilometre or so to the guesthouse in the drizzling rain. As we had feared, at that time of the morning the guesthouse was locked, so we collapsed, exhausted, on the porch.

I awoke next morning with someone shaking my shoulder vigorously. An employee, clearly alarmed at finding two strange women sleeping on the porch, was trying to rouse us. 'What are you doing here?' he asked.

'We've come to see Mr Boyce.'

'But Mr Boyce is not here. He went to Australia yesterday. For holiday.'

'Godammit!' said Donna, groggily.

We consulted our map and discovered that we had to get to a town called Muara Pahu, where we would continue west on a tributary to Mantar. What time did the boat pass by on its way to Muara Pahu, we asked. A variety of replies, ranging from 7pm to 2am left us none the wiser. Someone even ventured the unwelcome opinion that they never stopped at Kota Bangun and we would have to travel the twelve hours back to Samarinda in order to get another taxi!

Seven pm saw two solitary figures waiting on the dock by the guesthouse, rocking gently in the wake of passing boats. It was dark. It was drizzling. We had no guarantee that *any* boat was going to show up. By eight there was still no sign of the taxi. Nine-thirty came and went, and we were about to give up when Donna said she thought she saw lights approaching. I strained my eyes to see into the blackness, and we flashed our torches frantically in an attempt to attract attention. Ten minutes later, a huge, double-decker river taxi loomed out of the darkness and pulled up at the jetty.

We had tossed our bags onto the lower deck and jumped in after them before we realized what awaited us, and by the time we had fully assimilated the implications of what lay before us, it was too late. A sea of bodies covered almost every inch of available floor-space on the lower deck. Silent eyes looked up at us reproachfully. Every new passenger meant that much less space for everyone else. The air smelt stale and acrid; because it was night-time, the tarpaulins at the side of the boat had been pulled down, trapping the accumulated odours of hundreds of bodies, stale food and cigarette smoke inside. The top deck was even worse.

Unable to escape, we attempted to inch out a tiny area for

ourselves in the only space available, underneath a bare
lightbulb. It soon became clear why everyone had avoided it. Not
only did the light shine in our eyes; it attracted insects, which
dropped on us all night long. As if that wasn't bad enough, we
were plagued by horrible green bugs from the hold, which would
crawl over our skin to the point of intense irritation, but always
jump off as we tried to swat them.

We took it in turns to sleep – two hours each – while the other
sat up and tried to doze with her head on her knees. And,
inconceivable though it seemed, the boat kept stopping all
through the night to let on more passengers. When it was my turn
to sleep, I was repeatedly woken by the person sleeping next to
me tossing his leg over mine, or with someone's arm flopped over
my stomach. At one point I woke to find a bare foot pressed
against my face. It was the most wretched, interminable night of
the trip.

As dawn broke, we drifted into a small town where riverside
vendors served the passengers breakfast. This consisted of
anything from hard-boiled eggs to fried chicken and rice rolled up
in banana leaves. Donna and I were far too exhausted and
demoralized to feel hungry. We stared through bloodshot eyes, as
teeth were brushed in filthy river water with garbage floating
nearby. Had we followed suit, there is no doubt that we would
have become extremely ill. River dwellers develop immunities to
sickness at a very early age. If they survive the first few years of
life, they will probably make it to adulthood. Even so, both
children and adults suffer terribly from parasites and chronic
stomach complaints.

Fifteen miserable, uncomfortable, claustrophobic hours later,
we reached Muara Pahu, from where we would turn off the
Mahakam onto the Kedang Pahu River. Feeling like the victims
of a protracted hijacking, we gratefully disembarked and retired
to the Paradis Restaurant, where we sat down at one of several
tables. A quarter of an hour later, nobody had appeared to take
our order or even to offer us a menu. The tables were all laid and
the place looked ready for business. Eventually an old woman
appeared. She looked surprised to see us.

'Good afternoon. Can we have some food?'

'Oh no. No food.'

'But all the tables . . .' She shook her head firmly. '*Tidak ada makanan.*' (There is no food.)

We retreated to a *warung*, from where we witnessed a scene that could have come straight out of Buster Keaton's *The Boat*. Two men staggered to the river bank with a generator slung from a pole, which they carried on their shoulders. They had to take it across a succession of floating logs to a small boat. As they stepped onto the first log, it began gradually to submerge until they were soon knee-deep in water. As they continued – whether by momentum or stupidity I don't know – so the logs sunk further and further, until finally they were in water up to their shoulders! In a supreme effort, they somehow managed to hoist the generator over their heads and into the boat, which promptly capsized under the load!

We caused a minor sensation at the *warung*. A statutory part of any meal in Indonesia is a large colander stacked high with boiled white rice, and by this time we were both sick of it. All we wanted was some plain chicken soup – no rice. There was a stunned silence when we politely refused the colander, then an aghast 'You don't want any rice – are you sure?' Customers who wandered in were told the amazing story of the two foreigners who *didn't want rice* with their meal, and soon the little *warung* resounded with '*Aduhs!*' and other exclamations of disbelief. 'Much *aduh* about nothing if you ask me!' said Donna, draining the last vestiges of soup from her bowl.

As soon as we left the Mahakam, the river narrowed considerably, and the vegetation became denser. We had had to switch to a smaller boat, as the large river buses couldn't negotiate this tributary. Trees dotted the skyline; the most instantly recognizable being the kapok with its straight branches reaching out at right angles like ghostly fingers. There were coconut palms and banana trees laden with fruit, and sugar palms, wild ginger plants, tall rushes and nipa palms. But the dense jungle which I had expected to see so far up-river just wasn't there. Only the stunted wrecks of once-magnificent trees remained on the skyline; bleached white carcasses pleading with the sky.

212

We chugged on steadily all afternoon; *ketingtings* and canoes passed by loaded with bananas, pumpkins and fishtraps. Fish eagles soared way above us and, without warning, a pair of hornbills took flight from a nearby tree and flapped noisily overhead. These huge birds have long black and white striped tail feathers and an impressive curved bill, and hold special significance for the Dayaks, who believe them to be magical. The blunt, pale grey head of a rare freshwater dolphin appeared above the surface of the water, seemed to smile at us, then quickly disappeared again. Towns became fewer and the spaces between them wider.

While the boat stopped to load some papayas, I heard a mournful but tuneful birdsong issuing from some trees on the bank. A large brown and black bird with crimson eyes flew across the water. Donna tapped the captain of the boat on the shoulder and pointed. 'Is that a coucal?' she asked.

'Ya, coucal,' said the captain. This was encouraging. We hadn't guessed that we had an ornithologist on board. As we rounded another bend in the river, a brilliant yellow and blue kingfisher took flight. Donna looked at the captain expectantly. 'Coucal,' he said. We exchanged glances. Later on we saw a trogon – a beautiful red bird with a black breast – sitting on a branch, looking at us coyly from over its shoulder. As it flew off the captain looked at Donna. 'Coucal?' he ventured.

'No, it's a bloody ostrich,' she replied.

On and on we went, accompanied by the gentle caressing chug-chug of the engine, the high-pitched putter of a *ketingting* or the sound of cicadas whirring like crazed electronic toys. Hour upon hour passed in an intoxicating blur of river sounds and the unchanging landscape flowing past like a movie backdrop. 'Hey, look at that!' said Donna, sitting up and pointing to a large white arrow on a blue background at the side of the river. It was a directional sign pointing, incongruously, at nothing. It seemed oddly appropriate in the middle of this peaceful natural setting that the first man-made object we had seen for nearly an hour would have no apparent utility whatsoever.

Eventually we arrived in Damai, from where we would have to continue by *ketingting*. To get from the boat to the bank, we had to

negotiate a slippery thirty-foot tree trunk, into which notches had
been cut to form steps. If we fell, it would be into the glutinous,
sludgy mud below. I ascended the log first, waving my arms for
balance and feeling my way like a tightrope artiste. As I appeared
over the edge of the bank, a small child who had been playing in
the street took one look at me, burst into tears, and ran away
screaming!

We sat on the river bank and watched the children playing.
They were having a great time, leaping from the jetties into the
river, splashing about and shouting. After a while, we noticed
that an ever-increasing number of villagers had gathered on the
opposite bank to watch *us*. The jetties, trees and figures soon
became silhouetted against a dramatic backdrop of purples, pinks
and golds. As darkness engulfed the river, smoke from scores of
charcoal fires drifted across my field of vision; the river turned a
cool silver; oil lamps from the village and fishing boats twinkled
and shimmered in the water as droves of swifts and bats darted
and punctuated the air. Before long, the eerie wail of the muezzin
started and echoed across the cool, silent evening.

By 7am we were well on the way to Mantar, weaving our way
slowly between treacherous sandbanks as the river came to life.
The sun sparkled on the water, a few monkeys chattered from the
trees, brilliantly coloured kingfishers a foot long swooped from
branches, and swifts skimmed and dipped all around the boat.
The river was getting narrower and narrower and we saw few
people. As we rounded the umpteenth bend in the river, the
boatman pointed to a cluster of houses. '*Itu Mantar.*' At last! Forty
hours and almost five hundred kilometres up-river, we had finally
arrived. The *Kepala Desa* came to greet us. His name was quite a
mouthful – Pak Sionsanten Paneh – so he suggested we call him
Pak.

The longhouse dominated the village. It was a vast structure,
at least 150 feet long, built fifteen feet off the ground on massive
wooden piles, with a smoke-blackened roof made from banana
leaves and coconut fibres. The three entrances to the longhouse
could only be reached by clambering up notched logs like the one
we had had to negotiate at Damai. While Donna and I
progressed unsteadily upwards, clutching onto a fragile handrail

214

for support, the Dayaks sprinted up with ease, carrying armfuls of pots or baskets.

Stepping into the gloom inside the longhouse, I was instantly overwhelmed by a multitude of sights, sounds and smells. It was very dark inside, but shafts of light streamed in from openings in the walls and roof. Woodsmoke from kitchen fires mingled in the air with the eerie sounds of monotonous chanting. There was a general babble of voices, clatter of kitchen pots, and children's cries; while below, chickens clucked, dogs barked and yelped, pigs squealed, and cocks crowed continually. At first I saw things in brief flashes; a woman and her son grating coconut, small children playing tag, two women sitting together, one searching for lice in the other's hair.

The longhouse was like a self-contained village, with many families living and working in it together. Inside it was divided, lengthways, into two halves, with a main corridor at the front and rooms where individual families lived at the back. This corridor is the equivalent of the village street, where the Dayaks pound rice, weave baskets or textiles, sit and socialize and entertain, and where the children play together. The floor was made of interwoven pieces of split bamboo, which we found incredibly uncomfortable to walk on with our unhardened bare feet. At one end was a communal kitchen, where a frail old woman in a faded sarong crouched over one of the open fireplaces, tending a large cooking pot. The longhouse was blackened inside, and the smell of woodsmoke permeated everything.

Between the first doorway and the kitchen, sat the various instruments of an old, rusty gamelan orchestra. Composed almost exclusively of percussion instruments, the gamelan is tuned to two scales – one seven-tone, the other five. The music tends to be rather discordant to the Western ear at first, until one starts to appreciate its unique haunting qualities. A full orchestra consists of gongs, kettle-drums, cymbals, xylophones, zithers, flutes and an extraordinary two-stringed instrument called the *rebab*, which is like a cello or viola. In this – rather abridged – orchestra there were three ancient, worm-eaten wooden drums, which hung silently from the rafters, several massive gongs suspended from horizontal poles in the wall and a number of

215

smaller gongs scattered about the floor.

Most of the *Kwangkai* activities were taking place in a large communal area in the centre of the longhouse and, when we arrived, a rice ceremony was in progress to ensure that the spirits would have ample sustenance for their journey to the next world. Twelve men, dressed in white clothing fringed with yellow, sat facing each other in two parallel lines. Between them stood several brass dishes containing rice of various descriptions – fried, boiled, uncooked, sticky rice and so on. The *Wara* (Chief of the *Kwangkai*), who was distinguished by a bright red bandanna, led the ceremony and chanted some 'verses', while the others responded for the 'chorus'.

A pile of large brown pots with plates tied over the top had been placed by one door. These, Pak explained, held the bones of the dead. Nearby, a large box hung from the rafters. Its grisly contents were, apparently, the sixty-one skulls, which in happier times had been connected to the bones in the pots! The box was brightly painted and decorated with sequins, tassels and thin strips of curling rattan. Two carved hornbills with vacant, yellow faces gazed down from the roof, while dozens of plates and a few cooking pots dangled haphazardly from the rafters like strange stellar objects in a dark, cobwebbed sky.

'Pak, what are those, er, "flying saucers"?' asked Donna. The spirits of the dead were resting on them, he said. The previous night there had been a ceremony which had sent the spirits up into the roof. We never did find out exactly why they had been banished up there, but did ascertain that, later that day, another ceremony would be conducted to bring them down again.

Donna was in conversation with a gnarled old man dressed in a jerkin, a skirt and even a hat made entirely of bark. In days gone by many Dayaks would have worn garments like these. Most of the Mantar Dayaks were dressed in sarongs and T-shirts and wore rubber thongs on their feet. One of the women wore an eye-catching bright red bra with her sarong. She was obviously proud of it as I never saw her in anything else!

A baby swung to and fro in a sarong that had been knotted together at the top and suspended from the ceiling. The child was held securely in a sitting position, its legs sticking straight out in front and its tiny face peeking out, eyes tightly shut. As an extra precaution to ensure it wouldn't tumble out, another piece of material had been tied around the outside of the sarong, around its neck. It looked appallingly uncomfortable, but the child was fast asleep – or, possibly, dead!

Slowly making my way to the other end of the longhouse, I came to one of the three 'family rooms'. Poking my head gingerly inside, I saw an old woman squatting on the bamboo floor, cleaning out her cooking pot. Her black hair was swept back in a tight knot, revealing a serene, proud face, which was still very beautiful. She smiled at me. A small boy hid behind her, shyly sneaking looks at me every now and again from behind her right shoulder. We exchanged some words, establishing that we were both well and commenting on how unusual it was that it hadn't rained for so many days. I looked around the tiny room. It was only about twenty feet square; a minute space for the fourteen people the old woman said lived there. By far the largest item in the room was a large, iron 'four-poster' bed draped in mosquito netting. Heaven knows how many people slept on it. One or two beds were the only items of furniture I saw in the longhouse. There were no tables, no chairs; everyone sat and ate, and most slept, on the floor.

The room was extremely dusty and giant cobwebs, which must have been collecting for centuries, swept down from the roof. In one corner was a jumble of pots and pans, enamel bowls, plastic buckets, bottles and so on. By the door stood a giant pot. I had seen similar pieces for sale in antique shops in Jakarta for hundreds of dollars.

I had been so absorbed that I hadn't noticed the chanting had stopped and some evocative music started. The food in the brass dishes had been covered with giant green leaves and everyone had gathered around the gamelan instruments. Each 'stanza' that was played began and ended with a single drum being struck several times. After that, the tune – such as it was – would be picked up on the gongs and repeated seven times – a symbolic number for the Dayaks.

To the accompaniment of the music, the relatives of the deceased were wiping their fingers on the bottom of charcoal-encrusted cooking pots and then running around the longhouse in a ritualistic game of 'tag', trying to catch people and smear the charcoal on their cheeks, chins and noses. In minutes we had black smudges and fingerprints all over our faces! The old man in the bark costume was having the time of his life, sprinting after us like a youngster.

'That guy's going to end up in one of those pots, if he's not careful!' said Donna, dodging his wicked, blackened fingers.

The music was still droning on when we carefully descended the notched logs and went to the river for a swim. By now it was past midday and unbearably hot. I glanced at the still, murky, milk-chocolate-coloured river water doubtfully. It looked as inviting as a bout of mud-wrestling. I tried not to think what could be lurking beneath the opaque water. We had already seen crocodiles and snakes in these rivers, and the infamous leech scene from *The African Queen* flashed unwelcomely into my mind as I slid into the water. Despite its appearance, the water was wonderfully refreshing, and I was really beginning to enjoy myself when something large and bristly bumped into my back. I screamed, turned and came face to face with the bloated carcass of a pig, which was floating down-river. Caught off balance in the strong current, it was all I could do to prevent myself accompanying it downstream to Damai.

After lunch we returned to the longhouse for the ceremony to entice the spirits back down from the roof. A canopy of sorts had been fashioned by draping a number of brightly coloured sarongs over a wooden frame, and under this sat the prominent male family members. Behind them, a row of massive, dark brown pots stood overseeing the proceedings like aged retainers. In front, several large dishes containing food for the spirits had been placed, each tightly covered with green and red material. Donna and I sat to one side with the other women, who wore delicate head-dresses made from bark fronds tied around their heads, and dangling gracefully down their backs.

Everyone had mysterious bundles, wrapped in batik cloth, tied across their shoulders like backpacks. The shapes inside looked disturbingly familiar, but for now I couldn't work out what they were. The air was thick with pungent smells from some sort of weed the Dayaks were smoking. I asked a women sitting near me what it was. She replied that it was made from palm leaves and, in answer to my second question, yes, it made her feel a little funny! It was obvious that, whatever it was they were smoking, they were all getting 'high'. Most were already glassy-eyed and, after a few hours, had passed out completely.

Brandishing small sprigs of leaves and flowers, one of the Dayaks passed from one person to another sprinkling a thick white liquid over our heads, which quickly solidified on our skin, clothes and hair. Several of the Dayaks were covered with it, making their faces appear spectral in the muted light. The *Wara* went into a trance in order to communicate with the spirits, who would then speak through him. He looked magnificent in an elaborately carved wooden head-dress which had replaced his red bandanna. Brightly painted, with bells, tassels, squares of patterned material and pieces of bone hanging from it, it made him look like a cross between a Mexican *piñata* and a Christmas tree.

An old, old woman – her wispy hair thin and grey – crouched in front of the stack of pots that held the bones of the dead. Holding up her hands in a praying gesture, she began to chant and wail. The other women were silent. The men's voices rose in chorus each time hers subsided. As time wore on, she became increasingly emotional and started wringing her hands and swaying unsteadily back and forth. The air was full of the sounds of crying and sobbing and wailing. Eventually, she worked herself up to a crescendo of despair, the men uttered a final shout, and she got shakily to her feet and stumbled away into the blackness of the longhouse.

Donna and I looked on in a daze, hardly able to believe that we were really there – that the whole bewildering experience wasn't just an extraordinary dream. I looked at the women sitting around me. One grinned, displaying tiny red and green heart-shaped stones embedded in her front teeth. Another was leaning back against the wall with her eyes closed. Her hand, delicately holding her long cigarette, rested on her updrawn knees. Her face – so restful and serene – was one of the most beautiful I had ever seen.

The Mahakam River – the Dayaks

All around us the everyday life of the longhouse continued, despite the ceremony. Babies were nursed, dogs and cats picked their way between the bodies, food was being prepared in the kitchens, water collected from the river. Suddenly, a young girl next to me shifted her position on the floor and something inside her 'backpack' rattled. With horror, I realized what it was that the mysterious bundles contained – skulls! Looking uneasily from one neat bundle to the next, I could clearly see the contours of each skull outlined inside. The rattling I had heard must have been the teeth.

After two or three hours, the chanting ceased. Those who had lost consciousness earlier had now recovered sufficiently to get to their feet and congregate near the longhouse kitchen. Frantic squealing and squawking drifted up from below, as a sacrificial chicken and pig were carried into the longhouse. The unearthly gamelan music began again; those same monotonous phrases being repeated over and over again. Their repertoire didn't appear to be extensive! Each family member smeared some of the blood of the slaughtered animals on their foreheads and danced, or rather shambled, up and down the centre of the longhouse to the music.

The dancing was still in progress when, at dusk, we left the longhouse with Pak to see the graveyard, which was situated in a clearing a short distance from the longhouse. As we approached the site, we were assaulted by the foul stench of rotting flesh. I must have grimaced, as Pak hastily launched into an explanation. One of the bodies had been buried only for a few months and had not fully decomposed when they had dug it up. Macabre descriptions followed of how they had had to cut the flesh from the bones and this, mixed with the smell, was too much for Donna. 'I think you're on your own with this one!' she said, and walked off into the dusk. I forced myself to concentrate on the numerous tombs of Dayaks Past that were scattered around the graveyard. Several consisted of giant pots which stood on carved, wooden plinths. Others comprised beautifully carved wooden sarcophagi raised about eight feet off the ground. Pak seemed happy to stand in the fading light, and talk on at length. He was particularly voluble about some money which the government had promised to send to Mantar for the *Kwangkai*, but which had never materialized. But what with the appalling smell and the sudden appearance of clouds of blood-thirsty mosquitoes, I made what I hoped were polite excuses and left hurriedly.

Our request to stay in the longhouse caused quite a stir. No white woman had ever done such a thing before. We watched anxiously as Pak conferred with the village elders. Several times there were guffaws of laughter and amused faces turned in our direction. We smiled back encouragingly. Yes, we could sleep in the longhouse, but would do so at our own risk. With a discernible glint in his eye, Pak explained that that particular night was to be something of a 'free-for-all' and that he could not guarantee our 'safety' at the hands of the marauding young men who would be stalking the longhouse. I tried to envisage where all this frenetic physical activity would take place. Most of the longhouse inhabitants had nowhere private to sleep, let alone a bed to sleep on. We would risk it. The opportunity to spend a night in a Dayak longhouse was too unique to pass up.

It was peaceful in the longhouse when we arrived. People were sitting around in groups lit by oil lamps, waiting for the evening's activities to begin, and passing round gourds of river water to drink. Many of the children were already curled up asleep on the floor. We were ushered to the far end, where hand-woven mats had been put out for us to sleep on. Noticing a spot which looked as if it might be cooler, I suggested we might sleep there. As I moved over to it, to show Pak, I got the fright of my life. On the floor was a bag, which I had only half-registered and presumed to be full of rice or vegetables. Suddenly something inside it moved, and a long black thing started slithering out towards me. A snake! I screamed and leapt four feet backwards straight into Donna. Everyone roared with laughter, as a small, grey, macaque monkey appeared mischievously from behind the bag. The 'snake' was its tail.

To our left, an old man sat on the floor methodically fashioning a basket from strips of rattan. Beyond him, were two oblong 'tents', which served the double purpose of mosquito netting and providing some degree of privacy for the people sleeping under them. Except for the extended families who occupied their own rooms in the longhouse, this was how everyone else slept. Most didn't even bother with the tents, but just lay down to sleep in any unoccupied spot. A litter of black and white kittens scampered around our feet, children cried, children played, groups of men and women sat talking and smoking. The poor monkey, having been woken up, sat picking nits out of the hair of a sleeping man.

We had noticed a surprising scarcity of children – particularly babies – in the longhouse. Donna mentioned this to one of the women, who told us that Dayak women have a baby every six years. It seemed that they practised a form of birth control 'with wood . . .'. Despite prolonged questioning, we never did find out exactly what they did with it, but there was no doubt that it worked.

After an hour or so, the skulls – still wrapped in batik cloth – were taken out of their box and tied onto the men's backs. The gamelan struck up, sounding even more unearthly in the still of the night, and the men proceeded in a long line up and down the centre of the longhouse, moving methodically to the rhythm of the music. The boys were expected to join in and were learning the simple steps as they went along. It all seemed to be a huge joke, which suggested that the ancient traditions were not felt as strongly by the younger generations of Dayaks; and that perhaps in a few years they will have died out altogether – like the tradition of stretching the ear-lobes.

The dancing seemed to go on for ever. Periodically, the oil lamps were pumped to coax more light onto the proceedings. When the men had completed seven circuits, the women took over, repeating the steps exactly, their bark head-dresses flowing down their backs, some so long they reached their ankles. The oil lamps cast a sinister glow onto their faces as they passed; the batik backpacks rattled ominously. Gradually, as the night wore on, more and more people succumbed to sleep where they sat. It was well after 1.00am when the dancing finished, and the villagers who didn't live in the longhouse left for their respective dwellings. We were almost asleep on our feet and, despite the fact that a very bright oil lamp was hanging right above our sleeping mats, we fell asleep immediately. So much for the marauding young men, I thought to myself as I drifted off.

Gradually, I became aware of some activity very close to where I was lying. Reluctantly forcing my eyes open, I ascertained that it was still night-time, the oil lamp was still burning brightly, and Donna was sitting up. This wasn't right. Was *this* the long-awaited assault by lust-driven natives? If it was, I was fairly certain I didn't want anything to do with it. Dragging myself back to full consciousness, I became aware of two Dayak women setting down a large, brass dish on the floor. On this stood eight small bowls of fried, boiled and sticky rice, and some fried tapioca. I racked my groggy brain to remember where I had seen them before. After a few seconds, I realized that this was the same food that had been offered to, and blessed by, the spirits in the rice ceremony earlier that day. 'Room service!' said Donna, yawning.

I looked at my watch; 3.15am. One of the 'waitresses' was the woman in the bright red bra. She sat down beside us and poured some tea from a green plastic jug into two glasses, grinning broadly. I felt – and Donna certainly looked – like death, but this was a great honour. What sweet, kind people these were. How were they to know that the last thing we wanted was to be woken up after one and a half hours' sleep and offered inedible food which had been hanging around the longhouse for days – even if it *had* been blessed by their ancestral spirits! We decided that in order not to offend, we should try a small amount of food from each bowl. Unfortunately, I selected a piece of cold, fried tapioca, which was so inedible I had to slip some of it to the monkey and surreptitiously push the rest through the bamboo floor. Contented grunting noises from below indicated that the pigs at least were delighted with this manna from heaven at such an hour. The episode passed very amiably with much smiling and nodding until, eventually, the women asked our permission to take away the food. We gratefully agreed and fell back into a deep sleep.

I woke early to a general hubbub of noise; cocks crowing every few seconds, dogs scrabbling and yelping, chicks cheeping and people moving around and starting the day's activities. Clear early-morning light flooded the longhouse as I staggered to my feet to take a closer look at what was going on. The tents had already been taken down and the occupants were nowhere to be seen. The old man had disappeared too. Fires had been lit and were already smoking, pots steaming, children crying. A young woman entered the longhouse carrying a big basket full of bamboo water-containers, which she had just filled from the river. She put them down on the floor next, I noticed, to several brightly coloured plastic water jugs. Another was scraping cooked rice out of a massive, blackened pot with a huge wooden spoon. She offered some to me, but with a stomach still trying to digest lumps of cold fried tapioca, I declined.

Walking down to the river to wash, we noticed a large water buffalo contentedly munching grass with no notion of the fate that was to befall him later that day. He was tethered to a carved, painted totem pole – called a *blontang* – which would later be moved and put by the longhouse to show that a *Kwangkai* had taken place.

A fighting ceremony took place later that morning in the field in front of the longhouse. Two men, wearing loincloths and a swatch of material tied around their heads, lunged at each other with long sticks. They carried shields made from bamboo, with which they tried to stave off the attacks from their opponent's weapon. The fighting became quite vicious and, after it was over, one of the combatants showed us his injuries; three large, nasty welts across his chest. He clearly bore them with great pride and was very put out when I suggested that they must be painful and *tidak bagus* (not good). No, no, he replied, they were *bagus sekali* (very good).

Finally, the time came for the slaughter of the buffalo. The two dozen or so family members gathered, still carrying the skulls on their backs. The *Wara* and several other men held long spears. The sinister, monotonous notes of the gamelan filtered down from the longhouse, as one of the men set fire to the tip of the buffalo's tail. This sent it careering frantically around the field in terror and then, at a sign from the *Wara*, the men rushed at the creature, stabbing at it with their long spears. It was like some sort of haphazard bullfight and made the Toraja ceremony seem relatively humane by comparison.

It was unbearably hot; I was soaked with sweat and my head

pounded from the intense midday heat. This, compounded with the droning gamelan, the shouts of the Dayaks, the pounding of the buffalo's hooves as it tore about the field and the blood pouring from its wounds, made it an even more horribly affecting scene. Eventually, exhausted and wounded, the poor animal stumbled to the ground, and the men immediately fell on it and cut its throat. There was a terrific rushing sound as the breath escaped from its windpipe, and simultaneously the women (free now to mourn the departed) ran onto the field crying and wailing and throwing water and rice over the corpse. Ropes were tied around its back legs and its horns, and a macabre tug-of-war ensued, the men pulling on one rope, the women on the other. Eventually, with a scream from the Dayaks, the buffalo's head was pulled from its body and, in this symbolic finale, the souls and spirits of the dead were reunited and sent on their way to the Next World. The *Kwangkai* was over.

When Donna and I left, the entire village gathered on the jetty to see us off. The Benuaq Dayaks have a tradition that if you brush your departing guests' cheek and under their chin with water, it indicates that you hope you will see them again soon. By the time the *ketingting* puttered away from the jetty, things had become quite out of hand. Everyone was throwing water about, mostly at us, and several young men leapt into the water simultaneously, sending up a giant wave that soaked us completely.

As the boat weaved its way precariously around the sandbanks of the Kedang Pahu River, I sank back, exhilarated and exhausted. I was keenly aware that we had witnessed something unique and special; snatched a glimpse of a world that is rapidly changing, and may possibly soon disappear. How long would it be before plastic jugs replaced the bamboo containers and gourds entirely; before sarongs were replaced by blue jeans, as they had replaced bark clothing? Even that wonderful longhouse would be torn down in time to make room for smaller, more modern houses. In the past, Dayaks hunted pig and deer with blowpipes. Why bother, nowadays, when there is little forest left to hunt in, and when it is far easier to travel down-river in a motorized canoe to buy produce? Times are changing. Fast.

The Mahakam River – the Dayaks

Donna was very quiet as the late afternoon light vivified the colours around us. I guessed that she, too, was silently reliving the jumble of new experiences we had encountered over the past few days. What I had found special was the way we were immediately accepted and treated as equals, not as *'orang touris'*. Nobody bothered us with incessant 'Hello Misters' or pestered us with endless, repetitive questions. I shall never forget the sights, sounds and smells of the longhouse; even now, months later, I can't smell woodsmoke or hear a dog yelping or a cock crowing without the experience flooding back. I shall always remember the Dayaks' friendly smiles, and the serenity and beauty of their faces will remain with me always. It was a perfect way to close the lid on the treasure chest. Indonesia hadn't disappointed us. No value could be put on such a rare and wonderful collection of peoples, landscapes, textures and experiences.

After a long, long silence, Donna spoke. 'You know the most amazing thing, Annabel? They never once asked us how long we planned to stay or when we planned to leave.' She was right. We had been free to stay in the midst of these warm, hospitable people – presumably indefinitely. I wondered how the average British or American family would react to two Dayaks turning up unexpectedly on their doorstep wanting to stay for Christmas! How *I* would have reacted, for that matter? Such unconditional acceptance and hospitality isn't a 'given' to Westerners, who are taught to be mistrustful and never to expect something for nothing.

As we sat waiting for our flight to Singapore, we heard an announcement that a Merpati flight would be delayed. Merpati apologized for the inconvenience. We looked at each other and smiled. Was Tina on that flight with her pink pyjamas, or Djunardi – thumbing through his Maintenance Manual?

☆

Several months later, back in London, I was watching a TV programme about Borneo. I had been completely absorbed; temporarily transported back not only to the rainforest, but to that magic and timelessness that epitomizes so much of Indonesia. Suddenly the telephone rang, the usually familiar

226

'ring' sounding harsh and alien. I felt shocked, unsure where I was – as if I had been woken from a deep sleep – and involuntarily glanced at my watch. I had been jerked back to the realities of the modern world. Surely I had to be somewhere? Be doing something? This tiny episode seemed to sum up what the experience of travelling in Indonesia had been like. Travelling in a place where it is still possible to immerse yourself in age-old cultures, to lose yourself in a sense of timelessness, only to be yanked back to reality by some man-made intrusion; a world where the natural rhythms of the moon and the seasons are important – and so much more reliable than man-made schedules and timetables which seemed to be made only to be broken – or rather, 'brok'!

TRAVEL AND CULTURE BOOKS

"World at Its Best" Travel Series
Britain, France, Germany, Hawaii,
Holland, Hong Kong, Italy, Spain,
Switzerland, London, New York, Paris,
Washington, D.C.

Passport's Travel Guides and References
IHT Guides to Business Travel in Asia &
  Europe
New York on $1,000 a Day (Before
  Lunch)
London on £1,000 a Day (Before Tea)
Mystery Reader's Walking Guides:
  London, England, and New York
Chicago's Best-Kept Secrets
London's Best-Kept Secrets
New York's Best-Kept Secrets
Everything Japanese
Japan Today!
Japan at Night
Japan Made Easy
Discovering Cultural Japan
Living in Mexico
The Hispanic Way
Guide to Ethnic Chicago
Guide to Ethnic London
Guide to Ethnic New York
Passport's Trip Planner & Travel Diary
Chinese Etiquette and Ethics in Business
Korean Etiquette and Ethics in Business
Japanese Etiquette and Ethics in Business
How to Do Business with the Japanese
Japanese Cultural Encounters
The Japanese

Passport's Regional Guides of France
Auvergne, Provence, Loire Valley,
  Dordogne, Languedoc, Brittany, South
  West France, Normandy & North West
  France, Paris, Rhône Valley & Savoy;
  France for the Gourmet Traveler

Passport's Regional Guides of Indonesia
New Guinea, Java, Borneo, Bali, East of
  Bali, Sumatra, Spice Islands,
  Underwater Indonesia, Sulawesi

Up-Close Guides
Paris, London, Manhattan

Passport's "Ticket To..." Series
Italy, Germany, France, Spain

**Passport's Guides: Asia, Africa, Latin
  America, Europe**
Japan, Korea, Malaysia, Singapore, Bali,
  Burma, Australia, New Zealand, Egypt,
  Kenya, Philippines, Portugal, Moscow,
  Leningrad, The Georgian Republic,
  Mexico

Passport's China Guides
All China; Beijing; Fujian; Guilin,
  Canton & Guangdong; Hangzhou &
  Zhejiang; Hong Kong; Macau; Nanjing
  & Jiangsu; Shanghai; The Silk Road;
  Taiwan; Tibet; Xi'an; The Yangzi
  River; Yunnan

Passport's India Guides
All India; Bombay and Goa; Dehli, Agra
  and Jaipur; Burma; Pakistan;
  Kathmandu; Bhutan; Museums of
  India; Hill Stations of India

Passport's Thai Guides
Bangkok, Phuket, Chiang Mai, Koh Sumi

On Your Own Series
Brazil, Israel

"Everything Under the Sun" Series
Spain, Barcelona, Toledo, Seville,
  Marbella, Cordoba, Granada, Madrid,
  Salamanca, Palma de Majorca

Passport's Travel Paks
Britain, France, Italy, Germany, Spain

Exploring Rural Europe Series
England & Wales; France; Greece;
  Ireland; Italy; Spain; Austria;
  Germany; Scotland

Nagel's Encyclopedia Guides
35 volumes on countries and regions
  ranging from Albania to the U.S.S.R.

Passport Maps
Europe; Britain; France; Italy; Holland;
  Belgium & Luxembourg; Scandinavia;
  Spain & Portugal; Switzerland; Austria
  & the Alps

Christmas in Series
France, Mexico, Spain, Germany, Italy

PASSPORT BOOKS
a division of *NTC Publishing Group*
Lincolnwood, Illinois USA